THE ART OF MEDITATION

EIGHT STEPS

TOWARDS FREEDOM

THE ART OF MEDITATION

EIGHT STEPS TOWARDS FREEDOM

Robert Elias Najemy

Holistic Harmony Publishers
PO Box 93 Markopoulo
Greece, 19003
www.HolisticHarmony.com
armoniki@holisticharmony.com

© 1991 Robert Elias Najemy

Cover image - mandala -Louitgart Huntra

Cover Layout - Litsa Cheirouveim

isbn 0-9710116-8-0

DEDICATION

I offer this book to us - humanity.

That we may realize our true Divine Nature
and manifest it here on Earth
through thoughts, words and actions
permeated with Love, Peace,
Harmony, Truth and Righteousness.

TABLE OF CONTENTS

INTRODUCTION

I offer you this book out of gratitude for all that I have received from the technique of meditation. It changed my life from one without meaning to one full of creative, joyful activity. It changed my life from one of loneliness and separation to one of unity and love; from the selfish pursuit of personal pleasure to one of meaningful service.

I am thankful. And I thank you for your existence and thus the opportunity to put all these thoughts and experiences into words. Sharing something that is so important to me is always a pleasure.

I would suggest that you read this book through once and then return to the chapters, which interest you most, and reread them, especially the chapters about the details to watch for while meditating.

Whenever another book is referred to, it is by the same author, unless stated otherwise. You will find various styles of writing in this book as some parts were written about 10 years before others. This will not, however, be an obstacle to understanding or benefiting from what you read.

You will find that some points are repeated a number of times. This has been done purposely, because my experience has proven to me that such deep and important concepts are not easily absorbed by reading or hearing them just once.

I hope that this book will be useful to you and that you will create a life of love, peace, joy and creativity. May your life blossom into something ever more beautiful, and may you manifest the majesty which is hidden within you through this process of meditation and other spiritual techniques.

Robert Elias Najemy
August 26, 1991

CHAPTER 1

WHAT EXACTLY IS YOGA?

Various forms of meditation and inner concentration have been developed by most cultures and systems devoted to human health, harmony and evolution. The concept of coming into contact with an inner power, an inner voice, an inner knowledge or an inner guidance is common to all spiritual systems and religions.

These techniques, however, were used in the past mostly by the priests, monks, mystics and those with deeper inclination for spiritual growth. The most scientifically developed and effective system of inner concentration is probably the system called Yoga.

There is much confusion concerning the meaning of the word, and what exactly a person who practices yoga does; why he does it and what effect it has on him and his environment. Some believe that it is another religion. Others claim that it is a science of human harmony, while still others praise its wonderful healing powers on the body and mind.

The truth, of course, for each one of us is relative depending on our experiences, childhood programming, desires and needs. I will express to you the truth as **I see it** after 25 years of studying and practicing yoga and 20 years of teaching it.

My association with yoga has also brought me into contact with thousands of other teachers and students of this system in America, Europe, England, Australia, India, the Middle East and Greece.

YOGA IS NOT A RELIGION

It is a science of human development and improvement that can be used in any religious setting, and along with any particular dogma. It is a system of techniques designed to aid an individual in creating a world of inner and outer harmony, health and happiness.

These techniques will help each to **benefit more deeply from his own religious path.** A Christian will become a better Christian, a Christian in spirit and not only in name. A Hindu will become a better Hindu, a Moslem a better Moslem.

The same techniques of yoga, which will help a Christian focus more deeply, and clearly on the Christ, will help a Hindu to focus more deeply and one-pointedly on Krishna or Rama.

Yoga embraces the concept that there is ONE GOD who is worshiped through all the religious paths. It never asks a man to change his religious beliefs or worship some other God.

Yoga has no particular form of God or type of worship. Yoga is a system of techniques, which help each man and woman worship more efficiently, independent of his or her religion.

Yoga is like a car that is at the disposal of all. I can use it to go where I want, and you to go where you want. The same car takes each of us to where we want to go. Each chooses his own direction.

YOGA IS NOT RETREATING FROM THE RESPONSIBILITIES OF LIFE

Rather it is a preparation of the body and mind so that one can perform his duties more efficiently, more happily, more harmoniously, and more creatively. Any employer who would make a study of the efficiency, honesty and consistency of his employees who do yoga, would find that these qualities are present in them to a greater degree than the average of society.

WHAT, THEN, IS YOGA?

There are many ways to describe yoga. It is something different for each person according to his needs and goals.

1. It is a **Science of Human Development,** offering techniques for the harmonization and mastery of the body, bioenergy, senses and the mind.

2. It is a **way of life** which creates a state of inner harmony, as well as harmony with the environment around us. These guidelines for living are similar to the Ten Commandments of the Bible and will be discussed later.

3. It is a **method for the transcendence of human suffering,** leading to freedom from illness, pain and unhappiness.

4. It is a system for the **development of the inherent mental and supermental powers, which** are at present latent in man. (We use only one tenth of our brain - evolution has not stopped). We continue to evolve and yoga is an efficient system **for accelerating human evolution.**

5. It is a **path to Self - Knowledge** beyond the changing reality of our bodies and personalities.

6. Its ultimate goal is the transcendence of the mind and **union with God, the Universal Spirit living in all beings.**

WHY DO PEOPLE START PRACTICING YOGA?

People turn to yoga for various reasons according to their needs, issues, problems and goals in life.

1. The majority start **because they have some physical or emotional problem** such as headaches, high blood pressure, spinal problems, arthritis, constipation, drug dependency, insomnia, nervous tension, fears, anxieties; or they may have lost a loved one, or their wealth, or their job, or have some other difficulty in life. Yoga gives them a chance to help themselves.

It is not a drug that someone can take. Each person learns to develop his inner strength, to care for his body and mind properly, to cure himself and to develop his ability to face life, and to enjoy it.

2. Others start because they simply **want to learn to relax and be at peace with themselves.** They enjoy the inner peace that they feel during and after the practice of the various techniques. They find that when they **develop a daily discipline,** that this **peace and sense of well being carries over into most of the day.** They begin to change their attitude towards life.

3. Others come to **improve the quality of their bodies and minds.** They do not have any specific problems, but are interested **in greater control over their bodies and minds.** They develop this increasing control through regular practice of the techniques. As they progress they are given more difficult techniques. It is similar to studying any other subject. Whether learning to drive a car, to play the piano, to cook a good meal, to run a business, to do scientific research; **there are techniques that can help us learn to master those activities more efficiently.** The same is true with the mastery of the body and mind. There are techniques that can make the process much easier for us.

4. Fewer people come **for spiritual growth, in order to improve their character, to develop the ability to love more purely, to increase their self-knowledge,** and in general, to become free from the limitations of their bodies and their minds. Eventually they feel an increasing need for contact with the Divine. They want to feel the Divine in every moment, to break through the illusion of this temporary material reality and discover the Absolute Truth. They seek enlightenment and union with God.

5. Others may start out of curiosity and if they are not then attracted by one of the above mentioned motives, they soon give up the effort.

All motives are acceptable and one motive may lead to another. Also we often function from a combination of motives.

THE FOUR BASIC SYSTEMS OF YOGA

There are many systems of yoga, but they fall into four basic categories. All the systems have the same goals i.e., harmony between body, mind and soul, harmony between human beings, freedom from mechanical, unconscious, robot-like ways of thinking and living, transcendence of the limitations of the body and personality, the reduction of ego and selfishness and, eventually, the experience of the Divine in oneself and others.

Yoga offers various paths towards the same goals in order to facilitate the different needs, characters and inclinations of the various types of people. Each is free to follow whichever path suits him personally. Most people, however, find that a combination of the paths suits them more. There is a path for the practical person, for the doer, for the emotionally oriented, for the mentally and philosophically oriented; and a path for the development of will-power, which is useful for all the paths. You may choose according to your inclinations.

1. KARMA YOGA is also called the householder's yoga or the **path of action,** of activity in the world. One does not need to practice any special techniques or go to any special classes or retreat from life at all. One simply learns to serve without expecting anything in return and to act without being attached to the result of the action.

Thus, the Karma Yogi serves his family, helps his friends, offers whatever selfless service he can to society so as to lessen the suffering around him. He diminishes his ego by becoming free from his own needs and pleasures, so that he can offer something worthwhile to the society in which he lives. He does not worry about the others. **He does not worry. He acts.** There is a great difference between **action** and **worry.** Worry is worthless and brings negative results. Action with love and self-confidence can bring about great changes.

Thus a Karma yogi may run a business, fight a court case, drive a taxi, or bring up children. In each case he will use all his mental and physical powers to create the desired result, **but his happiness will not depend on the result.** His happiness depends on his knowing he is doing his best. His business may fail, he may lose his court case, his children may not act in the way he would like them to, but he is at peace. **He has done and is doing his absolute best and will continue to do so, but without anxiety about success or failure.**

He begins to feel himself as a cell in the body of humanity and starts to look around to see **what he can do to make the world a better place to live;** to help the poor, the orphans, the blind, the lonely, the ill. He may choose to direct his energies towards various movements such as those for World Peace or for Human rights. He corrects the world and himself at the same time. The key words here are **SELFLESS SERVICE** and **DETACHMENT FROM THE FRUIT OF THE ACTION.** The motto is «Service to Humanity is Service to Divinity». This is in alignment with the teachings of Christ in which He explains that He is in every being and that, whenever we help anyone, we are helping Him in reality. **Service is the path towards human unity through selfless action.**

2. BHAKTI YOGA is the **yoga of devotion, love and worship of the Divine.** It is the emotional path towards union with God. Yoga leaves the form of worship up to the individual. It encourages the Christian to worship Christ. The Hindus, Buddhists, Moslems and Jews will each worship in their own way. This is the path of complete surrender to the Divine Will. One tries as much as possible to have the name and form of the Divine constantly in his mind, i.e., the ceaseless prayer recommended by St. Paul, **LORD JESUS CHRIST HAVE MERCY ON ME.**

This path is expressed in Christ's words «Love God with all your heart, all your mind, all your strength and all your soul». And this commandment soon leads to the second, «Love your neighbor as you love yourself». Christ makes no conditions, such as; if he is a Christian, or a saint, or not if he is a sinner, or a communist or of another religion.

He tells us, also, to love our enemies - everyone without exception. Thus, while we must channel all our emotional energies into our worship of our chosen Ideal, at the same time we must keep our hearts and minds open to everyone else, no matter what their chosen way of worship or belief.

The Bhakti yogi soon starts to discover that **God is the inner resident of each and every being in creation** and consequently his or her love expands towards all. Ego and selfishness are slowly eroded by his love, which is like a light removing the darkness in his life. It is not possible to truly love God, without loving people. This path purifies negative emotions, destructive desires, the mind and the character. It is considered one of the more suitable methods of enlightenment in our present age. The methods of Bhakti yoga are prayer, chanting, spiritual discussion, repetition of the name of God and various traditional rituals, which may suit the individual.

A combination of Karma Yoga and Bhakti Yoga offer an individual in our society an opportunity to better his own life and the world around him simultaneously. It requires no techniques and no special training.

3. JNANA YOGA is the **path of wisdom,** understanding, discrimination and philosophy. It is the path, which few can follow. It requires a razor sharp mind that is always aware of the truth that we are not the contents of the mind, nor are we the body. Everything we see is just a temporary reality that is always changing and will soon pass.

The Jnana yogi gradually ceases to identify with his body, his emotions, and the contents of his mind. He begins to experience his Self as the WITNESS of all these changing phenomena, which are taking place in his body, in his mind and around him. He practices non-attachment to any particular person or situation.

He loves, but is not attached to. His love is felt as the experience of unity with the other being, but not a need to possess the other being. **There is a great difference between attachment and love.** They are opposites. Real love can exist only when there is no attachment, no need for anything from the other, not even his presence. Only then can one love unconditionally.

The Jnana yogi seeks to experience the Truth. He has heard from others that there is a more permanent reality behind this world, in which all forms are sure to decay, die and disappear. His logic confirms to him, as Socrates' did so well, that this must be true. But now he wants to experience it. There is a great difference between hearing, believing and **knowing by experience.**

The Jnana yogi usually does not concentrate on Holy forms. He seeks to know the formless, the unmanifest God. He seeks to experience God as the basis of every being and object which exists in this world. He sees everyone and everything as simply a temporary projection of the **one universal spirit.**

The Jnana yogi constantly struggles against the tendency of the mind to identify with pleasures and pains and various emotional states which cause him to lose his awareness of the Truth - that he is an eternal consciousness which is independent of all that is going on in his life. Life is a temporary drama in which he is playing a role for the time being, but the day will come when he will wake up, either through a spiritual awakening, or through the death of his physical body, and he will realize that all this was like a dream, that his true identity is not really a man or woman, mother or father, artist, businessman, scientist, politician, wealthy or poor, but that he is a soul who was just temporarily playing these roles.

The path of Jnana yoga by itself is difficult, but the truths that it offers us are very useful in keeping a peaceful and clear mind for facing the various tests of life.

4. RAJA YOGA is the **path of gradual control over one's self** through the development of discipline and will-power. It is a system that is useful to any one, even if he chooses to follow the other paths. It offers techniques for the harmonization and eventual

The Art of Meditation

mastery of the body, breath, emotions, senses and mind. Whatever we do in life, we do it with our body and our mind. So our efficiency in every action, in every effort is improved when the quality of the body and mind are improved and our control over them is increased.

Now, most of us have practically no control over our minds. We cannot relax, cannot concentrate, we cannot overcome obstacles such as tiredness, lack of energy, illness, negative reactions to heat and cold, emotional tensions, fear as well as our subconscious conditioning. Few people are masters of themselves and have control over their bodies, their mind, or their lives.

The Raja yogi gains control in a step by step process starting with the most material aspect of our existence, the body, and slowly working towards the more subtle, the mind. These are called the **8 steps of Raja Yoga.** We will list them briefly here and then discuss them in detail later in the book.

a) CONTROL OF BEHAVIOR is recommended for the individual who wants to become the master of himself. The key to all individual and social harmony is to «do to others as we would like others to do to us, and **not to do to others anything we would not like them to do to us**». If a person follows this one recipe for life, then he will have inner peace. His mind will be at ease knowing that there is consistency between his beliefs, his words and his actions. Thus the following five requirements are asked of the Raja yogi:

1. Not to consciously harm any being, with his thoughts, words or deeds.

2. To always **speak the truth.**

3. Never to take anything which does not lawfully belong to him through his honest work.

4. Not to envy or feel jealousy for what others have, but to be happy for them.

5. Not to unnecessarily waste energy on sexual activity either mentally or physically.

b) DEVELOPMENT OF DISCIPLINE is the second requirement of this path. He is asked to discipline himself in various ways:

1. The practice of various austerities and vows such as fasting, occasional silence, and in general the practice of a simple life without many unnecessary comforts, which weaken one's body and mind.

2. To maintain **purity of the body and mind.**

3. To **worship God** daily in his chosen way.

4. To study **the truth** of himself both as a personality and as a soul, through self-observation, reading and discussion.

5. To **practice contentment.** To learn to be at peace with himself, accepting what life has given him and not to be greedy for more and more material possessions.

The first two steps of Raja Yoga remind us to a certain degree of the Ten Commandments. They are guidelines which are found in all spiritual paths and help to set a safe and stable foundation for the spiritual structure which we are about to build. If the foundation is not well formed we could have problems later as we begin to increase the energy and power flowing through our bodies and minds.

c) CONTROL OF THE BODY is then developed through the use of specific exercises, some dynamic and others static. Breath control and deep relaxation are also used in this stage so as to develop the strength of the nervous system and harmonize the endocrine system. This is very necessary in order to succeed in the advanced stages of mastery of the emotional and mental energies. These exercises and techniques are also used today for therapy. The goal here is to develop a healthy and strong body that will not obstruct us in our daily life or in our spiritual quest.

d) CONTROL OF THE BIOENERGY is then achieved through the mastery of certain advanced breathing techniques in conjunction with concentration on energy centers in the body. This produces an excellent state of health and vitality and facilitates the eventual control of the mind. The breath, bioenergy and mind are very much interconnected. These techniques are very useful for learning to master the emotions, but are also dangerous to be practiced without expert guidance.

e) DETACHMENT FROM THE SENSES is now necessary as the mind is usually at the mercy of the various sensory inputs, which are bombarding the eyes, ears and other sense organs. One learns to disconnect the mind from the incoming sensory messages and allow them to go directly into the subconscious, without disturbing the conscious mind, so that one can concentrate on what one is doing. This frequently happens involuntarily as a result of intense concentration on some creative activity, i.e. painting, dancing, singing, playing music, gardening, knitting etc.

f) CONCENTRATION OF THE MIND ON A SINGLE POINT.

g) MEDITATION ON A CHOSEN OBJECT OF CONSCIOUSNESS.

h) ECSTASY OR UNION WITH THE OBJECT OF CONCENTRATION - GOD.

The first five steps are called **outer yoga,** because they have to do with the control of factors outside of the mind. The last three steps are called **inner yoga,** because they have to do with the control of the mind itself. These steps will be explained in much more detail later in this book.

Simplified, the last three steps have to do with learning to hold the mind on one object of concentration for a long time. Then one begins to experience deepening levels of that object until one experiences a oneness with that object. For example, we might start by concentrating on the name and form of Jesus the Christ. After some intense practice we will begin to feel Christ not as a man, with a form, but as an energy, as light, as a consciousness, as a vibration, as the Logos. In the final step we will lose our sense of self, our sense of individuality, separateness and there will be only the Christ consciousness. We will have then merged into unity with Christ.

Thus, we can see that yoga has something different to offer to each individual according to his own needs, desires and goals. It also seems apparent that it has much to offer to our society in terms of increasing the quality of health, mental peace, productivity, and the unity and harmony of society as a whole. It seems only logical that such a system, modified to suit specific needs, could start to be introduced in schools, offices, acting and musical companies, scientific research centers and various private and government organizations, as is already being done to some extent in America, Europe and Australia.

Now that we understand that meditation is the seventh step of one of the four major paths of spiritual growth, let us go on to discuss in more detail what meditation is and how it can be used.

CHAPTER 2

WHAT IS MEDITATION?

What exactly is the meaning of this word meditation that we hear more and more frequently during the last few years? Where has it come from? What is it for? How is it used? Who are the people using it, and how many are they? What are its effects on the human being, physically, emotionally, mentally and spiritually? What are its effects on society? What is the difference between meditation, prayer, positive thought projection and «mind control»?

Meditation can be described in hundreds of various ways. It would really take a number of books to answer these questions. Here we will give some brief answers in outline form and go more deeply into the subject along with «how to meditate» in later chapters.

THREE ASPECTS OF MEDITATION

1. Relaxation of the body and mind so that the mind is not cluttered with various unrelated and disturbing thoughts.

2. Concentration on a limited area of focus so as to begin to be able to control the functioning of the mind and direct it towards the "object" of concentration which one chooses. Thus, if I have chosen to concentrate on the concept of love, my mind will not wonder from that point of focus to various other unrelated thoughts concerning my daily life, needs, desires, the future and the past.

3. The eventual **transcendence** of the mind, thoughts and all identification with the body and personality, and the emergence into a state of supermental union with God (Universal Spirit).

These three aspects, RELAXATION, CONCENTRATION and TRANSCENDENCE constitute the basis of most meditation techniques.

WHERE HAS MEDITATION COME FROM?

The concept and practice of meditation exists in every religion, philosophy and system of spiritual growth. It is simply the process of learning to control the mind and direct it towards more positive and spiritual thoughts and objects of concentration. In the Greek Orthodox religion, the phrase «LORD JESUS HAVE MERCY ON ME» is used as a meditative focus for the purpose of staying in constant contact with Christ Consciousness and for the eventual ecstatic union with the Divine. The process of meditation has emerged out of mankind's continuing efforts to understand himself, to achieve self-knowledge, to improve his control over his mind, and to reach higher levels of consciousness.

WHAT IS MEDITATION LIKE?

Meditation is every action, or abstinence from action, which brings the mind into a state of contact with the inner self, so that an inner peace or silence is created. The meditative process climaxes in the transcendence of the ego and the mind itself, ending in a state of pure awareness; consciousness without an object of perception.

 Put more simply, during normal waking consciousness our minds are constantly in a state of activity, continually moving through moods, feelings, ideas, thoughts, perceptions of sounds, sights, tastes and sensual experiences. Every moment is filled with working, talking, thinking, analyzing, watching, worrying, solving, studying, dreaming and so on. The mind goes on continuously. We are like ships being tossed around by the waves of circumstances, with no control, at the mercy of the various stimuli, which activate our mental programmings.

One moment we are happy, elated over a new relationship, success at business, or school, or a well-cooked meal; joyful at meeting an old friend, or having bought a new dress to wear. In the next moment sadness flows through us - we are tired, depressed with life, bored with work, confined by our family, devastated by the heat, frustrated with ourselves, angry at others, or bitter about the hardships which life has put upon us. Life is an incessant flow of moods, thoughts and perceptions. An object of perception is always luring the attention of our consciousness.

Now the object of your consciousness is what you are reading. And in-between the lines it moves to the life experiences that are stimulated by the associations brought forth by these words. Then the past memories become your object of consciousness. And when you finish reading, at some point, you will look around the room and that will be your object of consciousness. Then you will wonder about the next few hours or the next days - what you will eat, the projects you must complete, the state of your relationships with family and friends, a planned vacation, your spiritual growth, etc. It's no wonder we are a bit confused, lacking in clarity, concentration and peace of mind. The ship of our mind is tired of bobbing up and down, in and out the never-ending waves of quickly changing mental impressions.

Cars, buses, trains, planes, TV, radio, movies, magazines and newspapers have improved the educational, financial and recreational aspect of life tremendously. We are more informed - more knowledgeable about the material world in which we live - than our ancestors. All this is at the expense, however, of our natural contact with our inner world. With so many mind stimulating inputs, our consciousness is constantly focused outwardly, resulting in a depletion of mental energy due to a deterioration of the connection to our inner source of peace, clarity and spiritual and mental power.

A NATURAL MEDITATION

Have you ever been to a quiet stream in the countryside in the spring where life is green and moist? You sit down on a rock and watch the running water. The sights and sounds of the flowing water and the growing plant life begin to work their mysterious way into your nervous system.

Gradually, with the simple repetition of the water's song and the harmonious beauty of the natural surroundings, the thousands of electronic impulses of your brain begin to discharge into the tension-absorbing air.

All of the concerns, problems and projects, which had filled your mind to bursting capacity, begin to disappear. There is nothing to try to figure out now, nothing to decide. The flowers silently console you with their perfect peace and harmony. The fresh air tingles in your lungs and your head becomes clear. You feel somehow sedated, as if the forces of nature have conspired to put you to sleep - to put you at ease. The wind massages your body with caresses of coolness as the sun unties your muscles with penetrating warmth.

There is nothing to do, nowhere to go, nothing to think of. Just lie back and absorb the peaceful vibrations which flow into every part of your being, whispering, «be at peace, relax my friend, all is well now».

A delicious sleep falls upon you; not really sleep but a half-conscious-half-sleep state, in which the trees and sounds and breeze begin to come inside and mix with all of the thoughts and feelings. It is as if the door of your mind has been opened and all of those conversations, actions and perceptions lying unresolved, floating at various depths in the sea of the mind begin to float upwards and outwards. Reality now is a mixture of the inner and outer.

The peace and security of being in the womb of nature, of letting go to the sun, to the water, the wind, the earth-draws out the stresses and frustrations. We swim semiconsciously at the level where the conscious blends into the unconscious.

We dance in our sea of consciousness, sometimes floating up to the surface catching the sensation of the breeze, or the warmth of the sun. Then we dive downward into a stream of upward floating thoughts, images, sounds - all the dislodged refuse from nervous stresses and unresolved problems.

We watch them as they float by and then dive deeper sensing by now there is something at the bottom of the sea that is attractive to us.

Occasionally we get caught by an upward floating sensation of worry, resentment, an image or an attachment, and before we know it, we are at the surface again thinking, wondering, worrying, being rocked by the waves of attachment.

But the dance goes on, we begin to sink again, for by now we see that we cannot really dive because diving is too intense - there is too much effort - we get hooked too easily on upward floating garbage. We instinctively learn the dance of the water, sinking, watching, letting go, being carried on the vertical currents of fresh water from the depths of our consciousness, like a seagull with wings spread gliding the air currents flowing against him without a movement, without an effort, letting the air do all the work.

By this time, we are no longer concerned about where we are going. The water becomes clearer, freer of debris. We have gone beyond the levels of stress release, past wreckages of old memories, relationships, failures and traumas. We have danced through the caverns of resentment and worry. The water becomes very clean, very still, very peaceful.

We are coming to the source of the life current, the source of the ocean, the spring of pure consciousness. Here we may encounter pure light or sound vibrational energy. Only subtle vibrations exist here. Only electromagnetic energy. Our bodies become filled - recharged with life. Our consciousness is renewed as we have cleared the way for a burst of fresh energy to flow up purifying the sea of consciousness, regenerating the mind, giving new life to every cell of our brain.

If we do not become enamored by the sensation of light, by the bliss of this energy which charges through our system, then we may sink a little deeper into the vast nothingness from which the spring of life flows.

Here there is not even energy; no body, no mind, no light, no sound - absolute nothingness - total vacuum - only tremendous potential unmanifest God, from which all life and material creation flows.

COMING BACK TO THE SURFACE

The sound of chirping birds greets you as you slowly float to the surface. The branches dancing in the wind wave «hello». The sounds of insects buzzing and water splashing salute you with a «welcome back friend, you are part of us now».

It takes a while to remember where you are. You were only gone 20 minutes, but it seems you have been in this spot all your life. The mind is clear, refreshed and in the present. There is nothing to do but take off your clothes and go swimming.

Have you ever been to this quiet stream in the countryside?

Most everyone has - either to a stream, or river, or mountain, or sea, or forest. And how well we feel when we return; how much more energy, clarity and newness we have to continue our work, to carry on with our life, to solve our problems. Somehow everything is more alive, more harmonious for a while; life is not so boring, difficult or overbearing.

It doesn't take long, however, to discharge all that energy and clarity. Once again we become upset, nervous and bored.

Can we go to the stream every day? It certainly would be nice, and life would be much less complicated. Of course for most of us it is completely impractical in terms of time, money and availability of such places - especially for those of us who live in the city.

Well, Mother Nature has a secret for us. We don't have to go anywhere at all. The stream of life; that place of peace, that source

The Art of Meditation

of strength and knowledge and harmony - lies right inside everyone of us.

What is meditation? It is nothing more than visiting this stream on a daily basis. Simply put, it is the sinking dance into our sea of consciousness, releasing the submerged stresses and coming to the point of inner stillness where there is no object of consciousness - but consciousness itself. Done regularly, this inward dance leaves us fresh, more alert, more relaxed, more creative, more healthy, and more in tune with ourselves and our environment.

The truth of these statements has been proved both subjectively and objectively through experimentation. Studies have been made on meditators and non-meditators over the years with respect to blood pressure, pulse, reaction time as well as with states of fulfillment and creativity expressed subjectively by the participants. Details will be given in the next chapter.

Hundreds of thousands of people today in all walks of life are finding that no matter what their goals, motivations, responsibilities or problems may be, they are able to act more clearly, more efficiently and more successfully with the aid of regular meditation.

Ultimately, the only way to know if meditation will be useful for you is to give it a try. To spend some time each day in the «dance of the soul».

CHAPTER 3

THE BENEFITS OF MEDITATION FOR INDIVIDUALS AND FOR SOCIETY AS A WHOLE

HOW IS MEDITATION USED TODAY?

People from all walks of life, in all the countries of the world belonging to all the possible religions, meditate for a wide variety of reasons. The same technique offers something different to each according to his needs and motives. Some of the motives for which people meditate today are:

1. To relax the body and mind and rejuvenate one's flow of energy in order to more effectively face the responsibilities of one's demanding and active life.

2. To heal illnesses (especially psychosomatic ones).

3. To overcome emotional problems.

4. To develop a more relaxed, and positive view towards life.

5. To develop a peaceful and more clearly functioning mind.

6. For greater ability tc penetrate into the core of problems and find inspirational solutions. This has been found especially useful by scientists and businessmen.

7. To tune into creative inspirations for artistic expression.

8. For freeing oneself from addictions such as cigarettes, alcohol, narcotics and tranquilizers.

9. To purify one's character.

10. To develop will-power.

11. As a method of self-observation and self-discovery.

12. To develop the latent powers of the mind.

13. To create a relationship with God.

14. To develop an inner relationship with God.

15. For spiritual growth, self-knowledge or enlightenment.

16. For transcending the identification of self with the body and mind, and experiencing spiritual realities.

17. For the ecstasy of union with the Universal Spirit, which is the essential reality of the universe.

Meditation has been and is being used for a wide variety of other practical uses, which there is no space to mention here. The possibilities are infinite, as the powers of the human mind are unlimited.

SCIENTIFIC RESEARCH ON
THE EFFECTS OF MEDITATION
ON THE BODY AND PERSONALITY

Numerous scientific experiments have given consistent results concerning the effects of meditation on a person's body and personality. Some of these effects are measured during the process of meditation, while one is sitting and concentrating. Others are made over the years, observing the changes, which occur, in one's physical and mental functions, as a result of years of regular practice of meditation. These results are from scientific research studies including people who meditate and similar control groups of people who do not meditate.

They have been made mainly on people who were performing Transcendental Meditation. I believe, however, that the results would be similar with most types of meditation.

1. DEEP PHYSIOLOGICAL REST is shown by a distinct **drop in the metabolism** rate, as measured by the oxygen consumption by an individual in meditation, waking activity, sleep and hypnosis. In meditation there was a sudden drop (16%) in oxygen consumption, whereas in sleep there was only an 8% drop (maximum) and in hypnosis a slight rise from the basic metabolic rate. These results indicate that the body and mind are established in a deep state of relaxation and rest which cannot be achieved even in sleep.

2. Another indication of the deep rest is that the **number of breaths** needed to be taken each minute during meditation drops from an average of 16 breaths per minute during normal restful waking consciousness to only 7 breaths per minute in the depths of meditation. This indicates that the body and mind are in deep rest and that there is much less need for oxygen.

Some people, when they first encounter this state in which they need less oxygen, become frightened because they suddenly realize that they have not breathed for a long time. They can rest assured that there is absolutely no danger. Whenever the body actually needs to breathe, it will give the message to the breathing apparatus to take in the necessary oxygen, without needing to think about this at all. This is a **completely safe and very beneficial state of consciousness.**

3. Good news for those with heart problems is that meditation is also extremely **restful and rejuvenating for the heart.** Studies have shown that meditators experience a more restful heart both while relaxing and during activity. This fact has been used by open-minded doctors who use meditation, along with exercise and discussion groups, to help their heart patients to rediscover their lost health and vitality.

One does not need, however, to become a heart patient in order to benefit from this aspect of meditation. Remember that the heart is a pump, which functions continuously. Like any other pump it will break down more quickly if it is over used and over stressed. Meditation is a powerful preventive tool for all physical and mental problems.

4. Another indication of the deep rest produced by meditation is the **significant drop in the blood lactate level** from 1.2mg/100ml to .7mg/100ml. The blood lactate level is a measure of the relative use and fatigue of the muscles. The lower the lactate level the more rested and rejuvenated is the muscle tissue.

5. Tests show meditation's deep calming effect through the **decrease in skin conductivity.** The skin's electrical conductivity is a measure of an individual's relative state of peace or tension. Tests have shown that the conductivity during meditation can **fall 300%** indicating that the individual has relaxed both physically and emotionally.

6. Brain wave measurements during meditation show a **higher incidence of alpha waves** indicating a restful alertness. There is a sense of peace and yet a wakeful awareness in one's environment. One might compare such a state to the relaxed alertness of a cat, who is completely relaxed, but ever ready to respond, if there be need.

7. Another scientific study showed that **meditation induces greater communication and interaction between the two hemispheres of the brain.** This brain wave synchronicity leads to a more wholesome and balanced way of thinking and acting. Many investigations are being done concerning the different qualities of functioning evinced by the left and right hemisphere. It is believed that the left hemisphere works more through logic, and that the right is more oriented towards creative free flowing thought. A harmonious balance of these two is obviously needed for a healthy and productive way of life.

Such studies also showed **increased communication between frontal and posterior portions of the brain.** Although we are not sure what this may mean, it is obvious that meditation allows an increased communication, and perhaps attunement, between the various substations of our brain.

8. Perhaps the best-documented and well-known effects of meditation concern its ability to **reduce blood pressure** in those with high blood pressure. A typical result is that during meditation one's diastolic blood pressure would fall from 15 to 13 and the systolic from 8.5 to 7. Such results would continue to remain in effect for hours after the meditation and eventually become a permanent reality after some years of meditation and proper eating, living and thinking.

These are only a few of the many changes that have been measured during the process of meditation. Now let us look at some of the more long-term changes, which were observed in meditators after some period of daily meditation. Remember that the results are compared to these meditators themselves as they were before they started meditating or to control groups of similar people who do not meditate.

LONG TERM PHYSIOLOGICAL CHANGES

9. In the long run both the **heart rate and breathing rate develop a slower pace** as the body experiences less mental-emotional stress and learns to waste less energy. The body becomes more relaxed and more efficient.

10. Persons who meditate experience much **more stable health.** They have less illnesses in general in their lives. This is true both in comparison to their lives before they began meditating and also in comparison to others of the same age bracket who live similar life styles but do not meditate. This indicates an obvious **strengthening of the immune system.** There have been a large number of scientific studies made recently concerning the relationship between mental and emotional states and the immune system.

It has become obvious to all that a person who is relaxed, has a positive view of himself and life will have a much stronger immune system than he would have had if he allowed his energy to run down or was plagued by negative thoughts and negative feelings.

LONG TERM PSYCHOLOGICAL CHANGES

11. Studies have also shown that those who meditate regularly **react more quickly and more effectively to a stressful event.** These studies paint the following picture. An average person who is neither especially relaxed nor overanxious requires a certain amount of time to react to a stressful stimulus. His stress will build gradually and then he will start to relax. A person who meditates regularly tends to react more quickly and then relax more quickly. Anxious individuals tend to react much more slowly and then their tension keeps building up for a long time after the event. They do not let go of the event but dwell on it for long after it has passed.

This experiment destroys the misconception that meditation makes a person uncreative and unresponsive. The truth is the opposite. He has a much quicker reaction time, because his mind is much more present and not so preoccupied by various problems, which exist only in the past or future.

A similar test showed that, **with the same stimulus, non-meditators took 5 seconds to react while meditators took only 3 seconds to react.**

12. Meditation also increases one's **perceptual ability and motor performance.** In an experiment with a speed and accuracy test in which each was scored according to both speed and to accuracy, meditators scored 7 while non-meditators scored only 2.5. This means that meditation will aid us in all of our mental and manual activities and tasks. The quality and productivity of our work will increase in every aspect of our life.

13. In Holland studies with high school students showed that those who meditated had an **«intelligence growth rate» of 28 points, while those who did not meditate had a growth of only 10 points.** This is one reason why meditation first made its largest appearance in the West through the students, who quickly realized that their mental abilities were deeply enhanced by this process called meditation.

14. Memory recall is also enhanced by meditation. In long-term memory recall studies meditators scored 52% while non-meditators scored only 32%. In similar studies on short-term memory recall, meditators scored 70% while non-meditators fell far short with only 37%. We can see that meditation is a powerful tool for developing all the mind's abilities. Rather than being a retreat from life it is actually a very practical tool for leading more productive and effective life.

15. Many **psychological studies have been made in work environments** concerning meditators and control groups of non-meditators. In the specific time period in which the study was made the meditators experienced a **40% increase** in **JOB SATISFACTION,** while non-meditators experienced only a 5% increase. Meditators exhibited a **50% increase in PRODUCTIVITY,** while non-meditators actually had a drop of 10% in their productivity. Meditators experienced a **65% improvement in their relationships with coworkers and a 45% improvement in their relationship with their supervisors.** Non-meditators in the same company experienced only a 10% improvement in their relationships with coworkers and only 25% improvement in relationships with supervisors.

Thus in the same work environment meditators were able to experience significant improvement in their feelings of satisfaction, productivity and relationships with coworkers and supervisors, while others in the same environment had significantly different experiences. We can see from this how subjective our reality can be and to what degree we create our own reality.

In another similar study, meditating workers experienced a 50% increase in job satisfaction, while non-meditators had only a 5% increase. **This increase in satisfaction is a result of a perceptual change on the part of the meditator and not due to changes in the work environment.** This is true for many aspects of our lives. We may believe that we cannot be happy with what we have, that we are in danger. But a perceptual change removes this illusion and all is fine again.

It is important to realize that this does not happen because the worker becomes apathetic and unconcerned. Remember that he has a 50% increase in productivity and 65% improvement in relationships with coworkers. This does not indicate a suppressed powerless character but rather a **positive attitude towards life** and work.

16. A large number of psychological tests have been done on those who have been meditating for various periods of time. A test made on those who had been meditating for only two months in comparison to non-meditators produced the following results:

a. In a test of **inner directedness** meditators scored 7 while the non-meditators scored only 2.2, showing that those who meditate either have an inherent sense of inner directedness or develop it through meditation.

b. When tested on a scale for **self acceptance** meditators scored 2 while the non-meditators averaged only **minus** 1. It appears that the inner contact developed during meditation helps a person experience a more harmonious relationship with himself.

c. A test for **spontaneity** showed the meditators to have a score of 2.3 while the non-meditators had **minus** 3. This again dispels the myth that meditation causes a person to become dry and unresponsive. The opposite is true. He or she becomes more responsive, more spontaneous and more creative.

d. In a test for **self-esteem** meditators scored an average of 2, while non-meditators had a **minus** 3. This additional self-confidence is an important part of any life endeavor, and a great asset in life.

e. In a test for the **capacity for intimate contact** with others, meditators scored 2.3, while the others scored only 2, again showing that meditation does not make a person more removed from others but rather it makes him or her more capable of intimate contact with them. This is a result of the fact that one feels more secure and has a better relationship with one's own self. Thus one fears others much less, and needs to play fewer social games which keep us apart.

f. In a test for how much **anxiety** a person has, meditators scored only 2 while non-meditators scored 8 evincing a much higher tendency towards anxiety than the meditators.

In other similar psychological tests it has been shown that, in comparison to non-meditators, meditators have **much less depression,** an **increased sense of friendliness,** and **decreased tendency to want to dominate others, more respect for others, greater emotional stability, greater staying power** in the face of physical or mental difficulties or stresses, **less rigidity** in their character and **greater SELF-ACTUALIZATION.** Concerning this last factor, meditators who started out meditating with a self-actualization factor of 30, scored 35 after 6 weeks of meditation and 50 after 4 months.

This is one of the most important gifts offered to us by our meditation. The gift is that we are able to manifest more and more of our inner as yet unmanifest potential on all levels: physically, emotionally, mentally, artistically, in relationship with mechanical tasks, creative endeavors, and even our financial needs. Our mind is more clear, productive and creative.

17. In line with the previously mentioned psychological tests, important studies have also been done on the effect of meditation on **prisoners.** Tests on prisoners who meditated in relation to themselves before meditating and in relation to prisoners who did not meditate produced the following important results:

a. There was a **marked decrease in psychasthenia.** They became much **healthier and more socially acceptable in their behavior.**

b. They evinced **less anxiety and less aggressiveness.**

c. They accumulated much **less offenses against the prison rules** and became inclined to **100% more positive activities such as sports, clubs and educational activities.**

OTHER LONG TERM PHYSIOLOGICAL CHANGES

Previously we had mentioned some of the physical effects of meditation on the body during the time period of the meditation itself. Now let us discuss some of the long term results on the body, as a result of daily meditation.

18. After 4 to 6 weeks of meditation, meditators with hypertension have found their **blood pressure fall** on an average from 15 to 13.5 and the lower from 8.5 to 7. This is obviously good news for hypertensive people.

19. A group of meditators who had been suffering from **bronchial asthma found significant relief.** Ninety four percent of them found **improved flow through the air passages.** Sixty one percent of them found **significant improvement in their breathing.** Doctors following up on these patients found the same results.

20. Meditators were checked on their **consumption of cigarettes** after starting to meditate. Of the 39% who smoked heavily at the start, the percentage dropped to 20% after 9 months and to 17% after 21 months. Concerning those who smoked lightly, 50% smoked lightly in the beginning. Only 25% after 9 months and it dropped to 20% after 21 months.

21. The same test was done on those who **drank heavily. They were 18% at the start.** After 9 months they had dropped to 15% and **after 21 months to only 5%,** a significant and important change in their lives. For those who drank only lightly the numbers changed less. They went from 55% at the start, to 42% after 9 months and back up to 45% after 21 months.

It seems that meditation is a great harmonizing mechanism, which works more intensely there, where we are most out of our balance without removing us from life or from contact with those around us.

22. Even more significant results were found in meditators who had been in the habit of using various types of drugs before they began meditating. There were significant drops in the use of all forms of drugs.

This test was made on 1300 persons who were users of some type of drug before they began to meditate. The first numbers are not representative of the number of people starting meditation who use drugs. The sample study was not done on an average group of meditators, but rather those who already used drugs.

The results are spectacular as you can see. The great power of meditation is that it gives us an inner source of security, power and satisfaction, so that we do not need to become or remain dependent on chemical substances, situations or persons. We become stronger, healthier, more self-accepting, more creative and more productive.

23. Other tests made on meditators show that they need much **less sleep to recover from sleep deprivation.** They tend with their normal sleep time to recover from various abnormalities in their sleep pattern. They do not need to sleep long hours to make up for what they have lost.

24. In a study on 408 meditators with a history of infectious diseases 70% showed a **significant decrease in the illness** they experienced after starting meditation.

25. In a similar study on 156 meditators who had a history of allergies, 56% experienced a **decrease or cessation altogether**

of their allergies.

26. In yet another study on people with **inflamed gums**, 45 persons started meditation and 26 who did not were the control group. Those who meditated improved considerably.

These results were found after only 25 days of meditation. The previous three scientific studies would lead us to the conclusion that meditation strengthens the immune system and thus our resistance towards disease. It is therefore a powerful healing tool in all cases in which the body has lost its balance.

27. In a study on insomniacs who started to meditate, the **time which they required in order to fall asleep dropped from an average of 75 minutes to only 15 minutes.**

28. A study on athletes showed that, after starting to meditate, there was an improvement in their performance on various athletic events as well as their intelligence as measured by intelligence tests.

29. In one other study it was found that meditation has the tendency to **normalize a person's weight.** That is if he is overweight, he tends to lose, and if he is underweight, he tends to gain.

SOME CONCLUSIONS
CONCERNING THESE RESEARCH STUDIES

The conclusion is obvious. Meditation increases whatever is good and life-supporting in a person. It strengthens our immune system, harmonizes our endocrine system and relaxes our nervous system. It creates health and vitality.

On a mental level it develops inner peace, clarity, self-confidence, self-acceptance, creativity, productivity and eventually greater self-actualization.

It makes our work environment more satisfactory, improves our relationships with coworkers, supervisors and subordinates. It makes us more creative, more responsible and more productive.

On a spiritual level it puts us in contact with our inner voice, with our inner strength, with our inner spiritual wisdom and love.

Think now, what would happen if many people in our society meditated? How would it affect our society?

HOW MIGHT MEDITATION AFFECT SOCIETY AS A WHOLE?

All indications and logical deductions point to the belief that meditation on the part of large numbers of people in our society will have a very positive effect. Let us consider, in the light of what we have already learned about the benefits of meditation, how meditation may affect some of the main sources of chaos, disruption and unhappiness in our society today.

1. CONFUSION - Few people today are not confused. Very few know what they want; what is right; what is wrong; what to do with their lives. Most are bombarded by so many opinions, desires, activities and responsibilities that they cannot think clearly. Sitting quietly for 20 minutes by himself everyday will help each individual to clear his mind, free himself from the haze of thoughts and emotions and become clearer about his life. He will be a more efficient member of society.

2. LACK OF INNER DIRECTION - People today are like sheep following the dictates of political leaders, religious leaders, TV commercials and in general the established view of what is success and failure, what is important in life and what is not. Thus people are like unconscious machines who are operated by the forces around them. They have no inner direction, no inner guide, even concerning the basic aspects of life such as: how to eat, how to communicate, how to live happily in harmony. Meditation will help people to reawaken to their inner sense of what is important and of value to them, and how to live harmoniously. They will become stronger, more satisfied from within. They will offer society a higher quality of human being.

3. LACK OF SELF-CONFIDENCE - When someone lacks self-confidence, he is not likely to perform any of his life functions effectively or well. He will not be a good worker, businessman, scientist, artist, politician or teacher. Neither will he be a high quality mother or father, or spouse. Self-confidence is essential for being effective at whatever task one has to do. Meditation increases one's self-confidence by putting one in contact with inner energies that were previously latent and undeveloped. Thus, as people meditate more, they will become more efficient members of society, in whatever role they play.

4. LACK OF INNER MORALS - Society today suffers from a serious lack of contact with inner values and moral behavior. There is a complete breakdown in the moral structure of society. People cheat, lie and use each other as if it was perfectly normal to do so. But they would not like others to do the same to them.

Thus there is a lack of consistency between what a man believes, thinks, says and does. His word has little truth, and thus little power. Neither do his actions.

The result is a society of people who are looking out only for themselves, often at the others' expense. There is little cooperation and harmony, and thus the whole system is falling apart economically and politically.

The harmonious functioning of any group of people depends on the basic law of doing to others as we would like others to do to us. When this is not followed, only disintegration and unhappiness can result - for all.

Meditation puts an individual in contact with his inner sense of morality. This inner sense of morality has always been, and will always be, in us, but we have lost contact with it. With meditation we become more sensitive and start to realize our oneness with the others and eventually become incapable of cheating, lying or doing harm to others. Meditation can help r**estore the natural moral**

The Art of Meditation

foundation on which the success and harmony of society are based.

5. LACK OF LOVE - We all suffer from lack of love. We all want more love than we are getting. The lack of love in modern society is responsible for the outrageous increase in divorce, mental asylums, cancer, psychosomatic illnesses, inner city crime such as theft, rape and murder and in general, the feeling of loneliness and isolation which runs deep in our society today.

If people had enough love in their lives there would be none of the above. It requires great inner strength, inner peace and inner contentment, and also love for ourselves, in order to be able to love others steadily. Otherwise our love will change to disappointment or anger the moment the other does something we do not like. Only a person with great inner strength and inner resources can love unconditionally. He must have no fear, no feeling of vulnerability.

Meditation helps one to begin the process of knowing his inner self, and of developing an inner peace that is not so vulnerable to external events. One begins to learn to love oneself and feel greater acceptance for himself and others. Meditation helps to remove the blockages to love, the ego-defense mechanisms of the personality. Regular meditation by the members of our society will make it a more loving and peaceful place to live.

6. NERVOUS TENSION - Nervous tension is the main "dis-ease" of our present society. It leads to all types of other diseases and emotional problems as well as conflicts in relationships, at work and at home. The problem with nervous tension is that it grows rapidly in a vicious circle. The more tension we have, the more easily we accumulate more of it. The more tense we are, the greater the probability that every little thing will bother us. On the other hand, the more relaxed we are, the less likely we are to get tense about events and issues. Also the more tension we have, the more likely we are to absorb the tension of others around us. When we are relaxed we can let their tension pass through us and remain unaffected.

Thus what we have today is a society of tense human beings walking around, each building on the others' tension, each releasing his tension on the other, spreading it around everywhere he goes.

This is, of course, very unpleasant, especially when you walk into an office and ask for some information and the employee bites your head off, because he has just been chewed out by his boss, who is upset about his daughter who disagrees with him about everything, and who is unhappy because her boyfriend is not interested in her anymore.

Meditation is a way of releasing on a daily basis the tension building up in us. In this way we can return daily to our natural peaceful state of body and mind, rather than build up tension from day to day. Thus we avoid many illnesses, problems and conflicts with others. Meditation offers society more relaxed, healthy, peaceful and clear- minded human beings.

7. LACK OF SELF-CONTROL - There is very little will-power or self-control left in people today. They can seldom manage to carry out their inner decisions such as to lose weight, stop smoking, control their emotions or develop a daily discipline. Gone are the days when people had the self-control to fast before the various spiritual holidays.

People have become slaves to their desires, and thus slaves to their senses and the distractions. We are not free to make a decision and carry it out. We have many voices in us. One part of us makes a decision to improve our lives and the various other parts of our selves distract us into following their own desires. There is no master voice to put order to our inner house. Without self-control, an individual can do nothing in his life. He will be a robot, a slave controlled by his various momentary impulses. He will never achieve his goals. His word means nothing. He may say that he will be there at a certain time, or that his product will be ready on a certain date, but because he cannot control his energies, he fails to do so. You cannot believe or trust a man with no self-control. He is neither a good soldier, nor a good employee and, of course, a very dangerous employer or leader of any kind. He is also not a very good parent.

Meditation is the process of learning to control the mind - the most difficult task on earth. We have gone to the moon and penetrated deep into the mysteries of subatomic particles, but we have made zero progress in understanding and controlling our minds. A man with self-control is the most precious gem that one can offer to society. He is like a diamond among pieces of carbon. But those pieces of carbon also can be formed into diamonds through various techniques of self-control such as fasting, prayer, vows and meditation.

A FEW CAN HELP MANY THROUGH MEDITATION

Thus it seems likely, from this short hypothetical analysis of the question, that meditation has much to offer society. And, in fact, in one study done in the small state of Rhode Island in America, they found that divorce, the incidence of cancer and crime rates dropped considerably when the percentage of the population, which meditated, reached 1%. It would be a wonderful service to society if those in power would start to make meditation more available to the members of society through TV and Radio documentaries, and programs in schools, and government and private agencies.

CHAPTER 4

PRACTICAL DETAILS CONCERNING MEDITATION

Just as with any other activity or process, meditation has a preparation, a process and an ending. This is true at least as long as we are not enlightened and our hours of meditation differ from our other waking hours. Let us discuss our preparation.

THE SPACE YOU SELECT

Meditation can be done in absolutely any place where our body is safe from apparent dangers. You can meditate in your bedroom, living room, kitchen, even in your bathroom if there is no better place. You can also meditate in a bus, a plane, boat or car, as long as you are not driving, of course. You can meditate in nature, in valleys, on mountaintops, at the seashore. All places are acceptable.

Perhaps, not all places will offer you the same conditions or the same results. Some places may offer you more peace or greater inclination to moving inwards towards the center of your mind. This is especially important for the beginner. As one develops more experience, his environment plays a less important role. Just as one who is learning to drive, needs a specially protected environment for his first trials, a person who is a beginner in meditation will benefit from a suitable environment.

We suggest that in the beginning you use the same room and the same space daily. That space will gradually become associated with the process of meditation and turning inward, and when you sit there, you will naturally become absorbed in that process. Each space tends to absorb the vibrations of the activity which takes place there. Thus a bar develops certain particular vibrations which are different from those of a church, or your living room, or a quiet place in nature. Select then the quietest place in your home; the place in which you feel most comfortable and are less likely to be disturbed by others or by their activities.

Since it is beneficial to have a window slightly open for oxygen, be sure that you are not sitting with your back to the draft. Place your face to the draft. You may or may not want to create an altar in this space. It is not necessary. You can meditate perfectly well without it, but some feel that it helps them to create a personal altar with a candle and some incense. Some who are religiously inclined, feel even better when they add an icon of their personal focus according to their religion and occasionally flowers or fruits of some type.

These physical objects are not at all necessary but are helpful in creating a more spiritual atmosphere for those who have such tendencies. As tradition has it, it is best to sit facing East. Others would have us sit towards the sun, wherever it may be. I would suggest that these are of lesser importance than your inner feelings. Sit in the direction, which suits you best. Some prefer towards a window, others towards a wall. Let your inner self guide you. You do not need to be limited once you choose. You can experiment in the beginning in order to find the place and orientation which suits you best. And once you have established this, you are always free to change it when something within you guides you to do so.

BE ALONE WHEN YOU MEDITATE

It is better to be alone when you meditate, unless whoever else is in the room is also meditating with you. Let your door be closed so that some one does not «happen» in while you are sitting there. It is best not to keep pets in the room with you. They are attracted by your peaceful vibration and have the tendency to sit next to you or even upon you. This is disturbing for our meditation.

The Art of Meditation

Remove the telephone jack from its plug if you are alone so that you are not disturbed during the process of your concentration. If others are at home with you, inform them that you will be concentrating or relaxing (whichever they will understand and respect more easily) for 20 minutes and that, if someone calls, to take his /her name and telephone number so that you can call later when you finish.

Why all these precautions? Being disturbed in the process of this concentration is like being disturbed from a sleep. It shocks your system and creates a temporary sense of imbalance. You will recover, of course, and no great harm will be done. But why not establish the optimum conditions whenever this is possible? When it is not possible to create such conditions, then let us learn to concentrate even in the most difficult situations. It is to our own benefit.

COMMUNICATE WITH YOUR FAMILY
ABOUT WHAT YOU WANT TO DO

Quite often when one starts out a new activity other members of the family feel threatened and sometimes fearful that their loved one is changing into something different from them. Some associate this with a retreating from life, or some weird, unnatural, secret activity. Some associate it with magic or with becoming some type of «walking vegetable» without interest in the family or one's responsibilities. Some family members feel left out and even jealous that we have an activity which does not include them (at least for the time being). Some just do not like to think that a family member will be closing himself off in a room alone without everyone else understanding what he is actually doing. Some believe that meditating means a change in religion.

In the case that there is some confusion or reaction in the family concerning this new activity, it is best to call them together or speak to them one by one, whichever you find most effective, and explain to them what exactly you are doing and why it is important for you to do this, and why you would be very grateful for their cooperation. Explain to them that this is no other religion. That you will not be leaving them or neglecting your responsibilities to the family. That you are experimenting with this method of inner concentration which has been proven over thousands of years to improve one's health, inner peace, mental clarity, productivity and creativity. Read to them some of the scientific studies that have been made in the last years on the results of meditation. Show them this because you want to help them feel less fearful and reactive towards the decision to try this out in your life, and **not because you want to prove that you are right or that they should also meditate. That is their decision, not yours.**

Explain to them that you believe that this method of inner concentration will help you to become a better person, more peaceful, more loving, more democratic, more able to consider the needs of others, which means that you will be a better member of this family and they will benefit from your changes. Explain that you are making an experiment and that all of the family can help in making the conclusions about its effect on you after some months have passed.

Most important of all, listen to their thoughts, fears and questions concerning what you are doing. Allow them to express what they are feeling. Do not be hurt by sly remarks, sarcasm or criticism. These are natural consequences to be experienced when you have decided to do something different from the majority. This is your test concerning your own self-confidence and self-acceptance. Any reactions that you receive from others are nothing more than reflections of your own self-doubt or fear of rejection.

Once you are very clear and sure that what you are doing is for everyone's best and you overcome the fear of criticism or rejection, you will notice that all will accept and, eventually, perhaps even participate in your new activity.

This does not mean that you need to speak unnecessarily about this. Communicate only when you sense that the others have a problem. Do not be ostentatious about this, or try to convert the others. You will simply be creating problems for yourself.

The Art of Meditation

THE BODY

You can choose between a variety of sitting positions for your meditation. In all positions the spine should be as straight as possible. In most cases it is preferable not to allow the back to rest backwards on some surface. It is impossible for the spine to simultaneously be supported by a wall or a chair and also to be absolutely straight. This does not mean that we should never allow our back to rest on some type of support while meditating. It simply means that we should sit as long as we can without any support so that our back muscles can develop strength so that we can eventually sit for long periods of time without support.

If, as beginners, we find that we are focusing more on our pain or discomfort than on our chosen object of concentration, then we will obviously allow our back to rest backwards on some type of surface, keeping it however as straight as possible in this supported position. When we use a back support of some type, we can keep the spine straighter when we place a small pillow or folded towel in the small of the back to straighten it.

You can choose from a variety of positions for your legs and can change position occasionally at first if they become a problem. The classic position is the half lotus, a crossed legged position in which the left heel is placed underneath the perineum, and the right foot placed upon the left thigh. This is usually easier if one places a pillow under the buttocks raising the level of the pelvis. One must be careful, however, to respect one's knees and not put them under great stress by sitting for long periods of time in this position without the proper gradual preparation of the knees, hips and other joints. Otherwise you could create serious knee or hip problems for yourself. If your body is sufficiently limber try this position out, but use good judgment, and listen to your body concerning how long you can sit in this position without stressing your joints.

Another sitting position is to simply sit cross-legged without placing one foot on the other thigh. It is, however, more difficult to keep the spine straight in this position. Sitting on a pillow will help. Still another possibility is to sit on one's knees «Japanese style». If this is not comfortable, a pillow can be placed under the buttocks or under the ankles, whatever makes you most comfortable. For those who experience discomfort in this position there are small «seiza benches» which have a slight forward tilt and serve very well for sitting on one's knees for meditation. Some of those who have problems with their knees find the seiza bench a solution because much less pressure is put on the knee joint.

A chair is a perfectly acceptable solution for whoever prefers it or finds other sitting positions uncomfortable. When using a chair let all of your joints, ankles, knees, and hips form right angles with each other and the spine be as straight as possible without using the back of the chair. If after some time you are disturbed by the discomfort of sitting without support very gently ease yourself back in the chair, and if it helps, place a small pillow in the small of the back in order to keep the spine straight.

PAIN AND DISCOMFORT

Whenever we try to keep the body in a position to which it is not accustomed it is natural for the muscles involved to react with discomfort or pain. In addition to this we may have various problems with our bodies which produce pain while we are attempting to focus on our chosen object of concentration. In such cases it is best not to change our position with the first «wave» of discomfort or pain - for they actually come in waves. If we ignore the first wave, it will subside and no harm will come to us.

We can learn in this way to become the detached observer, witness to the phenomenon of pain or discomfort. By being able to watch and not react to the first waves of pain we gain the ability to be detached from discomfort on both the physical and emotional level in our daily life. This allows us to function effectively in conditions which would otherwise be impossible for us. It also helps us detach our consciousness from the illusion of the body and its various phenomena. The same goes for the mind later on. We can also become detached from the phenomena of the mind. We will look at this point in more detail later on.

Thus when there is discomfort, just watch it. Imagine that it belongs to someone else, that you are observing something separate from your self. You will find that it will diminish greatly or disappear altogether. At times when a pain is becoming increasingly louder in its expression we can focus on it and allow our consciousness to become immersed in it rather than avoiding it or rejecting or resisting it. Allow yourself to feel it to its fullest and accept it as it is without resistance. You will be amazed that often this will cause it to disperse and disappear.

When your pain is being caused by your position and not by some other bodily factor, and you feel that you have observed enough «waves», then allow your body to change position with the least possible disturbance to your concentration. Do this with special care if you are meditating with others so that your movement does not disturb them. Continue your concentration until your time is up or you feel that you have completed that cycle of concentration.

WHAT TIME IS BEST AND FOR HOW LONG?

Any time is fine for meditation. The stomach should be empty, however. Thus it is best to meditate in the morning before eating or at least three hours after a meal. Of course, if someone eats only some fruit, he will need to wait less time.

Although meditation is beneficial at all hours, some hours are considered to be more conducive for a deeper inner contact. These hours are just before sunrise and just after sunset. If you cannot manage to be free for meditation at these times, then do it whenever you can during the day. It is best to meditate the same time each day. This creates an inner habit and the mind prepares for this inner focus because it is used to doing it at that time (in the same way that the stomach prepares to digest just before the hour it has been accustomed to receive food).

The duration of the meditation for a beginner is about 20 minutes at a time, twice a day if possible. This duration should be kept for about a year before increasing it significantly. It doesn't matter if occasionally we meditate for 15 minutes or 30 minutes, but our average should be about 20 minutes. Gradually over time with the help of a teacher, or someone more experienced, we can increase the time if we feel the need.

Avoid making a habit of cutting the meditation short. It is difficult to go deeply without sitting the full 20 minutes. Ten or fifteen minutes are barely enough time for the various tensions of the day to get released so that we can have a deeper concentration.

YOUR DECISION AND DISCIPLINE

Making the choice to meditate is in all probability the smartest decision you have ever made. It will totally change your life for the better. But making the decision is not enough. You will need to keep a vigilant watch over your mind and the various other voices, which exist there, which can undermine your clarity on this subject.

It is important to understand and be clear about why you want to meditate. Your reasons should be free from two basic emotional traps or games that we play constantly with our selves and others. One game is that of GOOD and BAD. In this game we say to ourselves that we are «good» when we meditate or when we do not over eat or when we do our exercises or when we help others and that we are «bad» when we do the opposite of these. This creates a vicious circle of feelings such as pride and superiority, when we do «what we are supposed to do» in order to be «Good» and guilt, fear, inferiority and self-rejection, when we do not do «what we are supposed to do». This attitude is not conducive to real meditation or real spiritual growth.

The other game that we play is that of PARENT and CHILD. We play both these roles within ourselves. The parent within us tells the child within us that we **must** meditate, that it is our duty and if we do not do it we are not acceptable. The child within us feels suppressed and, unhappy rather than joyful, when it sits to meditate. It sees its meditation and other very pleasant and beneficial disciplines as a **duty** that must be done in order to accept himself. This, like the previously mentioned motive, is not an effective one for meditating or employing other forms of spiritual disciplines.

These are not reasons to meditate. If we start out with these reasons then we will very likely feel restricted and suppressed and soon give up this so beneficial and pleasant experience because of these games we are playing with ourselves.

WHAT THEN ARE SOME REASONS TO MEDITATE?

One reason would be because I believe that it will help me to find inner peace or clarity of mind. I may believe that I will be able to manifest more of my mental and creative abilities. I may want to relax my mind and learn to concentrate. I may seek to get free from thought forms that obstruct my happiness and effectiveness in my daily life. I may want to experience my real self, which is beyond the body and mind. I may want to come into deeper contact with God and feel that bliss of union with Him or with my inner self. Perhaps I simply enjoy the feeling of freedom from thoughts, time and space. I may like the feeling of peace, unity and love for others that I feel after meditating. I may enjoy the increased awareness of colors, sounds and textures that I experience after meditation. I may want to use the inner focus as a place from which to create positive thought-forms about myself and others. I may want to get free from this illusionary world of time and space and experience the inherent unity behind this phenomenon of material illusion. I may simply want to cure myself of an illness or prevent any problems that might possibly occur as a result of accumulating stress. Or I may just want to be able to do my job with greater clarity, creativity and productivity.

Be clear about why you want to meditate. Be clear also so as to have discrimination when you hear the voices of your habits which prefer for you to do what you were used to doing at that hour, which you have now chosen for meditation. There are the voices of our desires that demand satisfaction and are not interested in our sitting quietly and our emptying our minds of them. There is the voice of laziness that prefers not to make an effort. There is the voice of the inner rebel that wants no discipline, no timetable.

You will have to be clear at these moments so as not to be distracted by these other voices which can easily dissuade you from what you really want within you and what is for our highest benefit - and consequently for the benefit of all those other subpersonalities who live within you.

CHAPTER 5

HOW DO WE MEDITATE?

There are as many ways to meditate as there are ways to dance. The result of each dance is the same - you come closer to and communicate with your partner - in the case of meditation - the soul. But each dance flows differently. Each meditation spontaneously expresses the inner music of the moment, which is never the same.

There are, however, some basic steps, which can take you to that union more efficiently. Although these steps can be described and understood intellectually through reading, this dance is one of the whole being; body, mind, emotions and spirit and can only be learned through experience.

It is also helpful to have guidance from someone who knows the dance and has performed it often. These explanations and guidelines will not be enough for most to begin meditation. Most would do well to seek out someone who has had experience as a meditation instructor.

Once, however, you know the basic steps, then it is up to you to improvise on your own, to learn how to glide like the seagull on the currents of your mind. This mastery will come only through regular daily practice. It is as simple as any other dance. All you have to do is to let go and flow.

Here are some general guidelines, which apply independently of the type of meditation you are learning or using.

1) **Body Position**

As we have already mentioned, the body should be in erect **and relaxed stillness.** The spine must be perpendicular to the Earth. The stomach should be empty. A check should be made of each part of the body that it is relaxed and not tense. Check especially the muscles in the abdomen, neck and shoulders.

If sitting on a chair, the feet are flat on the ground, muscles relaxed. If on the floor or rug, legs are crossed in either lotus or half lotus position (this enables the back to remain straight for longer periods of time). A pillow under the buttocks is helpful. The arms are resting on the knees with the palms relaxed opened upwards. Check the shoulders to make sure they hang naturally and are not tensed upwards. In this position the body will be of the least distraction and you will not be weighed down by discomforts and tenseness.

2) **Movement of Breath**

The rhythm and volume of the breath are directly related to our state of mind. A nervous or anxious mind produces irregular breathing rhythms. Anger generates rapid, short breaths. In a relaxed state our breath is deep, rhythmical and longer in duration. We may reverse this process and affect the mind through breath control.

Relax the abdominal muscles and begin breathing with the diaphragm in long even inhalations and exhalations. Nothing should be forced. Do only what comes easily and naturally. If you are not used to breathing with the diaphragm, then spend some minutes each day on your back practicing this breath. It will develop gradually. With time the breath will be longer in duration; slowly and evenly in and out. There is no need to retain the breath. Keep an even relaxing rhythm. (In later stages of meditation you may be guided to retain breath. This is not suggested in the beginning).

It will be necessary to start the process consciously at first with a certain control over the mechanism of breathing. After a while this

The Art of Meditation

will take place automatically as you sit down to meditate or relax, just as you are now breathing automatically without thinking.

Eventually you will want to learn the "alternate breath" technique in which we alternatively breathe in through one nostril (holding the other closed) and then exhale out of the opposite nostril (now hold the other one closed). This technique is described in our book "SELF THERAPY", but you would do well to have an experienced yoga teacher check your position and method.

This technique is a very powerful means of creating balance and harmony in the bioenergy and the nervous systems. Scientific tests have shown that breathing only through the right nostril stimulates the left hemisphere of the brain, and that breathing only through the left nostril stimulates the right hemisphere. Thus, by breathing alternatively through one and then the other nostril, we create a harmonious balance in the nervous system.

This corroborates the intuitive findings of the practitioners of yoga, thousands of years ago, who named the technique "that which cleans the energy channels". The energy channels are directly related to the flow of nerve energy and the quality of mental impulses. Alternate breathing harmonizes, purifies and calms this bioenergy flow in the body and the mind, thus creating an excellent inner atmosphere for meditation.

Concerning the breathing ratio and its gradual evolution, we suggest that you refer to our book "SELF THERAPY" or to an instructor or person experienced in guiding others in breathing techniques or in meditation. Until you find such a person you can work with one of these simple ratios using whichever suits you most.

a) Equal Breath (1:1) in which the inhalation and exhalation are equal in duration.

b) Double Exhalation (1:2) in which the exhalation is double the duration of the inhalation. (For example, if you count to 3 inhaling, then you count to 6 exhaling. Or 4 inhalation and 8 exhalation).

c) Triangle Breathing (1:1:1) in which the inhalation, the retention and the exhalation are all equal in duration.

d) Square Breathing (1:1:1:1) in which the inhalation, the retention (with lungs full), the exhalation and the suspension (with lungs empty) are all equal in duration.

Choose any of these ratios which suits you best and breath slowly, counting silently within your mind in order to keep one of these ratios. Have someone check you if you have any doubts.

Perform this conscious, slow, rhythmic breathing for about five minutes as a prelude to your meditation. After this five minutes of harmonizing your energy, leave the breath to continue on its own without your conscious intervention.

PRAYER OR INVOCATION

Although it is not absolutely necessary, most meditators prefer to make an invocation, or small prayer, as an introduction into their meditation. These words mentally spoken give a spiritual direction to the mind and lead the mind into a more spiritually oriented state. These words could be a traditional prayer such as the Lord's Prayer or the Great Invocation. Or they could be whatever you sincerely feel at that moment.

You could simply express your purpose for meditating. You could ask for help in overcoming your mind. You could express some beliefs that you would like to strengthen. You could pray for help in your growth process. You could send light or love to people who have need for help. You could pray for world peace. You could ask for protection in your life. Or you could simply resign yourself to the Divine Will asking God to do with you, your body and your life whatever serves His purposes best. You could ask to become a pure instrument of the Divine Will, a source of love, light and harmony for all. You could ask for purification of whatever hinders your manifestation of your inner love and beauty. You could ask for nothing and just express your gratitude for all that you have, including your problems and difficulties which offer you so many opportunities for growth and evolution. Or you could simply have an informal conversation with God, as you would with any other close friend, explaining how you are doing and expressing your feelings.

Find your own way to enter into meditation. You do not have to use the same way each time. You do not have to do this at all, but I believe you will find it enjoyable and beneficial. Try it and decide for yourself.

THE PROCESS OF MEDITATION

There are hundreds of systems of meditation but the ultimate result of each is the same. They are all different ways to sink into the sea of consciousness, gliding through more and more subtle depths, along the stream of upcoming inner movements, coming eventually to the source of that sea - the point of pure consciousness - the void. The sea is the same, the source is the same, and the result is the same. Only the ways to travel are different.

Basically that which makes one system different from another is the "object of consciousness" and not the process of concentrating. The process of meditation in all systems of meditation is the same. That which differs is **what we choose to concentrate on -** we will call this the **object of consciousness** or object for short.

Our consciousness in its purest state is without any object. It is free, unlimited, undefined, unattached to any particular form, result or event. It is the eternal witness for all forms and events. It is divine and free. (In order to understand this more clearly we suggest that you read our book "**UNIVERSAL PHILOSOPHY**", as there is not sufficient space here to go into details concerning this subject).

Our consciousness is like the empty television screen or movie screen that is lit up but without any forms appearing on it. It contains all and infinite possibilities because any form whatsoever can appear upon it. The form that appears on it will be the object of consciousness and when that changes the object will have changed.

Thus in meditation we choose an object of concentration which helps us to get free from the incessant, involuntary and uncontrolled flow of thoughts, feelings, desires and impulses which flow through our mind disturbing our inner peace and clouding our clarity of vision.

By focusing on this "object" we flow through the layers of the mind into the depths of our consciousness. Some objects of consciousness, which are suggested by the major schools of meditation are; the breath, a word with spiritual meaning (mantra), an inner image, an inner light, an inner sound, the body energy, body sensations, the witness - our consciousness itself or the void. We will discuss each in detail later on in this book.

In each case, the light, the word, the breath, being the witness, the image, the sound, the body awareness or the bioenergy; each serves as an object of consciousness (a dance partner). By concentrating on, or sensing, this object of consciousness we use it as a type of submarine with which to make our descent through the gross levels of the mind into the more subtle vibrational essence which is the true nature of our eternal being.

Each journey we make into the calmness of our soul brings us one step closer to experiencing that same peace in our daily life. It is as if we are dropping anchor to the solid ocean bottom so that we are not tossed around so easily by the winds and waves of life. With time we grow more calm, more centered, more relaxed. It is as if we are building a direct pipeline to the spring of fresh creative energy at the bottom. We grow more intuitive, more creative - more alive.

The specifics of your meditation will depend on your teacher and his preferred technique. Hopefully it will be the technique that is suitable for you. The only way to know is to practice it daily for **at least six months.**

You may find that, as the years go by, you will be attracted to other techniques. Or you may stick with the same one throughout your life. Ultimately, it makes no difference - because if you are sincere, serious and regular - any technique will take you there. In the end

The Art of Meditation

you will make your own way. It is best, however, not to change your object of consciousness.

It must be understood that no two people will experience meditation in the same way. There is no use in comparing meditative experience. Although the place we are moving towards is the same, we are all starting from different places and will logically travel through different waters to get there.

Some people will have visions, others will see lights, others will hear sounds, some will have pains, some will have realizations, body feelings, smells, warmth, cold and some will see, hear and feel nothing. Each experience is as valid as the next. The person who has visions is no better off than the one who sees nothing.

Furthermore, no one person will have exactly the same meditative experience twice. So it is useless to search after past meditative pleasures. There is never any benefit to try to have experiences described to you by others. In fact, in meditation, there is really no value in trying or searching after anything. Just let go and glide like the seagull, dancing with your object. Some good advice, I heard one time was, "Don't meditate - let yourself be meditated".

HOW TO MEDITATE

We still haven't discussed how to meditate. As I have mentioned, this would be best learned from an experienced meditator. But there are some helpful hints no matter what method you choose.

Having placed the body in the right position and breath in proper rhythm, you can begin to take one of the possible "dance partners" as your object of consciousness.

Begin to focus on the object. Do no force your concentration. Be gently focused, amused with it as you would be focused on an interesting TV program. When we force our mind to concentrate, it reacts as would an unruly child. It has been said that the "mind is like a wild drunken monkey stung by a bee". You can imagine how much such a monkey would jump and move around. The more you force it, the more it will react.

On the other hand, if you leave your mind completely free, you will never learn to guide and control it so as to get free from it. Most beginner meditators have a tendency to try too hard. So let your concentration be natural and gentle like watching a program which interests you. You have full concentration without force or effort.

The mind will become attracted to other thoughts, feelings, and desires. It will think about the past and program the future. It will create complicated dialogues, scenes and situations as it focuses on whatever it is concerned about. At times it will be overcome with images and sounds which seem totally unrelated to yourself and your interests.

Every time we discover that the mind has left the "object", we gently with love, patience and understanding bring it back to the object. It will leave again. Again with patience, again with **love,** again with **understanding** we bring our mind back to the object. This may happen hundreds of times in our 20 minutes of "concentrating". Even after a hundred times, we forget the previous hundred and again with patience, love, understanding and **perseverance** bring our mind to the object of concentration.

You will begin to experience a relaxation of body and mind systems and will commence sinking into the mind. Thoughts will come, and sounds outside you and bodily discomforts will bring you to the surface of the mind, thinking again. When this happens it is absolutely self defeating to worry or become frustrated or feel that you cannot meditate. This is a perfectly normal part of the meditation. Just accept that you have been seduced by your thoughts or other distractions. Let go of the thoughts and let go of any feelings of failure and simply begin to dance with your object again. Naturally place your attention on the object and let the process begin again.

This requires very fine balance of control and letting go, which will come with time. The extreme of forcing the mind to concentration so that the mind defies relaxation through its own intense effort is

The Art of Meditation

useless. The other extreme of allowing random thoughts for a half-an-hour is an equal waste of time..

It is a dance of **controlled letting** go or **spontaneous concentration**, which will develop gradually. Whenever you find yourself distracted, simply relax and begin again as if for the first time.

Thoughts and other inner impulses like sounds, images, pains, sensation of temperature, feelings etc. are all, for the most part, the expression of released tensions or energies which have been previously stored in the mind and body. The process of meditation begins to untie these stresses and release these energies so that they may float to the surface in the form of thoughts, images, pain, heat, etc., and be released.

So we must allow them a certain room for expression, especially in the beginning. Do not hold on to them and do not try to stop them. Simply feel that you are an empty vessel and allow them to pass through you. Watch impartially and begin to place your attention on your object again.

With time and practice the overall content of thoughts and distractions in meditation will diminish - although there will always be cycles of more thought consuming meditations. They should be accepted as necessary stress-releasing experiences that make the deeper meditations more possible.

Having moved through the levels of stress we come to the dance of the soul. This is the dance which takes place upon one's eventual arrival at the point where the object of consciousness becomes so subtle - so vibrational - so pure - that everything becomes still. In other words, after some time of dancing with the object, a certain stillness will take command, in which not only will the thoughts disappear, but also the dance partner. The object is no longer our dance partner, no longer the object of consciousness.

The object of consciousness now is consciousness itself, our soul. The manifestations or symptoms of this state are subjective to the individual - a sense of expansion (no space) - a sense of eternity (no time) - a sense of complete stillness (the void). There is often a feeling of bliss.

Often, especially at first, this experience is so unusual that we immediately become overjoyed about it; or fearful of it; and are hence no longer in it. We think, "Now I am transcending - Hey, I 'm doing it - this is beautiful"; and we ride these wonderful thoughts right back up to the surface again. For some, the absolute stillness and lack of familiarity becomes so terrifying that we rush to the surface gasping for anything familiar to fill our consciousness with.

Then we begin with the "object" again continuing until we feel our time is up. With experience we will be able to accept the normality of this state of pure being and sustain it for longer periods of time. Let the meditation go on as it will for whatever time it feels comfortable.

At first it may be useful to check the length of time, so that you begin to create an inner alarm clock which you can set when your time is limited. As we have already mentioned, a reasonable schedule for the first years is 20 minutes twice a day. Once in the morning before the daily activities and again before the evening meal seems to be a popular rhythm among meditators. Always wait a few minutes after ending the meditation before getting up. Your metabolism, will have dropped and it might be a shock to the system to exert yourself immediately. Let your activity grow slowly.

The most important suggestion to a person starting meditation is BE REGULAR. If you lack discipline you will make up any excuse - time, noise, no space etc. There is no such thing as lack of time - there is only a lack of priority and motivation. The day has 24 hours. We are talking about a total of 20 to 40 minutes.

Once you have disciplined yourself, it's not a tragedy if you miss one here or there. But do not let missing a meditation become a habit. Some will be able to find time only once a day. If this is the case, at least be regular with this once a day.

The Art of Meditation

THE PROCESS OF UN-STRESSING

Occasionally, one may feel a bit unsettled or uncomfortable after a meditation. This will happen at times when a large amount of inner stress has been released and is still in the process of leaving the system. One solution is to sit or lie down for a while with your attention on the parts of the body where you feel the most sensitivity, tension or pain. Relax and allow your attention to float onto the next blocked part of the body. Soon the tension will disappear, and you will feel fine again.

We have already briefly mentioned this process of un-stressing. As it is a common experience to many **but not all** beginners, let us discuss it a little further. Not being able to deal consciously with every stress, with every event, or with every feeling of fear, hurt, injustice, pain, guilt or rejection we tend to hide these feelings in our subconscious mind. This allows us to deal **somewhat** effectively with our present needs and responsibilities without being overwhelmed by these negative feelings. This, however, is something like sweeping the dust under a rug so that we do not see it and so that no one else sees it. Although it does not show, the dust is there.

Another example would be that of a house in which there is a fire in the bedroom. Imagine that you live in a house in which there is a long corridor between the living room and your bedroom where you have also stored all of your valuables and whatever is important to you. Imagine also that one day you find that there is a fire in the bedroom, but that you do not feel that you have the ability to handle this fire at the present and you close the door and ignore it and pretend that there is no fire. Gradually the fire burns its way into the corridor and still you ignore it and pretend that it does not exist because it pains you to realize, or believe or admit that it exists. You feel ashamed of this fire and it makes you feel inferior, weak, hurt and out of control. Thus we pretend that there is no fire and that all is fine. But how long can one go on pretending before the fire gradually burns its way into all the rooms of the house destroying it entirely?

The bedroom and the corridor represent our subconscious mind which have many valuable resources for living our lives and which are also a connecting link with our inner or higher self. The fire is the sum total of negative feelings, which we cannot handle and which we keep locked in the subconscious.

As long as these unresolved feelings are locked within us, they will destroy our nervous system, immune system and endocrine system from the inside just as the fire will destroy the house from within. These feelings will destroy more than our health, however. They will undermine our feelings towards ourselves, our feelings and relationships with others, our success in our various endeavors and, most of all, our happiness and inner peace.

Thus, it is absolutely essential that we not be afraid to open that door to the subconscious and begin to allow that fire to evaporate out into the atmosphere. We can then remove the debris which exists within and which fuels that "fire". This process of letting these subtle tensions out is called **un-stressing**. Each person experiences it in some way. We have already mentioned some possibilities; pain, discomfort, unpleasant emotions, greater sensitivity towards others' negative feelings or behavior, feelings of fear, or lack of control. We may feel more cold or heat in our bodies. We may find that we have a greater need for sleep or have some sleepless nights at first.

No importance should be given to these and other symptoms of stress release. If you have some doubts, however, consult your doctor or meditation instructor. Most meditative experiences in these first days are the result of energies being released from the subconscious. Some experiences may be pleasant and others unpleasant. Our attitude should be to witness both the unpleasant and pleasant with the same detachment. Do not give a lot of importance to various visions, even if they have spiritual content. They are not the goal of our meditation. Observe them with an accepting attitude. Also try to have the same accepting attitude towards any unpleasant experiences.

These experiences usually last only a few weeks or months at the most. If they continue on beyond this period of time, seek guidance. There are some things however which you can do in order to create a state of balance during this process of change.

GUIDELINES FOR SAFE PASSAGE

1. Do not meditate more than 20 minutes at a time twice a day. If the symptoms of un-stressing are too much, then cut back to once a day until they are reduced. If they still continue, cut the period of time to 10 minutes once a day. If they still persist, then stop meditating and seek guidance from an experienced meditation instructor. Do not let these words of caution frighten you. Less than 1% of the people who start meditating have such reactions. They are never actually harmful to the person, but can be annoying and disturbing to him and his family. In the end, however, he will be "cleaned" inwardly with much more mental clarity. He will be grateful that he has passed through this process. For safety' s sake, however, we prefer that people not push this process of un-stressing to an imbalanced state so that they can continue to conscientiously perform their responsibilities towards themselves, their families and the society in which they live. Thus, this is not cause for alarm, but simply for logic, discrimination and balance.

2. Do not seek after experiences. Many beginners, because of their self-doubt and need for some type of proof or self-verification seek after "experiences" in meditation. They feel that a meditation is successful if they see the Christ, or lights, or colors, or shake about or cannot function in "the material world" after their meditation. This has absolutely nothing to do with meditation. Meditation is a process in which we come into harmony with all levels of creation, including the material world, our families, our work and our responsibilities. Seeking after experiences, and talking about them, is just another social game that we play in order to gain recognition from others. We try to prove that we are more "spiritually advanced". Even if we have such experiences, it is best not to talk about them to others. Let them be our inner treasure, our inner communion with the higher levels of consciousness within ourselves (if in fact that is what these experiences are all about). In many cases they are simply energies which are being released and thought forms which are manifesting. That does not mean that real spiritual experiences, in which we have contact with higher spiritual planes of reality, do not exist. It simply means that few of these first experiences are such, and that even if they are, it is best not to talk about them, unless we want some type of guidance concerning them from our spiritual guide.

3. Learn to analyze your emotions and the beliefs which create them. Learn to become the witness of your emotional mechanisms and to be able to function independently of them when they are extremely negative. Learn to communicate your feelings clearly so that you do not need to suppress what is going on within you. I would suggest that you read the book "Psychology of Happiness" as a guide to putting your emotions in order before beginning to meditate.

The process of the stress release is similar to releasing the pressure from a pressure cooker. When we look at the cooker we cannot tell if there is pressure in it or how much pressure might be in it. If we touch the weight on the top lifting it to one side a small amount of steam will escape. This is stress release. If we take the cap off completely while there is great pressure, then we will have a small and probably unpleasant explosion of steam. This occurred because we did not act intelligently. We removed the cap completely without allowing the energy to escape gradually in small doses.

Thus, one who meditates in small doses, 20 minutes once or twice a day is in no danger. Those who have problems are usually those who overdo it. They are victims of our misled thinking that if 20 minutes is good then 60 minutes is even better.

Be regular and act intelligently.

WHAT TO DO IF YOU EXPERIENCE
INTENSE UN-STRESSING

The following techniques will help you to balance and calm your energy if in spite of all these guidelines you in fact are in the 1% of those who have some serious problem.

1. Have frequent contact with water. Take two or three showers a day. In addition wash your hands, face, neck and if possible your feet frequently throughout the day. Let the temperature be that with which you feel most comfortable, but finish with a little cold water.

2. Stop meditating until you feel balanced again.

3. Practice deep relaxation techniques with positive imagery. (Unless these too generate too much energy for you)

4. Walk in nature and let its peace flow into you.

5. Find someone **experienced in bioenergy massage** or spiritual healing techniques to help you balance your energy.

6. Eat whole grains and **avoid sugar, drugs and meat.**

7. Drink **herb teas** that have a **calming** and **balancing** effect.

8. Sleep more if you have the need.

9. Do dynamic exercises rather than static ones.

10. Work with your hands; preferably with plants.

11. Avoid negative stimuli such as movies or TV programs or books that disturb your emotions or create fear.

12. Have warm, affectionate contact with your loved ones.

13. Have faith that all that is happening is exactly what you need for your evolutionary process. Trust in that process and be the witness to whatever is occurring within and without you. You will be much clearer, much freer when this process is over.

14. Engage in various creative activities such as dance, singing, playing a musical instrument etc.

15. Do all of this and simultaneously **seek guidance from your meditation instructor.**

I repeat that these guidelines should not put you off from the idea of meditating. It is like saying that no one should ever drive because 1% of them might have some problems while driving, so that it is better not to go anywhere. If we are intelligent and use our logic, and do not go to extremes, we will have **no problems whatsoever** and we will have a wonderful spiritual journey.

SOME KEY THOUGHTS

1. Meditation is a **natural process** of coming to inner silence.

2. One cannot try to meditate **- let yourself be meditated.**

3. The process is one of **controlled – 'letting go'.**

4. Follow the changes that come from within.

5. All meditative experiences will be different - do not compare.

6. The value of meditation lies in its **harmonizing of body-mind-soul.**

7. Let the **inner silence be a springboard for a creative life.**

8. Accept responsibility for creating your reality.

9. Accept the ego structure - but become liberated from seeking security outside of the soul.

10. Let go of attachments - **identify with the nature of the soul.**

The Art of Meditation

CHAPTER 6

THE POWER OF VIBRATIONS

Meditation is basically a matter of focusing on higher vibrations, which affect and transform the vibrational frequencies of our minds and bodies.

We are affected by the sights and sounds around us. Sounds, smells, sensations, tastes and images enter into our minds through the senses and affect our mental state. These inputs are all various manifestations of vibrations. In fact, all matter, energy and thought are types of gross or subtle vibrations. All of these vibrations exist in the sea of pure consciousness and appear and disappear like waves on the surface of this sea.

Our consciousness, our true self is that pure consciousness through which all these waves or vibrations are waxing and waning. However, because we identify with the body and the mind, we experience the effect of these vibrations on the body and mind. Vibration is the basis of all the manifest world. This fact, which is now being discovered by nuclear physicists, has been considered an obvious truth by the wise for thousands of years.

St. John the Evangelist corroborates this in the opening words of his Gospel. (John 1.1.). "Before the world was created, the **Word** already existed; he was with God, and he was the **same as God.** From the very beginning the Word was with God. Through him, God **made all things;** not one thing in all creation was made without him. The Word was the **source of life,** and this life brought light to mankind. The light shines in the darkness, and the darkness has never put it out".

"This was the real light - the light that comes into the world and shines on all mankind".

This basis of Christian thought is in complete agreement with the Hindu concept of the Holy Sound AUM (AMEN) which is the sound through which creation takes place; through which the divine manifests itself as the physical world. It is the vibration through which spirit projects itself into mind, energy and physical body. It is the one vibration from which all other vibrations, gross and subtle, are born. It represents the ONE, which has temporarily become the many. This ONE primeval vibration is the self-creating, causeless sound flowing out of the silence.

The purpose of our lives is to reunite with the ONE from which we have "apparently" split off. It is this reunion which we are all seeking in our search for happiness through possessions, objects, achievements and relationships. By tuning into, and aligning with, this basic divine vibration, we bring our own personal vibration into closer harmony with the One vibration, which is the cause and basis of all beings. Through concentration on the repetition of various basic vibrations, we shake off the unnecessary ego-centered matter, which dampens our possibility of vibrating in harmony with ourselves and our environment.

The words we hear and speak very much affect our mood, mental state, beliefs, physical health and spiritual progress. The same is true of the light, colors and images with which we surround ourselves. We have all felt the inner joy of feeling the light and warmth of the sun after a number of cold, dark, cloudy days. The sun is the source of life on earth. There is no food, no light, no warmth, no health, no joy or happiness without the sun. It is no wonder that many cultures worship the sun. We may imagine that it is the physical manifestation of the divine, the provider or the life giver.

Darkness represents ignorance, blindness and the lower side of

The Art of Meditation

man. Of course, God is ultimately the creator of (and therefore beyond the duality of) Light **and** Darkness. But most religions and individuals have chosen light as their path towards God.

We say "he is in the Dark" when one does not know the truth. We call a man's weakness his "dark side". Final spiritual realization is called ENLIGHTENMENT, for the inner light is turned on and the individual does not need the external light any more. He knows the truth from within. Light represents wisdom, knowledge and truth.

Pure White Light is one of the more basic Divine Vibrations. Pure White Light is to the visual realm what the AUM is to the audio realm. Just as the AUM differentiates into all sounds, the white light differentiates into all colors.

Thus, in our search for reunion with the ONE , we can use the various colors and sounds, images and melodies as channels to work toward the simplicity and perfect completeness of the white light and AUM which contain within them all possible manifestations.

On a perfectly white wall you have the possibility of creating absolutely any image you desire. If the wall is colored or already has images on it, then you are limited in what you can do. Our true spiritual nature is pure undifferentiated white light. The ego personality is a particular changing pattern of colors and images momentarily projected onto this permanent white background. We can use certain sound and light vibrations to help us tune into the pure Divine vibrations within us.

A candle is often used to symbolize the inner light of wisdom within an individual. Truly, we feel more relaxed, more peaceful in candlelight than we do with electric light. Candles have been used for thousands of years to create a spiritual atmosphere.

Let us now concentrate on the possibilities of sound and how it can create various states of mind and body. Sounds can be gross, or subtle, harmonic or non-harmonic., melodious or non-melodious, stimulating, relaxing, balancing, irritating, healing, uplifting, painful, pleasant, or even fatal as in the case of certain sound weapons which have been developed.

In its highest use, sound can create ecstasy in which the individual loses his awareness of his separate ego-identity, and becomes the music, or the sound vibration. This is the purpose of sacred music and sacred dance. This is the path of letting go of the mind and logic and experiencing God through union with His vibrations. The same may be observed in the musical-dance approach of the Greek Anastenaria of northern Greece, who walk on the hot burning coals after creating an inner concentration through music and dance.

CHANTING

Perhaps the most available method of tuning into the Divine Vibration is through chanting. Chanting, either alone or preferably in groups, has many wonderful benefits on all levels.

1) It helps to release pent up tensions - especially anxiety, fear, and anger, which get locked, physically into the chest and solar plexus area. Chanting "throws out" these tensions and negativities.
2) Chanting gets the bioenergy moving in the body and mind. It breaks down the physical and mental blockages and pumps the energy around the body. There results a corresponding exhilaration.

3) Chanting brings healing vibrations to the various parts of the body and mind. It is now a scientifically proven fact that certain vowel vibrations such as "A,E,U.O,I" and the consonant "M" have healing effects on various organs and parts of the body.

4) Chanting brings about changes in mood towards higher, more joyful, pleasant feelings.

5) When we chant together, we unite our voices in the same harmony, melody and rhythm. This brings us closer together, helping us to overcome mental differences and join our hearts in song. Light represents wisdom, but sound represents love. Sound, words and song, are the medium through which love is expressed.

6) When the vibrations and words used are oriented towards the Divine, then by sympathetic vibration, divine qualities are awakened within us. This is easy to understand. If we hear military marching music, our feelings of national pride and defensiveness are awakened within us. If we hear love music, we feel romantic. If we hear dance music, we want to move and dance. In the same way, if the music is spiritually oriented, then a spiritual mood is awakened within us. The conditioning of our mind will depend on the type of music we listen to and sing.

7) When we allow our heart to get carried away, and overcome our self consciousness, we can rise up into an ecstasy of joy, love and gratitude in which we feel great love for God , all beings and creation itself.

HOW WE USE CHANTING VIBRATIONS FOR SELF-HEALING AND SPIRITUAL GROWTH

Here are some practical hints as to how to get started.

All chanting has its best results when done in a straight-backed position either sitting on the floor or on a chair. When making simple, single-toned sound vibrations, one should take a deep, complete inhalation, using the lungs to their full capacity (without of course, forcing, exaggerating or doing anything unnatural). Then open the mouth and vocal cords fully and let the sound flow out easily, harmoniously, soothingly with the fullness of your being. Don't hold back in hesitation and self-consciousness.

Imagine yourself to be a great opera singer (or a potential one) and let go of any worry about what the others think. As long as no one is sleeping, you will not harm anyone with your pouring forth of your Self through these vibrations. Rather the opposite is true. When you get used to it, and chant in a relaxed and confident way, you will fill the atmosphere with pacifying and harmonizing vibrations, which will completely change the mood of the room and surroundings.

Chanting, in this way, in the same room everyday, creates power in that room. Any sensitive individual who walks into the room will automatically relax and more easily find his inner center. He may not be consciously aware of what is happening, but he is being healed by the vibrations that have become part of the energy of that room.

The vibration flows out full throatedly but peacefully and harmoniously until the lungs are completely emptied and then one takes another complete inhalation and repeats the sound. In this way the exercise also purifies and develops the lungs and bioenergy. The effect of these vibrations is much greater with the eyes closed and the attention directed inwardly. One can start with five repetitions of each sound and then increase slowly doing 7,9,12,15 until one reaches 21 times.

The AUM is broken down into its constituent parts, A,U,M.

1) Start by making the sound AAAAAAAAAAAAA in the manner described above 5 times. The AAAAAA vibration affects the area of the body from the diaphragm to the feet, but it is especially beneficial for the organs of digestion and elimination. While making the sound, one can concentrate on feeling the vibration in the abdomen, or even in the specific organ which needs healing energy.

When the problem is with the kidneys or liver, the sound HA,HA,HA,HA, can be made in a forceful and dynamic way so as to stimulate these organs even more effectively. This HA,HA,HA,HA,HA, can easily eventually become **laughter, which** is perhaps the most healing vibration of all.

2) The sound UUUUUUUUU focus on the area of the chest and neck, having an effect on the lungs and heart.

3) The sound MMMMMMMM vibrates in the area from the neck to the top of the head. It relaxes the nerves of the neck, head and all the nervous system. If one concentrates inside the head there will be a calming effect on the mind. If the ears are closed up with the thumbs, then the effect will be even more dynamic.

4) The AUM can then be chanted in its whole form as the monosyllable OM. Here we can concentrate on God, the unmanifest who lives within us. This is traditionally done 21 times every morning to start the day, but can be done any number of times which suits you.

5) The OM can also be silently concentrated on as a continuous vibration within one's mind. This then becomes a meditation on the "OM" which links us up with the Divine. This is the same sound made in the Greek Orthodox Liturgy by the charters who create the background sound of "OOOOOOOOOOO" while the others chant the Liturgy.

6) As vibration becomes more differentiated it breaks down into rhythm and melody. One can chant these vowels and vibrations freely, allowing the voice to raise and fall in pitch in familiar or self-created melodies and rhythms. This can be a wonderfully energizing and uplifting experience. Just let go of all self-consciousness and make up your own free flowing melodies according to your mood at the moment.

7) As vibration becomes even more concrete, it manifests as words and mantras, which symbolize different qualities, beings and objects in creation. Each word symbolizes what it stands for, and, when used, brings that which it stands for into one's life. Thus the chanting of "LORD HAVE MERCY" will bring the Lord and His Grace into one's life. The word "Alleluia", which means praise to God, can be chanted in a variety of melodies and rhythms. It encompasses the basic vowel sounds, while at the same time inspiring a spiritual focus.

When these chants are accompanied with devotion and visualization of that which the words represent, the inner transformation is even greater. Consider the Greek Orthodox chant **"O, Giver of Light and Salvation, illuminate the garment of my soul"**. If one, while chanting this imagines the Light of the Christ flowing into his body and mind (which are the clothing of his soul), this combination of vibrations, melody, word-symbols, devotion and imagination can create a significant transformation in

The Power of Vibrations

the consciousness of the individual.

Let us let go of our blockages, our fears, our self-consciousness, our "intellectuality" and reserve, and enter into the joyous worlds of vibrations, and chanting. Let us relax our minds and open up our hearts with song, so that love may flow up from the heart into the mind resolving all differences and conflicts between us and the world around us. Let us join together with others in song and experience the Joy and Happiness and Health that we deserve in life.

PRAYER

Prayer too, like chanting, is a powerful means of focusing on higher vibrations in the form of words that seek to describe the Divine and ask for help in communicating with the Divine.

We will discuss Prayer in more detail later on. Let it suffice to understand at this point that:

1. Vibration is the means by which the Unmanifest Absolute becomes manifest in our world of forms, beings and events.

2. Vibration is the means by which we can transcend our low level of perception and thinking and manifest our higher self.

3. Vibration is our telephone connection with the Divine.

4. We can focus on these vibrations on many levels, physically, emotionally, mentally and super-mentally.

CHAPTER 7

CHOOSING AN OBJECT OF CONSCIOUSNESS

ABSOLUTE

I

LOGOS

WORD

I

SOUND   LIGHT

I   I

OM   WHITE

I   I

SYLLABLES   COLORS

I   I

WORDS   FORMS

I   I

PHRASES   IMAGES

I   I

CONCEPTS   OBJECTS

SOUND   **LIGHT**

DEVOTIONAL   &   NONDEVOTIONAL
RELIGIOUS   &   NONRELIGIOUS

The above diagram will help us to understand more clearly the following discussion concerning choosing and working with an object of concentration for our meditation.

In the previous chapter we discussed how the Logos is the means by which the unmanifest becomes manifest. We can see from the above diagram that this happens basically through two channels; through the channels of sound and of light.

Following the channel of sound as means of expression for the universal consciousness, the basic syllable OM (amen) becomes all the syllables, which then are developed into words, then words into phrases, and phrases into sentences which express concepts, concepts which already exist in their unmanifest state in that one universal consciousness.

Through the channel of light, we move from the more subtle to the more concrete through white light, to the spectrum of colors, forms, images, and finally the objects we perceive.

Thus any name, word, concept, color, form or object, which we might choose, for our concentration, will simply be another expression of that one universal being with whom we are trying to reunite.

The fact is that we too are natural projections of this one universal consciousness. We have simply lost the awareness of this truth and our mind experiences separation and alienation from the people and world around us. As a consequence we live in fear and suffering. Through meditation we can begin to experience this oneness with all, and thus oneness with this causal energy of all life.

All objects, including our own body and our personality when concentrated on and experienced at deeper and deeper levels of their existence will lead us to an experience of God, the one being behind all beings.

Although any object will eventually take us there, if we concentrate on it deeply enough and allow our consciousness to follow it through its transformations to its highest level of existence, not all objects are equally as effective, and, of course, not all objects are equally effective to different persons, each with his unique psychosynthesis.

Most schools of philosophy or of meditation declare that their object of meditation is the best and most effective. This is obviously something that will be relative to the individual. All schools and their systems are good and will bring the desired results we are searching for. One does not need to become fanatical in order to benefit from a system. Remember that the **process** of meditation is, for the most part, the same in all schools. The only real difference is the object used for concentration.

These "objects" may include holy words such as the name of Christ for Christians or, if someone is Hindu, the name of Shiva, Krishna or Rama. In some cases we might concentrate on a phrase or prayer focused on this spiritual being such as "Lord Jesus Christ Have Mercy on us". Or it might be some spiritual value such as Love, Peace, Truth, Righteousness, Unity, Acceptance, Faith etc.

Some other school may encourage us to mentally focus on a light (white or colored) and to let the mind become absorbed in that. Others tell us to let this light move around in the body and imagine that it is purifying it.

Another system is to focus on the form of our ideal being, which for Christians would be Christ. We can imagine him in front of us, within us or even "in miniature" within our heart.

Some schools instruct us to focus on an inner sound or inner light, which manifests when we concentrate. Other systems encourage us to focus on the energy centers, feeling the energy in those centers and allowing it to flow more freely within that center and towards the other centers.

Others say that it is best to just be aware of the bodily sensations in general while allowing the awareness to flow from the head to the toes and back again in a continuous circle of awareness. A very old and basic system is to simply watch the incoming and outgoing breath.

Some schools teach their students to concentrate on words that have no connection with a particular form. Two such spiritually charged words are "OM" and "SOHAM". The "OM" is a symbol, which represents the Universal Divine Consciousness, and "Soham" means that "I am that consciousness". Both of these help us to focus on the divine without form.

Other schools teach meditation as the development of positive thought forms, in which we imagine positive realities for our selves and others. This would best be called positive thought projection or visualization and not meditation.

And then there are the schools which suggest that we have no object of consciousness at all but rather that we simply witness whatever comes up in the body or in the mind and release all identification with that, thus letting it disappear. In such a case the object of concentration is our consciousness itself or the void, the emptiness from which all flows forth.

All of these and other objects of consciousness can and will lead us to union with the Divine Consciousness, which is the causal reality behind each of them. Through concentration on them our mind begins to identify with those higher realities and to penetrate through them to their source. In coming into contact with their source, we come into contact with our own source. Throughout this process we begin to experience more and more all of those qualities and benefits, which we mentioned in the earlier chapters of this book.

Most of these objects fall into four basic categories. Refer again to the chart at the beginning of this chapter. Two paths belong to the sound channel and two paths to the light channel.

THE DEVOTIONAL PATH OF SOUND

One path is that of **sound with devotion.** This is similar to the various traditional religious paths. One chooses the name of God, according to his traditional religious upbringing and uses that name as a focus in his meditation. He repeats this name over and over. He has this name and all that it represents steadily in his mind. When his mind wanders elsewhere, he brings it back to this name and remains focused on that.

On this path this concentration might be started with a prayer towards his chosen spiritual focus i.e. Christ for Christians. Or at times this concentration on the name might turn into a prayer or communication with Christ. One may use the phrase, "Lord Jesus Christ Have Mercy On Us". The continual repetition of this prayer will empty the mind until there is nothing else in the mind but this awareness of the presence of Christ and this connection with Him. (Persons of other religious backgrounds will use other names or prayers accordingly).

THE TRANSFORMATION OF THE OBJECT

There is a phenomenon that must be explained at this point. What we are about to explain here holds true for all objects of concentration and not only for that which we are discussing here.

The object of concentration is experienced differently at the various levels of awareness or consciousness. This means that we will experience the object differently at various stages of our meditation, depending on how deep our concentration is and how free we are from the material level of duality. The higher our consciousness rises in the meditation the less concrete, the less physical the object is. It is the same object but perceived from a higher spiritual viewpoint.

A few examples might help here. Imagine that you are looking out at a street scene from the basement of an apartment building. You see very little, your perception is limited to a very small portion of the street. Now imagine that you look at the same scene from the first floor. You see it differently. Now you are on the fourth floor. You see this scene in perspective with a much larger reality. Go up to the twelfth floor and things are quite different again. And if you are in a skyscraper which has 70 floors? How different things are now. The object of your concentration has not changed at all, but our perspective has. You see it from a raised level of perspective. The same holds for the higher spiritual awareness with which you observe the object in your meditation. The "object" has not changed but you perceive it at a higher or deeper level.

Another example is that of ice. Imagine that your "object" is ice. As you focus more deeply on it, it heats up and transmutes into water. Your further concentration heats it up even more and it transforms itself into steam. Focusing even more intensely on it causes it to break up into its composite components, the gases of hydrogen and oxygen and we perceive a completely different reality. Imagine that further concentration caused these gases to expose their ultimate reality, which is energy that has taken the form of matter.

Thus we start with ice and we end up with energy. The "object" is the same. We are simply experiencing this physical object in its most subtle inner reality which is energy.

In the same way, when we focus on the name Christ or love or any of the numerous previously mentioned possible "objects", they begin to transmute in our consciousness into more and more subtle aspects of their inner reality.

Take, for example, a meditation on Christ. We start by focusing on His name or perhaps His Image. Gradually, in the increased awareness of the meditation, we begin to experience Christ not as a man as we are accustomed to when our mind is focused on the material world. We might experience Him as one of His attributes such as Divine Love, or Peace or Strength. Or we might experience Him as a benign Energy, or Consciousness, or Power, or Light with or without form. Or we may experience Him as a vibration, as the Logos, or as Divine Consciousness encompassing and permeating us and all beings. We may experience Him as the Cosmic Being, the essence of all that is.

A beginner to meditation may fear that, in such circumstances, he has wandered off the "object". He might try to bring back the

The Art of Meditation

original concrete name or form of Christ into his mind. We explain all of this to you so that you will not be alarmed and so that you will allow your "object" to evolve naturally in your mind.

Be mindful that this transformation is different from changing "objects" of concentration during the meditation. What we have described is different from changing voluntarily during the meditation from Christ to a flower or to an energy center or to the word Love. When this happens as a natural outcome of the concentration, then this is the natural transformation of the "object" into its various subtle realities. It is best not to make such changes consciously, or purposely.

Remain with your "object" through all of its spontaneous transformations and, when you discover that you have been caught up in thoughts or various distractions, return to the "object" at whatever level of its manifestation is easiest for you to tune into. If, for example, you have become totally engrossed in thoughts, you will most likely want to return to the concrete name or form of Christ (or your chosen "object").

If, however, you have slipped away, but are still focused on a higher level awareness, it may suit you to return to one of those transformations such as the Christ energy, Christ love or that vibration, wherever you may have left off.

The same holds true for the repetition of the phrase "LORD JESUS CHRIST HAVE MERCY ON US". As we repeat this phrase over and over and concentrate on its meaning and the basic realities behind these words, then we may find that the phrase itself transforms itself in our mind. There is a basic rule that the higher our spiritual perception the less duality we experience and the more aware of the unity of all things we become. (Those interested in learning more details about this prayer may want to read two books by Bishop Kalistos Ware, **"The Power of the Name"** and **"The Orthodox Way."**

Thus as we focus on this phrase we may begin to become aware of the LORD, or of JESUS CHRIST, or of the process of MERCY. We may become aware of our subtle connection and unity with CHRIST. Thus the words may become more abbreviated as our focus becomes as simple as "LORD" or "CHRIST" or "MERCY". Or in some cases we may feel very comfortable with the continuous repetition of the whole phrase. There is no right or wrong here. We are simply to remain focused on our original "object", whatever form it may naturally take.

Again, we warn you about making changes purposely or intellectually. We are "dancing" with this word or phrase, but **we are allowing it to lead us.** We are holding on to it and letting go of our own preconceptions, needs or desires. We are seeking to "not exist", so that the only thing which remains is the reality of the word or phrase we are focusing on.

This then is the highest experience in meditation, the cessation of our separate personal existence. We merge with the "object" and there is no longer a meditator, the object and the process of concentration. There is only the object. Now there is only one reality, one factor, and all time, space and interaction disappear. There is silence. There is peace. We have become peace. We have experienced the source of creation. We have experienced our real self.

Finally, it does not matter what object we choose. Each and every object is a projection of that one subtle consciousness which we are seeking to experience. We are looking for our real selves and this is the way to find it.

In this first path of devotional sound we can use any name or phrase or prayer or invocation which inspires us and helps us to connect in this way with higher levels of our own being.

THE NONDEVOTIONAL PATH OF SOUND

On this path we choose to focus on any sound, word or phrase which does not represent a particular human form. For example we might select the word "OM" (which represents the unmanifest formless God) or "SO-HAM" (which means I am He, I am that

The Art of Meditation

Divine Consciousness). Or one might choose one of the higher human values or qualities such as Love, Peace, Harmony, Unity, Purity, or some phrase such as "I am spirit", or "I am Love", or "All is Divine", or "All is One". Another possibility is to listen carefully within so that one hears the natural inner sounds that appear within the mind when there is deep concentration. One can follow such a sound to its source.

All that we have said about the gradual transmutation of the "object" applies here also. We may start out with a certain word or phrase which has specific meaning and, as our concentration deepens and our awareness changes, we begin to experience the energy-mental-emotional-spiritual reality represented by those words. For example, Love or Peace cease to be words we are concentrating on and become vibrations - emotional-mental experiences. They become states of consciousness which embody those qualities. The more we focus on these qualities or truths, the more they begin to saturate increasingly deeper levels of our mind. We begin to embody these qualities in our daily life. The mind becomes saturated with the quality of Love or Peace or with the truth that "all is Spirit" or that "all is God". This creates a transformation of character, which is very pleasant and beneficial for ourselves and those with whom we come into contact.

THE DEVOTIONAL PATH OF LIGHT - FORM

Some people work more easily with words, and others with images. Those who are more optical in their inner world may choose the form of God or some other spiritual form as an inner "object of concentration". One could choose Jesus or the Cross, or some scene from Christ's life. Persons belonging to other religions will choose the forms that suit them best. The same processes and truths hold true here. We may start with the form of Jesus. It is better to choose a particular image or scene that inspires us most, and not change continuously our chosen image for concentrating.

The image may, however, begin to transmute. Christ's physical form may become one of light. We may begin to perceive the inner spiritual energy, light, consciousness, which expressed itself physically through that form 2000 years ago but now exists as totally independent of that form. The form may lead us to its qualities of love, peace, righteousness, sacrifice, or forgiveness. We may experience the grandeur of that spiritual power. We may feel it enter into us or surround us. We might experience that high spiritual vibration, which we call Christ Consciousness or Holy Spirit.

Any of these transmutations could lead us to that total peace, to that ecstasy of union with Christ such as the ecstasy we experience when we achieve union with our loved one. In this spiritual union with Christ we may remain in this bliss until the mind is pulled outward again by thoughts and needs.

Do not be influenced by the possibilities described to you here. They represent one possible evolution of experiences out of thousands of possibilities. Do not try to create these specific possibilities which are described here. Do not feel that you are not meditating correctly if your experiences are different. Every meditation is different. Every meditation is perfect; it is exactly what we need at that moment in order to move forward with our particular unique psychosynthesis. I have described some possibilities here so as to help you understand that some transmutations of the object are natural and not to be suppressed. On the other hand, such changes are totally useless when done intentionally or intellectually.

THE NONDEVOTIONAL PATH OF LIGHT

On this path we can focus on light or color, with or without form. We may choose to imagine the sun shining in our mind, or the flame of a candle. We might focus on a ball of light or a dispersed light. We may choose a particular color or we may simply focus on the light appearing in our mind when our concentration deepens.

Just as with the previous paths, this light may go through various changes in size, quality, intensity, color, or patterns. It may become a different kind of light than any we have ever experienced in the physical world.

Again we caution you not to make any changes in your object purposely. Imagine that it is a horse that you are riding and allow it to take you wherever it will. Or imagine that it is a river upon which you are floating and have total faith in wherever it is carrying you.

CHOOSING AN OBJECT

I would like to share some guidelines concerning the choice.

The "object" must be concrete enough to hold our mind's attention and, simultaneously, be subtle enough to be able to transmute itself through our concentration into a higher manifestation of its existence as we have already explained a number of times. Thus, theoretically, a bottle of wine, if focused on deeply enough, could bring us into contact with the source of its existence, which is that universal consciousness. But this would work for very few people. The void on the other hand, might be that which is closest to the universal divine consciousness and requires the least transmutations to bring us to that experience. But the void would fail to keep most meditators' attention - at least when they are beginners.

The example of television may help us to understand this. If we are watching a fast moving program, with plenty of images appealing to our lower centers such as sex and violence, we have very little difficulty in concentrating on what is happening. We do not yawn with disinterest. We do not get up to do something else. The object of concentration is concrete and interesting enough to hold our attention. But it is unlikely at that moment that the scenes we are watching transmute themselves into the higher spiritual reality of which they are a projection. They do not bring us the feelings of peace and unity which are indicative of that higher stage of consciousness.

Now, if someone changes the channel (the object), and there is a symphony orchestra playing a classical piece, fewer persons would be glued to the screen as before, but there are more possibilities of feeling that divine harmony through this new object.

If the program ends and there is simply a white screen, it is unlikely that anyone would stay and be entertained by this monotonous field of white light.

Thus, you will want to choose an object that is concrete enough to hold your attention but, at the same time, subtle enough to guide you into higher states of consciousness. I repeat that it doesn't matter what you choose. All will lead you to the same transcendental experience. What is important is to be regular in your practice. What is also extremely important is not to approach this activity with the same programmings that have ruined our social and professional lives. Do not force your concentration. Be relaxed. Be patient. Understand the nature of your mind and, when you realize that it has become distracted, guide it again with love towards the object. You are not going anywhere. You are already where you want to go. You simply have not realized that you are there. Accept every meditation as perfect. Do not judge yourself on the basis of your meditative experiences. Do not compete with others. Do not fight with your mind.

Just keep coming back to the object with patience, perseverance and love. Be gentle. There is no time. There is nowhere to go. Anxiety about spiritual growth is the same as anxiety about any other worldly activity. It does not help. It is a result of a lack of faith. A lack of faith in ourselves. A lack of faith in life and others. A lack of faith in God and the Divine Plan.

So approach your meditation **without attachment** to the result. **Let yourself be meditated.** Imagine that you are a mound of clay which is being shaped and transformed by a higher being.

In closing, I would like to share with you an interesting excerpt from a text by Greek Orthodox Metropolite of Demetrias, who is now the head of the Greek Church, on the **TOPIC OF GOD IN ORTHODOXY.**

"The means by which man may approach God has always held the interest of thoughtful persons.

The Art of Meditation

"In the West, where religious notions have been deeply permeated by Roman ideas, an attempt was made to develop a particular kind of theological thought which, by means of logic, tried to present the subject-matter of the faith in a systematic manner, accessible to the human intelligence. The "natural knowledge of God", as it is called, made use of philosophy, especially the Aristotelian logic, to achieve an initial approach to God. However, as the Western thinkers themselves admit, this rationalization of the faith fostered the presently prevailing atheism, and it opened the way to the formulation of a theory about God's death.

"Atheism in the West is the natural symptom of the Western attitude, and it is the result of a long thought-process which has tried to contain the infinitude of the Divine's attributes within the narrow limits of the human intellect.

"Contrary to this, Eastern theological thinking operated in a completely different manner and followed a different path which, apophatically, leads to participation in God. It is not, that is, so much the reason which can grasp the infinitude of the Divine essence, as it is the emotion which commands a distinctive power for achieving this. The East did not try to dress the question of the existence of God with the garb of logical proof. It turned, instead, to the method of personal experience, i.e. to man's participation and communion with God. It did not view God as an object foreign to man, nor man as an independent unit on earth. It taught, in the language of the Fathers, that the topic of God is, in its essence, the topic of man, man's nature and his destiny. The incarnate God of love, includes the human nature and man can become a "godfilled living being".

"The Divine discharge divinises man, and the "creature in the image" of the Creator takes on an ontological character even while in the midst of the human existence itself. All the above-mentioned are components of what is called the mystical or apophatic theology, and are the features of the Eastern spirituality and our Orthodox approach.

"It is thus apparent that in the realm of Orthodoxy, faith is not processed and standardized. One labors in vain if he thinks that with the sole resource of his limited human thought he can put to sea in the ocean of the divine activities. The truth is not so much knowledge, as experience of reality - the gift and revelation of God. Because God is indescribable, inexplicable and unnameable. According to St. Symeon the New Theologian, God is "visible and invisible, going and coming, disappearing and suddenly appearing". We do not know the essence of God. However, we can approach His effects and His actions, though only a minute portion of these. St. Gregory the Theologian says that "it is only a fraction of what is reaching us and just a tiny glimpse of the great light". Thus, nobody can express God by means of logical categories but in accordance with the degree of his participation in the divine life, each one of us can know something of God.

"This apophatic method of the Eastern mystics is founded on the Holy Scriptures, which teach that God does not deliver Himself to the human senses, but only reveals Himself. Of His own Will, He discharges Himself and incarnates Himself; He ceases being a transcendental power and willingly gifts Himself to man, and, thereby, He endorses the human nature which He puts into its natural framework. In the final analysis, the vision and the knowledge of God is a gift of God consequent on man's collaboration. This means that it is purposeless to seek proofs or indications regarding the existence of God. In fact, such proofs or indications do not exist. However, there is something else which is more essential and more valuable, and that is the vitalizing presence of God in the world. This fact needs no proof, and is similar to light which, when it exists, its presence is luminous. Only a blind person does not see it, or someone with diseased eyes cannot stand it. For all others it is enough that it vitalizes and warms. Therefore, the problem of God, as we have said, is basically the problem of man. Whoever would approach God, must first of all know himself, must study himself, must control himself. If someone is spiritually blind or diseased, he does not have the possibility of approaching God. That is why the Lord said, "Blessed are the pure in heart, for they shall see God (Matt. 5.8)". And this purification is the result of repentance and ceaseless prayer. To those who stand incredulously and inquisitively, before the topic of

The Art of Meditation

God, the Church offers, simply and convincingly, the approach of "come and see". And that is the best path leading to the appearance and the vision of God. "The Church does not offer solutions and logical answers. The Church itself is the solution, because it is a place of light and truth for the sake of man".

ELEFTHEROS KOSMOS (newspaper) 26.2.81.

CHAPTER 8

OTHER OBJECTS OF CONCENTRATION AND METHODS OF MOVING INTO MEDITATION

In the previous chapters we have already mentioned some very valuable "objects of concentration" for our meditation. Here we will mention a few more as well as some techniques or visualizations that you can use in order to move into a meditative state more easily and then begin to focus on your regular object. These introductory techniques are not designed to be meditations in themselves (although in some cases they can be) but rather as a way to develop inner concentration and a spiritual orientation in the mind so that we can then begin to focus on our chosen object of concentration. We will refer to these methods then as "Objects" or as "Methods of moving into meditation" accordingly. You can use them as they suit you best.

ALIGNING THE BODY

The first step in preparing for any type of meditation is to establish the proper conditions in the body. Assume your favorite position. Make sure the body is comfortable and the spine straight. Then check the key points. The legs, abdomen, are they relaxed? The upper back, shoulders and arms, are they relaxed? Straighten the neck, relax the cheeks, temples, eyes, forehead. Let the spine become even straighter and relax any parts of the body which are still tense. Move on into your meditation. This is common to all meditations.

FOLLOWING THE BREATH

The breath can be used both as a means of moving into meditation and as an object of meditation. We have already mentioned in a previous chapter how to use slow, rhythmic, deep breathing (especially the Alternate breath with breathing ratio) as a means of increasing and harmonizing the bioenergy for a more harmonious meditation. Here we will focus on the breath as an "Object".

We simply watch the breath, as it comes in and flows out. We experience its movement through the nostrils, perhaps down into the lungs and then back up again and out of the nostrils. Or we simply remain focused on its movement in and out of the nostril. We do not control the breath. We do not breath deeply or in some specific rhythm, unless this occurs naturally without intervention. We are simply the witnesses of our breath. If it stops, we simply notice that it has stopped. If it is rapid, we notice that it is rapid. If it is deep or shallow, we just observe this. We make no judgments that "this is good breathing" or "bad breathing". We simply witness without evaluation or judgment or control. This meditation creates a deep peace and can be done even while we are in activity, while working or waiting or walking, we can watch our breath without trying to control it.

POSITIVE VISUALIZATION

Visualizing positive realities and wishing well for ourselves and others is an excellent way to create a positive mental state conducive to meditation. One can take a few deep breaths or use any method for relaxing his mind and begin to create positive mental images concerning himself, his loved ones, humanity and the world as a whole.

One common method of moving to deeper levels of concentration is that used by the system called "Mind Control". We sit with the spine straight and breathe slowly and deeply. After a few minutes we take in a deep inhalation and upon exhaling we imagine the number three to flash on and off in our forehead three times. Then we take another deep breath and with the exhalation we imagine the

The Art of Meditation

number two flash on and off three times in our forehead as if there is a screen there. Then we take a third inhalation and on the exhalation we imagine the number one flash on and off three times in the same way. Then we count mentally backwards from 10 to 1 relaxing our body and mind more deeply with each descending number.

We can then imagine that we are transported to a place in nature (real or imaginary) which creates a feeling of peace and security within us. We are now in a more relaxed and concentrated state of mind and can effectively visualize, or imagine, the positive realities that are important to us. Before giving a few examples, I would like to point out that it is not necessary to actually be able to see what we are visualizing as you now see this book and your present surroundings (although some people do see with the same clarity when they visualize). It is sufficient to have the idea, the concept or the feeling of what you are visualizing. If you can see it clearly, however, this is fine also.

Thus, before focusing on our object of meditation we can send light and love to all of our loved ones, or to people who are ill or have problems, or to peoples around the world who are suffering for some reason. We can imagine ourselves changed, transformed in the way we would like to be, with self-confidence, self-acceptance, love for others, inner peace. These positive thought-forms will gradually transform the mind as they sink into the subconscious on a daily basis in this way. They will simultaneously establish a mental atmosphere conducive to meditation.

This is an answer to those who ask if they can mix mind control or positive thought projection with meditation. The answer is obviously yes, but we must make a distinction between the two. We must know when the projections have stopped and the meditation begins. During the meditation itself, we will not want to make any projections or introduce positive thoughts. We are simply following our object and allowing ourselves to change with it.

During the meditation we have no earthly goals, nothing to correct or change or improve. We have trust in whatever changes are occurring as a result of our surrendering to the object and uniting with it. This is the difference between positive projection and meditation. In projecting, we have attachment to certain positive realities that we want to create for ourselves and others. In meditation we surrender to the Divine Will and just flow with the object. In projection, or in prayer, we are asking that creative power of the universe to act on our behalf, to do something for us on the material, emotional or mental level. In meditation we are simply seeking to merge with that power and let it transform us independently of our preconceptions as to how we and the world should be. In meditation we transcend the mind and its preferences and let God's will decide what will happen. In projection, and most often in prayer, we ask for what we believe is best.

Both prayer and positive mental projection, however are excellent methods of attunement and evolution, and are also valuable as methods of moving into meditation. We will discuss prayer in more detail later.

LOVE MEDITATION

This can be a method of moving into meditation, or a meditation in itself. It is a visualization technique that can become a meditation on the quality and vibration of love.

1. Once we have established our body and mind in the correct states, we bring to mind a person whom we have loved deeply in the past or love now in the present. We want to set up a point of reference, which is for us, a symbol of the greatest opening of love that we have felt. That could be for a person, for a pet, or even for God. We first bring the point of reference to our mind and, while focusing on it, remember the feelings of expansion, happiness, tenderness, gratitude, caring and closeness which we experienced through the love which we felt. As much as possible we seek to experience those feelings emotionally and physically, especially in our heart center in the chest.

2. Once we have established these feelings of openness and love, we allow the image of this particular person to disappear and we bring

someone else into our mind, and seek to feel the same openness and unconditional acceptance towards him. Once we feel that opening we bring still another person to mind and open ourselves to him with the same intensity and closeness as the first.

3. Once we have worked on feeling love and unity with the important people in our lives at this time, we then bring our own selves, our body and personality into focus and develop the same feelings of love and unconditional acceptance for ourselves, exactly as we are at this stage of our evolutionary development.

4. Then we bring into mind a person with whom we have difficulty in opening up or communicating, or towards whom we harbor negative feelings, or who harbors negative feelings towards us. We seek to transcend our fear, resistance and negativity and feel the same opening and closeness with him that we have felt for the first person (our love reference) and the others.

5. Having mentally developed a feeling of unity with all of these persons in our life, we can then turn our awareness to God (however each person imagines this universal being) and feel an opening of love and gratitude towards God. Then we can feel the flow in the opposite direction, the flow of God's love and blessing for us. We can feel this flowing into our heart center, or into our forehead or into the top of our head.

6. We can remain in this feeling of love and union with God and with whomever or whatever comes into our awareness. Surround every thought, every situation, every pain, every feeling, every phenomenon, which appears in the mind, with Love.

THE TRIANGLE PROJECTION

The system called "Triangles" is a worldwide unified field of positive mental projection in conjunction with the **GREAT INVOCATION** participated in by millions of people. There are main offices in the UN building of New York and other offices in various capitals of the world where one can register his participation. One can participate, however, without registering officially.

Once we establish the body and mind in the proper state, we bring our two friends, with whom we are working this triangle, into our minds. These two persons will need to be persons who understand and desire to work similarly for the same purpose. They will do what you are about to do every day. It is not necessary for you all to do it at the same time or in the same place. It is sufficient that each does this every day (this includes you of course).

Bring the other two "corners" of your triangle into your mental awareness. You could mentally see them as you are seeing this book at this time. Or you could imagine them as "presences" or energies sitting or standing in relationship to you so that the three of you create a triangle. Repeat their names in your mind as you feel their presence and energy connect with you. Now imagine a connection of energy, light or feeling - connect your heart center with their heart centers, so that there is a triangle of energy at the level of your heart centers. Then do the same between your forehead centers and imagine a triangle of light connect the three of you at this level.

Imagine then that you unite and that the three of you become one united energy. This united energy then takes its position in a network of millions of such lights (each of which is comprised of three cooperating persons) which surround the earth. As you imagine this network of lights surrounding the earth like a beneficial protective aura, you repeat the Great Invocation, which was written through Alice Bailey during a session of inspired automatic writing.

The Great Invocation

**"From the point of light
Within the mind of god,
Let light flow into the minds of men.
Let light descend to earth.**

**From the point of love
Within the heart of god,
Let love flow into the hearts of men.
May Christ return to earth.**

From the center where
The will of god is known,
Let purpose guide
The little wills of men.
The purpose which the
Masters know and serve.

From the center which is
Called the race of man,
May the plan of
Love and light work out.
And may they seal the
Door where evil dwells.

Let light and love and power
Restore the plan on earth."

As you repeat each phrase let your mind create images which represent that which you are invoking. Imagine that what you are saying is happening. You can repeat it verbally or mentally, whichever you prefer. Focus on the basic energy of each paragraph of this prayer.

1. The first focuses on the awakening of all humanity through the light of knowledge of spiritual truth.

2. The second calls for this awakening to occur through the love, which does exist in every heart, which needs only a little encouragement.

3. The third stanza calls for the surrendering of the personal will to the divine will, which knows what is best for the whole.

4. The fourth stanza awakens us to the reality that no changes will take place without our united effort. Great spiritual leaders can show us the direction, but only through our unified effort will harmony be created on Earth.

This is an excellent method of moving into meditation. It brings one into a space of inner alignment with these higher truths. Meditation is much deeper once connected in this way.

But this technique has many important qualities of its own, even if it is not used as an introduction into meditation. We gradually become connected, through subtle spiritual lines of energy, with all those other beings who are working together on a spiritual level for a better world. We become connected to the Divine through our goodwill and desire for the good and our desire to be useful and cooperate with others for that purpose. We begin to experience "universalization" as we feel that we are a small, but important, part of the body of humanity. This helps us to overcome the excessive importance we give to our ego and leads to feelings of brotherhood towards all. **Our ego is reduced and our unity increased.**

By repeating these words everyday we become more attuned to our inherent urge for goodness, love and unity. Our values become clearer and we are more guided by spiritual values in our daily interactions. Our daily visualization implants all the more deeply into the collective unconscious of all of mankind and of creation, the values and reality of love, peace and harmony. Our every thought affects the whole. Our minds are connected to the cosmic mind, and, through the cosmic mind, our thoughts affect all other beings to some extent. (For a more in-depth explanation of this read **"The Miracles of Love and Wisdom"** and **"Universal Philosophy"**.)

LIGHT MEDITATIONS

There are a wide variety of meditations on light with and without form. We have already mentioned some. This one is particularly effective and beneficial for beginner meditators. Establish the correct state of body and mind with the methods we have already explained.

1. Now imagine light in your forehead. It could be the flame of a candle, the sun or simply a formless light. Let this light expand and fill the entire brain cavity, immersing your brain in the light essence. When we say imagine light, you do not necessarily have to

see a light. You may feel the presence of light, or have the idea, the concept of light or the vibration, the feeling of light. You may work with any of these.

2. Now allow any of these manifestations of light move down into your neck area and permeate that area. Then allow it to flow into your shoulders and then into your arms and hands. Each step in this process should take place slowly and naturally without rushing. Let that awareness of the light be established in each area before moving on to the next. You do not have to stick with this series of body parts, you can move in any order that suits you. Some people choose to imagine that the light purifies each part of the body and renders that body incapable of participating in actions which degrade one's consciousness.

Move in this way into the chest cavity and into the heart center. Then down into the abdomen, allowing the light to permeate and relax all the muscles there and especially the solar plexus and navel. Then allow the presence of light to move down into the legs creating relaxation and harmony there.

3. Once all of your body has been permeated in light, you can check if there is any area that still feels tense or isolated from this unifying presence. Allow the light to move into those remaining areas. Then imagine the light expanding, so that you visualize, or feel, an aura of light around the body. Now the light that was within you is also around you. Feel yourself immersed in this light and the light immersed in you. Feel that your physical form is disappearing, dissolving and that you have become a field of light - energy.

4. Then imagine God as a much larger or infinite energy field and imagine the unification of these two fields - our self as light, energy or consciousness with God as light, energy or consciousness. Remain in this blissful union for as long as you can and return to it over and over again when your mind has been distracted.

This can be used either as a method for entering into meditation or as a meditation in itself, in which the object is your energy union with God or the awareness of yourself as light or energy. At the end of this meditation you can visualize this light energy going out to all those who have need. Imagine that it permeates their physical, mental and spiritual bodies bringing forth the inherent harmony existing within each of them.

THE CANDLE MEDITATION

The candle meditation can be used by those who have difficulty in concentrating at first. The advantage is that we have our eyes open and the "object" is more concrete and entertaining.

1. We sit in any straight-backed position, and place a candle about 20 to 30 centimeters in front of us at about the level of our nose. We focus gently on the flame, letting its image fill our mind.

When we discover that our mind has been pulled elsewhere, we gently, with patience, bring our awareness to the flame and its attributes. We seek to be totally present, without thoughts about past or future. The flame becomes our only reality. We keep returning to that.

Be careful not to strain while watching. Remember that this is a gentle watching as we would watch a river flowing without tension. We watch the flow of light from the wick. We are not trying to prove something or achieve something, we are simply seeking to be present, to be at peace, to be with the flame and nothing else.

2. After about five minutes of this let the eyes close and visualize the flame in your mind and watch it mentally in the same way. When you lose your inner concentration open your eyes again and continue in the same way with the external flame that is before you.

3. Move in this way between the external and the internal flame staying in the present moment, focusing on the light. Eventually the inner light can lead you to the previously described light meditation. This is an excellent meditation for those who have difficulty in concentration and also a good method for students of all levels for increasing their ability to concentrate.

The Art of Meditation

NATURE MEDITATIONS

We can meditate on any object in the same way that we have described for the flame meditation. Especially beneficial, pleasant and uplifting are meditations on the beings and scenes in nature.

1. We can choose to sit before a flower, a tree, the sea, a mountain, a rock, or even an insect, if it will sit still. We can allow our awareness to be totally absorbed in the form we are observing. By letting go of the past and the future we can tune in to the inner essence of that being and experience a totally different dimension of its existence. We can realize its inherent divinity and role in the universe and our subtle spiritual and material interconnectedness with this being. We can experience the beauty and perfection of creation, which will lead us to a realization of our own beauty, perfection and inherent divinity. We might even lose our feelings of separateness and experience the ecstasy of union with all that surround us. This may happen with the eyes open or with the eyes closed, whatever happens naturally.

2. During such a meditation we may be moved at times to close our eyes and experience inner realities which have been stimulated by our concentration on nature. We can allow ourselves to be free to move in and out. At some point this may not exactly be a meditation, but rather a **contemplation** on the nature of things, as thoughts and realizations come into our minds. At other moments we may flow into meditation again as we transcend our minds and experience rather than think or realize mentally. Both processes are beneficial.

A word about external objects of concentration. They are very beneficial for developing concentration and for attuning ourselves to the material world. But one would do best not to create a dependency on an object outside his mind for his ability to come into contact with himself. Such meditations, or contemplations, or reflections are very important for our rejuvenation and attunement with the rhythms of nature, which should also be our rhythms, but it is best that our object for daily meditation be an inner one, which does not require a special environment or a special time or external apparatus. We are freer in this way.

CONTEMPLATION ON CHRIST'S LIFE AND TEACHINGS

We have already mentioned some types of meditations on Christ's name and form, and also the prayer "LORD JESUS CHRIST HAVE MERCY ON US". These visualizations, which you are about to read, can be used as methods of entering into any of the Christ meditations, which suit you most.

One visualization is similar to the contemplation techniques used by some Christian monks. We bring a scene, event or teaching from Christ's life into focus. We concentrate on it dwelling on the message or lesson, which can be received through His words or His actions or some event.

After some contemplation, we create a phrase in the mind which for us is our message or lesson at this moment. At some other moment the same words or event may offer us a totally different message. This is especially true of the parables because they can be understood at so many different levels.

Once we have established a clear phrase in our mind, which represents the message we have tuned into, we move deeper into the message and find **one word** (which may or may not be a part of the message) which represents this message. This will usually be a spiritual value such as love, peace, forgiveness, faith, service, sacrifice, humility, strength, fearlessness, devotion etc. Once we have established this word, which sums up in a way the message we found in the original teaching, then we begin to focus more intensely on this word.

Focusing on this word, this value, we gradually become attuned to its inner quality or energy. We begin to feel the vibration of this value such as love or peace etc. permeating our body and mind. As our concentration increases, this vibration or quality permeates our whole being, we are immersed in it and become transformed by it. We remain in this bliss returning over and over again to the energy of this quality that is vibrating in our being, or focusing on the Christ in the way which suits us.

SURRENDERING TO CHRIST

Another way of moving into a Christ meditation is to imagine Jesus standing in front as you sit with your eyes closed in your meditation position. Feel His presence, His energy, His vibration, His love, and His peace as He is standing before you. Let these energies come forth and pass into you. Now mentally imagine that you bow forward and place your forehead on His bare feet. Feel His energy pour into your forehead and purify your mind. Mentally create the feeling that you are surrendering your will, your desires, your needs, the results of all your actions, your body and your life itself to the Divine.

Once you feel that this part has come to a completion, mentally come again into the meditative position and imagine the Christ in front of you radiating his energy towards you. At this point we have some options:

1. Imagine that Christ's rays of energy permeate your heart center and then your forehead center and saturate them with this divine energy. Remain in the sensation of this energized state.

2. Imagine that Christ's form becomes very small and moves toward you and establishes itself in your heart. Imagine that Christ is in your heart. You decide if He is sitting or standing there. Imagine that He is emanating His love, peace and power from within you. Remain focused on this, or move into your preferred meditation.

3. Imagine that Christ moves behind you and stands behind your back with you sitting in your meditation position in front of Him. Now imagine that He places His two hands on the top of your head and passes His blessings and energy into the top of your head. Let this energy fill your brain and then move down into the rest of your body. Let this energy continue expanding until every aspect of your being, including your mind, are immersed in this vibration which is flowing in through the top of your head.

These Christ meditations can be used as a method of entering into meditation independently of what object of meditation you are accustomed to using. If you belong to some other religion, you may use these methods of focusing with the form you are accustomed to worshiping

GOD IS IN EVERYTHING

This is another excellent method of moving into meditation, or it can also be used as a meditation in itself.

1. Once you have established your position and the correct state of mind, bring a plant (one you know or an imaginary one) into your mind. Remember that this plant is a projection of the one Divine Universal Consciousness. Say mentally to yourself, "God is in that Plant". Bring another plant to mind, and see the intelligent force in all beings expressing itself through that plant. Do this again with another species and remember that this is one of God's many forms.

2. Now do the same with various kinds of animals. See each one as an unique material manifestation of the one Divine Consciousness. Remember to choose each time at least one type of animal which you fear or dislike. Then do the same with some types of insects.

3. Now bring some persons you know and remind yourself of the same truth, and try to feel it. See each person as divine and feel the same respect and love towards him that you would feel toward God, if you were able to meet Him. Christ told us many times in various ways, that God is the consciousness in every being, in the prisoners, the poor, and even in our enemies.

4. Be sure then to bring into your mind people with whom you have difficulty in communicating, or towards whom you have negative feelings, and remember that they too are unique manifestations of the One God.

5. Bring your family, parents, children, siblings and spouse to mind and see them too as divine beings.

6. Then bring your own self, your body and personality and realize

The Art of Meditation

that these too (you cannot be the only exception on the earth) are manifestations of divine consciousness, and feel the love and respect towards yourself that you deserve.

At this point you can move on to your regular object of meditation, or continue on in this way, remembering that whatever comes into your mind is a manifestation of the divine. Persons, events, places, thoughts, feelings, pain, problems, situations are all manifestations of the only cause for whatever exists, God. (If these concepts are foreign to you I would again suggest that you read **"The Miracles of Love and Wisdom"** and **"Universal Philosophy").**

MEDITATION ON THE ENERGY CENTERS

This meditation will be described in detail in another chapter. We will give just a small description here, because it can often be used in combination with the other forms of meditation.

The energy centers are certain points in the body where the bioenergy is more intensely focused. These points are along the spinal column. They are not physical and cannot ordinarily be seen by the human eye. These energy centers are stations, through which the higher spiritual energies are transformed into certain types of more gross energy necessary for action, thought and existence in the physical body. Each center colors this pure cosmic energy with the quality of that particular center, just as a colored film colors the otherwise white light passing through it. Each center has to do with another quality of human energy, with other motivations, other needs and desires. Each center is a "sub station" for the soul, through which energy is distributed to the various organs, limbs and all the cells of the body. When this energy leaves the body, the body dies and begins to decompose.

Our thoughts and feelings are very much affected by the energy center which is most activated at a certain moment. These centers are stimulated by various external factors, such as what we eat, what we see and hear, what company we keep and the places we frequent. They are also stimulated and fed by our conscious and subconscious thoughts, needs, desires and feelings.

The process of evolution is accompanied by the rising of this energy towards the higher centers, which are colored by more spiritual tendencies, needs, feelings and thoughts.

By focusing on these centers, we can energize them and create more harmonious connections between them. Focusing on them also helps to activate a purification process in which they throw out whatever is held in them which is preventing our evolution. It is for this reason that one needs to be careful not to overdo such meditations on the centers. Too much concentration can start a purification – un-stressing process (like that which we mentioned in chapter 5) which might bring about unpleasant reactions which we may not be ready to handle given the present circumstances in our life such as responsibilities towards family and work. If one lived in a monastery, he could take more risks with such techniques.

For this reason, I would suggest the following guidelines:

1. Practice concentration on the energy centers **only under the guidance of an experienced teacher** and **after the necessary inner cleansing** (physically and emotionally).

2. Do not overdo it. More is not better.

3. You can use it more safely when using with other objects of meditation. For example **focusing on love, light, or the Christ** in the heart center or the forehead center. In this way we imbue these centers with the spiritual vibration of the object of concentration.

4. During the first years **do not focus on the three lower centers.**

Work first on awakening the heart center and then the forehead center. When you are well-established in love (the result of the awakening of the heart center) and Spiritual discrimination - wisdom (the result or work on the forehead center) then begin to work on opening the other centers.

The Art of Meditation

The concept here is that these centers are like flower buds that are still closed and thus manifesting only a small portion of their potential. As they become energized, they flower and much more of their previously hidden potential is available to us.

This subject is a large one and we have given you little information because we believe that whoever wants to follow this path must necessarily have a teacher who will guide him step by step.

INSIGHT MEDITATION

This is a very ancient meditation which can be used as a method of moving into meditation, or as a means of smoothing out tense energies, while one is in meditation (especially when one is making too much effort,) or even at the end of any meditation, so as to smooth out the energy and create balance. Independently of these possible uses, in combination with other "objects", it is a powerful meditation in itself.

After establishing your position and state of mind, begin to observe the various parts of the body. One method is to allow your consciousness simply to become aware of the parts of the body which make themselves more evident through feelings, sensations or even pain. Just become aware of this part and accept it as it is. Do not try to relax it or change it. Notice its condition and accept it. The same can be done concerning feelings or thoughts passing through the mind. They can be recognized and accepted. It is like watching the contents of a river flowing between its banks. You are on the banks. When you see the movements of water or some leaves, you do not reject them or become attached to them. You notice them and let them flow. You do not say this is good and that is bad. Sit in the same way on the banks of your consciousness and just watch the various phenomena such as physical feelings, discomforts, pleasures, temperature, tiredness, desire, an insect on your cheek, wind on your face, thoughts which come about the past and the future. None of these concern you. You do not reject them. You do not resist them. You acknowledge their existence and allow them to continue their flow. You are not concerned or affected.

The same meditation can be performed in a more methodic way called "sweeping". We allow our awareness to sweep through the body in a systematic way feeling, acknowledging and accepting the state of each part of the body before we move on. There are many methods of "sweeping". I will presently mention only one here.

Bring all of your awareness to the center of the top of your head. Feel and accept the sensations or state of that part of your body. Now feel the area, which would be a ring around the center of the top of your head. This would be a band about two centimeters in width. Feel, acknowledge, accept and then move. You now move onto a similar band about the same size or a little larger which is further out from the center. After stopping, feeling and accepting, your band moves down over the forehead and encompasses the forehead, temples and back of the head at the level of the temples. The band continues to move down the face as you feel simultaneously the front, sides and back part of the face and head according to the level of the downward moving band of awareness. It moves down into the throat region, where you are simultaneously aware of the front, sides and back portions of the neck. The band then grows larger and moves down to encompass the shoulders, upper chest and upper back. It continues to move downward in sections touching all parts of the chest and abdomen. It then moves into the legs, moving down one leg at a time, or both legs simultaneously.

Once arriving at the toes one can begin moving back up again toward the top of the head, passing through each area in the same way with the band of awareness covering the front, sides and back of the body at each stage of its upward movement. This can continue for the complete duration of the meditation as your awareness moves up and down continuously feeling and accepting and moving on.

There are many variations of this sweeping technique. Some prefer to move only from top to bottom. That is once they arrive at the toes their awareness jumps up to the top of the head again and they start moving down again. Others prefer to move only upwards. Most need to work separately with each arm and leg before being able to

The Art of Meditation

work with them simultaneously. Most parts of the body need to be worked on, "opened up", if you like, to our awareness with more slow and concentrated work on those parts of the body before one can have the intimate awareness necessary to sweep in this way. It is often beneficial to be guided by someone at first.

This meditation has special healing powers and is an excellent technique to be employed when one is ill or has some damage such as broken bones or pain. This opening of the body to the mind's attention and acceptance brings healing power into all parts of the body. As already mentioned it is an excellent way to enter into any meditation. It is also very helpful after any meditation to make a few passes through the body so as to relax and bring harmony to the energy flow. This is especially important for those who tend to try too hard when they are meditating. It is also a way to balance the energies or work with pain while in the process of any other type of meditation. After a few passes we can return to our original "object".

NOT THIS, NOT THIS

This is perhaps the king of all meditations. It has no object of concentration. It rejects all mental objects and phenomena as illusion and as not being that for which I am searching. What am I searching for? MYSELF, my real identity. It is very simple, I ask the question "Who am I?" or "What am I?". The truth is, however, that anything that I can observe cannot be my real self, because I have to be something other than what I am perceiving in order to perceive it. I cannot be the perceived since my consciousness must be positioned outside of the perceived in order to perceive it. When my eyes see a car, they cannot be that car. My eyes cannot see themselves. They can see only a reflection of themselves. Can we trust this reflection? We want to see the real thing. Being aware of the changes taking place in the eyes, I cannot be my eyes.

1. We establish our proper position physically and mentally. We begin to search for our real identity. We can start with our legs. "I am not my legs". I exist without my legs". We feel our abdomen and realize that to be able to feel it we must be something other than

that to feel it. We move on to the chest. This is not my real self, for I perceive it and thus I must be something other than that in order to perceive it. I am not my arms. I exist without my arms. I am not my face or head for I am aware of them and thus must be something else which is aware of them.

2. Then we move on to more subtle aspects of our reality. I am not the sounds I hear, the sensations or pain I feel. I am that which is hearing or sensing those. Yet I am aware of sensing them and, thus, I must be something even more subtle which is aware of that part of myself that is perceiving those sensations.

3. I am not my thoughts because I am aware of them. I am also aware of a consciousness, which is aware of that part which is aware of the thoughts. This all might seem very confusing. But it is not, when you practice it. Neither do you have all these thoughts. After the first few times it all becomes totally automatic. Your mind simply disperses every object of consciousness as not "me", not what I am looking for, not the truth, just a temporary wave on the ocean with no permanent reality.

In this meditation, whenever the mind falls on any mental or physical phenomenon, it allows it to dissolve, to disappear. It is as if your awareness itself is like those "ray guns", so predominant in science fiction movies, which make their target disappear instantly.

We are eventually left with awareness itself as our object of consciousness. Each will experience this awareness of witness differently. Some may experience void, others some type of bliss or states without time or space, in which their existence has no size.

I would suggest that this is an advanced meditation technique and not useful for most beginners. I would suggest that you leave this for a few years, and pick it up later if it feels right to you. Most require a more concrete object of concentration in the beginning.

JUST BEING - NOT TRYING

The supreme meditation, however, is not to meditate at all.

The Art of Meditation

Inherent in any verb (and thus also in the verb "to meditate") is a sense of effort or trying, of seeking to achieve something. This feeling of seeking is, however, the antithesis of what meditation is all about. The process of meditation is a natural elevation of consciousness, until it transcends the world of dualism, and the world of time and space. When this transcendence takes place there is no separation. All is one being. All is God, All is divine. We are back in the Garden of Eden, as we were before we "ate from the fruit of the tree of knowledge of good and evil".

Thus, real meditation is just being. It is a total acceptance of the perfection of all things. It culminates in the union with all that surrounds one. But, since the mind would never experience this on its own without some help, so we are forced to fight fire with fire, or remove a thorn with another thorn. Since the mind is the problem, the fire, the thorn, then we are forced to turn it upon itself in order to overcome its reign and end its illusion. Thus we turn the mind upon the mind telling it not to allow its "other part" to get out of line, or get lost in its endless thoughts about the past and future. We train it to avoid senseless negative thinking. We educate it into tricking its own self out of existence. From this is born the feeling of effort or success or failure in meditation. All of this, however, is a part of the illusion; but a necessary part of the illusion. The mind cannot be overcome otherwise, and there is no liberation or real freedom for a person who has not transcended his mind.

Thus the final goal is this one act; the cessation of action, the unification of doer, object and doing. Effort itself is an obstacle to this, but at the same time it is the only way to arrive there. Thus one must meditate to arrive, but one needs to understand when and how to give up all effort as he approaches. It is like climbing up to the top of hill so that we can see everything. There we no longer need to climb, unless we are so used to climbing and trying that we cannot stop. Meditation then is a delicate balance between control and gentle effort combined with a letting go, a surrender of every effort.

This same balance of effort, without attachment to the result of our actions and the surrendering to the Universal Will is also the key to life itself and every other effort we make.

In choosing an object of concentration you may want to return to and read again chapter 7, before going on.

CHAPTER 9

SOME GUIDELINES FOR THE JOURNEY INWARD INNER CONTACT, OR HIDING FROM THE WORLD ?

The long-range goal is to carry this peaceful and clear state of being into our daily life, as a center from which we act and react. If all our thoughts and actions can come from this place of pure consciousness, unaffected by our conditioning, then we will be always in harmony with others and the world around us.

Eventually there must be a merging of our meditative states with our practical daily life activity. Meditation is useful for harmonizing our body-mind-soul complex. If the body, mind and soul are in perfect balance there is no need to meditate. Life itself becomes meditation.

Some people turn to meditation and other spiritual disciplines as a healing drug to soothe their problems and neurosis or to substitute other drug addictions. This is perfectly normal, for it is often through life's sufferings and hardships that we are forced to become aware of our soul; which is the only true healer. If we did not have these problems we might never be motivated towards moving in a spiritual direction.

Meditation can help us develop an inner source of serenity, self-confidence, self-acceptance, and also greater faith in God, nature and life itself. This inner serenity should gradually lead toward an opening to life. We may, however, pass through a period of closing in. This is similar to the caterpillar who retreats from the world into its cocoon so that it may become transformed into a beautiful butterfly, which, when it comes out, offers so much joy to the world.

Meditation then can be a temporary refuge or "Spiritual cocoon", through which we might need to pass, in order to experience our inner self-transformation. It should, however, not become a hiding place from the world or its problems.

Some on the spiritual path have a history of maladjustment, dissatisfaction, confusion or high anxiety states. It is through these conflicts with the world and themselves that they are led to the truths of life. In breaking out of the stranglehold, which society and material attachments make upon us, we are left open and unsheltered by the usual standards and norms. We go through periods of self-doubt and confusion and alienation from the rest, who seem to be content with what has become so meaningless to us.

A SENSE OF ALIENATION

This is one of the possible pitfalls to the beginning meditator. A sense of alienation from society. In meditation, we find a place of peace - a state, which we can visit every day, where no one bothers us, where there are no problems.

It is easy to begin to prefer this state of peace over the state of anxiety that occupies our consciousness much of the time. It can soon become a way of hiding from the world, a method of shutting people out. Knowing about this reaction may not prevent it from occurring anyway, because in some senses it must happen as a natural part of the growth process. As one begins to focus on the inner impulses or inner sense of motivation and morality, there is a natural need to shut out the external forces of conditioning for a while. As one becomes more directed from within, one must necessarily let go of some of the social voices one was depending on for direction.

Unfortunately, while we are passing through this adjustment, we have a tendency to place the blame on society, on our family, government, educational system, religion etc. for having "suppressed" us for so long. We may react with feelings of condemnation and of alienation from the groups we were once part of.

As our interests change, we may feel the need to reject those who still are motivated by those interests which were previously an important part of our lives. We usually do this because we reject those same interests now within ourselves and we fear that we are not free of them. We also fear that we are not free of temptation from others.

We also tend to reject others because we want to make ourselves feel superior to them, more spiritual, better than them. This is a result of our insecurity and inability to accept all parts of our selves. We reject in others, that which we reject within ourselves.

TAKING RESPONSIBILITY

The meditator can avoid the bitterness, loneliness and resentment, which sometimes accompanies these changes, by accepting responsibility for his or her life. No one forced us to be controlled by the ways of thinking and living around us. Nothing happens to us by accident or as a result of "circumstance". If we take responsibility for our actions we will learn from what we experience. The concept of personal responsibility for one's reality has deep spiritual roots, which cannot be discussed in detail here, but the reader is encouraged to investigate this subject more deeply, in the books **"The Psychology of Happiness"**, **"Universal Philosophy"** And **"The Miracles of Love and Wisdom"**.

If we feel alienated, it is not because others are unfriendly. It is because we are changing and feel differently. We are the cause of all our problems. Accept the changes that are taking place in your life as changes which are taking place within you and are being then reflected in your environment. You would do well to be alone once in a while in order to clarify and sort things out within. It's the best way to get to know yourself.

ALONE OR LONELY ?

Being alone occasionally is beneficial, feeling lonely or alienated is the problem. Have patience as you come more into your new inner orientation. You will find new people who you can relate to, or you will relate to old friends in new ways. Be sure to remember that it is very confusing to your family and friends, who are not changing, to watch your life and values growing in a different direction. They will probably feel insecure, and perhaps even jealous, about your new interest which they may fear will be taking your attention away from them. Remember to reassure them of your love and interest in them.

Let us take responsibility for our actions and try to remain balanced in our growth. We will inevitably, through trial and error, go through extremes, like solitude or eating only certain foods, or wearing certain clothes. We should keep in mind that the purpose of life on earth is not only to realize our spiritual nature, but also to merge the spirit with the mind and body.

Hence, there is no need to change our lifestyle radically, unless we truly feel from within a new motivation guiding us. It would be a mistake to try to emulate the stereotyped monk or yogi, unless that is what we truly feel inside.

FOLLOW YOUR INNER GUIDE

Many beginners on the spiritual path have a superficial idea of what "spiritual" is and try to emulate that with the right clothes, foods, vocabulary, lifestyles, etc. Everything is spiritual when it is done with love for God and humanity.

Drastic change is unnecessary, unless we find that our present mode of living is extremely dissipating or contradictory to spiritual growth. Once one begins meditation, these destructive actions will begin to diminish on their own. For example, if you feel less desire for meat - then eat less meat. But don't try to give up meat to be spiritual. This ultimately is the same as following the dictates of society, it's just another society; the spiritual society. Follow your inner guide.

In all fairness I must say that some teachers or systems will require you to give up certain habits i.e. drugs, sex, meat etc. They are quite proper in asking this - because at certain levels of meditation, detachment from such cyclical desires is necessary. If you find that you cannot follow those guidelines then practice another form of meditation which does not require such purification. If you feel you want to give it a try - then give it a good try of at least six months or a year and then decide if it feels right for you. Of course in no case should drugs ever be mixed with meditation. If you want to start meditating you will need to give up use of narcotic drugs.

DETACHMENT

Detachment from the cycle of desire and temporary fulfillment is both a necessity to and an outgrowth of meditation. As long as we are caught in this endless oscillation between wanting something and fulfilling it, then we will always want it again. We will then be limited as to how much we can focus inwardly because we are too caught up in the ego and illusory needs and problems.

Gradually we must learn, and eventually experience, that at the soul level we need absolutely nothing - except perhaps **to Be** and **to Create.** But we are on the Earth and in the body so we must deal with the objects of attachment every day.

There is nothing wrong with making love. It is the attachment, the need for it, that binds us to the body. Money is a powerful resource that can help many people. Being attached to it for security binds us to the illusory value of matter. Being famous can be a very powerful tool for raising the evolutionary level of mankind, or it can be a pitfall of false ego identification and vanity.

There is nothing evil about money, sex or any earthly pleasure - the problem is in the attachment - in the state of **dependency** on such an object of consciousness as a source of security or meaning.

Gradually all security and motivation must come from the higher centers of consciousness. Only then can one truly act with purity. Only then can one love without the selfish need of being paid back with the same.

EXTERNAL OR INTERNAL SECURITY

The major blockages to deep soul contact in meditation are inner stress, ego identification and desire attachment. They result in tensions and rigidity in the body and mind structure. If we are full of emotional and mental tension, then our meditation will be primarily an experience of stress release, rather than residing in inner silence.

This is perfectly okay. It is possible, however, to work out the gross tension with various exercises and breathing techniques, so as to increase the quality of the time spent in meditation.

In terms of our analogy of diving into the sea of consciousness, the exercises release those more obvious tensions hovering near the surface of consciousness, so that during the meditation one is able to sink more easily with less debris in the way and, thus, is able to reach the finer, more subtle areas of consciousness.

Exercises and breathing techniques are beneficial for releasing already accumulated stress. But the ideal situation would be to think and live in such a harmonious way so as not to create the tensions in the first place.

Having a relaxed body through daily exercise will help. When one is relaxed, then less situations are stress producing. When one is tense, most everything becomes a source of irritation. So one can get on either circle of action. By relaxing, less events cause difficulties and one becomes more tolerant or, perhaps even happy in spite of what is happening.

The main source of our tension is our identification with our personality and our ignorance of true-life values. Only the ego has problems, not the soul.

Our difficulties come when we forget about the strength, potential and eternal nature of our soul, and look to strengthen our frightened little ego by surrounding ourselves with many illusory securities.

THE SHIP OF OUR EGO

When we deny or are not aware of the power within us, we are like that ship mentioned earlier, which is being bounced around on the sea. We look to the world around us for something to hold on to for security. So, we throw lifelines out everywhere. One to a relationship, a lover, friend, husband or wife; another to a job - a sense of professional dignity and meaningfulness. We hook lines into money and material objects to build a security structure that can disappear with a momentary tremor of the earth, or a fire, or war. We are like spiders weaving a web-like structure all around us - eventually chaining ourselves down to a rigid and limited lifestyle, which rather than protect us, chokes us spiritually and mentally.

In such a case our "ship" will be very "safe". In fact it won't move at all, we will be stuck, completely stagnant, unable to move out of the web of identifications we have spun around ourselves. This would be fine in a static world; but this world is changing and with ever increasing greater velocity. The nature of life is constant change, and we must be prepared to deal with that. Nothing remains the same. We must always be ready to adapt and respond to our environment. And this is where the problem arises. Soon the "supports", to which we have fastened our security lines, begin to move and the ropes snap, or we imagine that they are going to snap and become very fearful that we will be lost or drown if they do.

Our basic mistake is that we fail to realize that all of these "supports" to which we have tied ourselves, perhaps even chained our selves and depend upon are not at all stationary but actually bobbing up and down on that same rough sea of life that we are seeking refuge from. Nothing "out there" is stable. All is changing. What is here now may not be five minutes from now. Our only real security comes from having faith in our ability to navigate the sea of life without help from others if that is required at some point. We can also feel a deep sense of security by believing in the sea itself (Life, nature or God) and that it is benign and ultimately wants only what is best for us - our evolution and self realization. We will experience inner security when we have total **faith in ourselves, in Life, and in God.**

Otherwise we are vulnerable to various changes. A lover may leave us. A spouse may die. Economic conditions may result in our unemployment. We may lose our professional status. War may break out. We may lose our possessions, our financial security. An earthquake, flood or fire could change our lives drastically.

We spend so much time worrying about keeping these security lines tight, that we actually cause them to snap more quickly. Whereas, if we had more faith, we could flow with the events and would be much more in harmony with the forces at play around us.

Each of these crises-situations offer an opportunity to let go of that line of tension and put our faith in our own inner self instead.

WHAT CHOICES DO WE HAVE ?

If one loses a spouse or a child this is truly a most sad and even terrifying event. A mate and child is for most of us our strongest emotional attachment. But if separation occurs what choices do we have?

We can go into deep depression, feel bitter and resentful towards God and the world for having been so cruel to us. Our self-pity increases and we don't really care to live any more. Or we can very quickly cover up the hurt, fill up the gap, by immediately sending out a new security line, finding someone else to depend on or someone else to live for.

A third, and more realistic, solution is to accept and express the pain and sorrow of the event. But then eventually let go of it and, instead of sending out more lines of dependency into the world, begin to look into ourselves and experience our inner strength and ability to cope. Each crisis is an opportunity to become stronger, more aware, and more alive.

Nothing in the material world is lasting or solid enough to depend on. Only inner lines of strength will give us the security and flexibility to grow and function in this rapidly changing world.

The Art of Meditation

LIVING IN THE WORLD

This is the point at which every "realist" brings up the argument: "Are you saying we shouldn't get married, or love, or have money or a place to live? If we didn't have professions the world would fall apart. Are you saying we should all leave everything up to faith and do nothing to improve our lives?"

No, I am not saying any of these things. What would the world be like without love and marriage? And there is no need to live an underprivileged life when the earth has so much to offer us.

The problem lies in the **attachment** to these identifications for our sense of security. We can love without being dependent. We can have a profession without relying on it for our sense of importance. We can live in a political, religious or social system without thinking it is the only right one, and that we would not exist if it changed. We can continue to be happy even after our vast fortune disappears.

The soul, inner self, God, the source of life are the only anchors which are firm enough to hold our ship in place through the storms of life. In a storm a ship needs to be flexible to move with the currents, otherwise it will be crushed and will sink.

STEADFAST FLUIDITY

One time, while in the Rocky Mountains of Colorado, I came upon a stream. I became immediately hypnotized by its rhythmic flow and sat for hours looking mindlessly into the ice clear liquid flowing over a bed of rounded gray and brown rocks. My eyes fixed on the whirling dance of the water grass attached to one particular stone. The water rushed by these green hair-like creatures, massaging them into an infinite variety of flowing movements. These fine and delicate grasses, although firmly rooted to the stone at their base, let go and allowed themselves to flow and turn in any way that the force of the water guided them.

One simple thought came to my mind "This is the way to live life. To be firmly rooted in discipline and discrimination, but at the same time to be loose, flexible and responsive to the changing forces around us".

This type of living and thinking - although foreign to us at this point, is one of the necessary steps for us to make in the process of our evolution. Such an attitude creates a very minimum of tension and a maximum of harmony.

EXTRICATING OURSELVES FROM ATTACHMENTS

Meditation is a process of freeing ourselves from our excessive and self-destructive attachment to external sources of security, pleasure, satisfaction or affirmation. This process obviously comes into conflict with those deep-seated attachments and the fears and ignorance from which they come forth.

What can we expect then when we start meditating?

To understand this, we must look at what meditation does in terms of spiritual growth, and, for that matter, what spiritual growth is.

Spiritual growth is traveling the path from the ego to the spirit within. That is, the road of evolution in which the individual consciousness unfolds in greater and more harmonious expression as it evolves. A gradual opening up of the channel between the spirit and the personality occurs, bringing greater identification with the inner source of mind, so that the higher self can enter and function more freely and effectively on the earth plane.

Every action of our life is part of that journey on the spiritual path back to our source. Every moment is an opportunity, a crossroads, at which we can take a step forward, or remain asleep at the wayside.

WHY IS THIS HAPPENING ?

Our spiritual growth is not reflected in how long we can meditate or in what exercises we can do, but in our attitude, thoughts, actions and interactions every moment of the day. Meditating for a half

The Art of Meditation

hour each morning and then getting up to spend an half hour on the phone complaining about our children, spouse, or friends gets us nowhere. **Hours spent in the delicious peace of meditation are useless if our attitudes and values remain selfish and irresponsible.**

Growing spiritually means taking responsibility for creating our reality. Everything that happens to us is a function of our own actions, thoughts, needs, emotions and beliefs, past and present. This realization is our main protection from problems along the spiritual path. By accepting that we are creating the events that are occurring around us, we are able to ask "Why is this happening to me? What can I learn from this? How can I grow more mature and stronger through this experience?"

In this way, we are getting closer to the real source or **cause of the flow of events,** and thus can more effectively change them (if we don't like them) and more easily flow with them when we cannot change them.

The obvious answer which often becomes apparent to "why is this happening?", is that these dramas, in which we find ourselves, are self-created so as to wake ourselves up; to force us to let go and flow along the river to our inner selves.

Example; You are very much in love and just cannot bear the thought of living without your loved one. Even a few days apart leaves you lost and depressed. Everything has been all right until now because your friend likes to be depended on and also needs you as much.

Now there cannot be anything wrong with love. For, surely, it is the most powerful healing force in the universe. But the inner self recognizes that you are undermining your own strength and self image by ignoring your inner power by believing you must have your loved one to be happy or to continue existing. It is obvious that, with such a strong dependency, you cannot travel much further along the path because you are not recognizing what you really are; a spirit which is immortal, and self fulfilling, dwelling in flesh. On this higher level, inner level, **one is in love with all humanity.** If one wants to continue along the path towards cosmic identification, then this over-fascination with a particular individual must relax.

Should we stop loving? Obviously not. There is nothing in love that keeps us from moving along the road to our souls. It is the dependency, the need, and the disbelief in ourselves that slows us down. It is entirely possible to be married, have many children and also accept and express the creativity, strength, the immortality of one's soul.

Returning to our example; the soul who is the director of our reality (at least as much as we allow it to be), can see that the only reason we came here to Earth in the first place, and occupied these bodies, was and is to continue along the spiritual path and bring the spirit and the flesh into harmony. Everything else we do and strive for must be seen in that perspective, as another step towards knowing ourselves and expanding human potential.

Our inner self may get rather tired of waiting while we ignore it and search everywhere else for happiness and satisfaction. Life, for a person who ignores his soul, is one of constantly attempting to seek external gratification, security and pleasure, through food, sex, money, possessions, social relationships, prestige, fame, professional success and even spiritual achievement. In other words, the ego is like a little child lost from its parents, looking everywhere but at home, for that love and security which is always there.

WAKING UP

So, our inner self decides to wake us up a bit, to cut those "balls and chains" which we are dragging along the path with us. This is often a rather painful and disturbing process, especially if we do not understand that this is a **process initiated from the depths of our being for the good of our spiritual development.**

In such a case we might face the loss of some source of security, pleasure or affirmation. This will be the crucial moment of testing, from which we may leap into increased awareness and move more freely and quickly along the path, or desperately grasp at another "ball and chain" on which to depend. We can accept what is happening and find inner strength, and discover that we are complete within ourselves in a rebirth, a fresh new opportunity to start a more open and dynamic way of life.

Thus, meditation is an accelerator of spiritual growth. When one practices meditation and other spiritual practices, he is in effect saying to his inner self, "okay, I am consciously deciding that I want to know you. I want to grow, to expand my awareness, to know God, to continue down the path of evolution, to become free from illusion and the unhappiness it creates".

As we have mentioned, all of life is spiritual, and true spiritual growth takes place through the interactions with the people and events in our life. Everyone is on the spiritual path. We simply don't have any other choice; that is the only reason we have come here to planet Earth. But there are many ways and velocities at which to travel.

One can move along with the crawl of humanity, not daring to break away from the norm, and stand up and start walking. They avoid making decisions for themselves, lulled by the mass sleep consciousness, following the various forms of social programmings concerning what brings happiness, success and what has importance and value in life.

Some choose to walk alone. Walking alone sometimes leads one to certain spiritual practices. This often happens when those who walk alone become very unhappy and confused at the beginning. They are different and don't find comfort or security in the mass games and dramas. In their search for something more deeply satisfying they come upon an assortment of spiritual vehicles, as we may call them with which to travel the path more quickly. One may choose some combination of philosophy, psychology, meditation, dietary changes, serving others, exercising, breathing techniques, prayer etc. No matter what vehicle one chooses to take, he or she is necessarily going to be moving faster than before.

But this means that the chains of security and attachment will have to be broken more quickly, for they cannot be dragged along at such high speeds of growth. So, this is how meditation can sometimes create problems. By doing regular meditation we are setting ourselves up to become liberated from our identifications and attachments. This is sometimes a difficult or painful process. We may pass through periods of confusion as we are caught between our conflicting needs for both external grasping and internal centering.

In the case that one's spiritual growth process does bring him to an internal crisis, the insurance policy which will cover one for recovery from all accidents along the path is an acceptance of the fact that life is a school, and that it is always giving to each of us exactly what we need for the next step in our growth process. As Richard Bach expresses in his book "Illusions" , "a problem never comes to us without a little gift in its hands". Any problem that comes to us is actually an invaluable opportunity for our spiritual growth process. This does not mean that we need to search for, or create, problems. They will appear if and when we need them.

When one meditates twice a day for 20 to 30 minutes, there is a very small chance if any that one will release inner blockages and stress at such a rapid rate that a life crisis would be created. On the other hand, life crises are an integral part of every person's life regardless of whether he meditates or not.

SOME AIDS TO MEDITATION

There are some beneficial activities that help prepare the body and mind for meditation and which supplement and enrich the process of spiritual growth in combination with meditation.

We will mention some of them briefly here. Some will be explained in much greater detail further on in the book. Others are explained in much more detail in our other books (given in brackets) and we will refer to them where appropriate.

Here are some possible techniques and concepts, which might help us make this transition and act as "catalysts" to the dance of the soul.

1) Deep Relaxation - Body Awareness

Developing the communication between conscious awareness and body sensing. Learning to relax the body in parts and as a whole. (Refer to our book "SELF HEALING").

2. Exercise

Methodically releases body and mind tensions through stretching postures and breath. Creates a more fluid and relaxed body and mind. (SELF-HEALING).

3) Dance - Creative Movement

Breaks down body-mind rigidity and puts one in contact with inner forces and forces of nature. The same possibility lies within all forms of creative expression, i.e. music, painting, crafts, scientific discovery, singing, etc.

4) Chanting and Prayer

Repetitious singing of simple tones and prayers serve to orient and tune the personality to larger cosmic forces. Also it is enjoyable.

5) Facing Ourselves

Learning to see our ego identifications, accept them and go beyond them. (Refer to the books **"The Psychology of Happiness"** and **"Miracles of Love and Wisdom"**).

6) Breathing Techniques which balance and increase the energy flow in the body and mind, allowing us to sit more easily with the spine straight and to attain higher levels of consciousness.

7) Contact with Nature is an important part in our process of attunement with our universal self, which is expressed so concretely in the beauty harmony and perfection of nature.

8) Service to Humanity

By attuning our individual will to the good of all humanity, we come more into harmony with the forces of nature which provide support for human growth and survival. As we serve others, we are taken care of by the forces around us. We gradually become freer from the ego and its tendency towards ego-centeredness, which is the basic obstacle to our spiritual growth (**"Universal Philosophy"**).

9) Detachment and Discrimination

The most powerful companion to meditation is an attitude of detachment from the objects and relationships, which bind the mind into thinking we are the body. Discrimination between the soul and the body will help us to reach higher levels of meditation much more efficiently. Detachment from the body and personality is a basic prerequisite for spiritual growth. (**"Universal Philosophy""**).

CHAPTER 10

THE ENERGY CENTERS AND EVOLUTION

We briefly mentioned in the previous chapters how health, happiness and clarity of mind are all basically a function of how abundantly and harmoniously our energy is flowing through the body and mind. Thus it would be useful for us to discuss briefly the seven centers from which this bioenergy radiates out to all the body, nourishing all the cells and organs of the body with this life creating and sustaining force. The quality of this energy flow has a profound effect on the quality of our meditation, as well as our thinking and feeling processes. A low or disturbed energy flow can lead to fear, depression and negative thinking, or anxiety and agitated thoughts all of which are obviously obstacles to our spiritual growth and happiness in general.

The existence of these centers was discovered thousands of years ago by mystics and yogis who, while in meditation, penetrated into the deeper realities of the body and the mind. They actually saw these seven centers like vortexes of energy which were in continuous pulsating motion. Throughout the years, individuals, gifted with the ability of supernormal sight, have seen and reported the existence of these centers. They have also reported that the quantity and quality of energy flow, as well as the color of the light being emanated, change according to the physical, emotional and mental state of the individual.

In recent years very interesting scientific tests were made by a doctor at the Belview clinic in New York, concerning the ability of such "psychics" to diagnose diseases and other physical problems, by interpreting what they saw at these energy centers. The doctor's name is Shaffica Karagulla and the book which she wrote, which documents the results, is titled "<u>BREAKTHROUGH TO CREATIVITY</u>" - DeVorss Publishers. This very interesting book reports on the incredible accuracy (usually about 80%) with which these psychics were able to diagnose the cause of the patients' problems by interpreting the conditions of these energy centers.

Doctor Karagulla and the psychics sat in the emergency ward of the hospital and observed the patients coming in. The psychic reported to the doctor what she or he understood to be the problem and the doctor wrote it down. Neither the patients nor the doctors in the emergency room were aware of what was going on, for doctor Karagulla and the psychics were sitting in the entrance lobby, and the diagnosis which was made was done as the patient passed by. This is an amazing phenomenon that could help many people to recognize the existence of these energy centers and their connection to our physical and mental condition. This is definitely a realm for much more research in the future.

As we mentioned previously these centers are located along the spinal column. They are not actually a part of the spinal column. They are not nerves, but actually the energy system, which is the causal reality of the nervous system. If there was no bioenergy, the nervous system would stop functioning. There are thousands of tiny lines of energy which flow out from these centers. They are called **nadis,** and they distribute the energy to all the cells of the body. If we open up the body, we will not see these energy centers, but if we photograph it in an electromagnetic field, we will probably be able to see them on the print which is created. Such work is being attempted both in Russia and in the U.S.

These are both centers of energy and also centers of consciousness simultaneously. They are centers through which consciousness becomes manifest as energy and through which energy is directed to the body and the mind. They are centers through which the soul or the higher self communicates with, and supports, the body and mind. As we evolve, this energy flows upward, the higher centers are activated and we become more conscious and intelligent, more connected to our higher self. Let us discuss these seven centers.

The first center is found in the area at the base of the spine. It governs the legs, and the genital organs, and, to some degree, the process of elimination of wastes. If there is a disturbance in the energy flow at this center there will be problems in these areas. On the other hand, if there are problems in these parts of the body, a corresponding disturbance will be created in that energy center. These centers are also connected to our emotional and mental bodies, and thus our negative thoughts and feelings can create a disturbance in any center and this can, in turn, be manifested as a physical problem. Many emotional problems are transferred to the body in this way. This energy system communicates its state of harmony or disharmony to the body through its effect on the nervous and endocrine systems.

The first center has to do with the need for **security and survival.** A person who is functioning from this center will feel basically insecure and most of his actions will have survival and safety as their motive. The psychological aspect of all these centers is discussed in more detail in the book **"Psychology of Happiness"**.

The second center is located some centimeters below the navel. This center regulates the energy flow to the organs which hold and eliminate the wastes from the body. It also governs the reproductive organs. This center governs our need for sensual pleasure. A person who is functioning basically from this center will be seeking continuously to satisfy his need for pleasureful experiences in various ways; through food, drink, sex, coffee, cigarettes, and, in general, drugs of various kinds. Such persons tend to get easily addicted to substances, people or stimulating situations. This is often at the expense of their health and real lasting happiness.

The third center is located in the area of the solar plexus and has to do with the flow of energy to the organs of digestion and absorption; in the stomach, duodenum, small intestine, liver, gall bladder, pancreas, and the adrenal glands. This center and, thus, these organs, are very much affected by our emotional states. Accordingly, our problems with digestion, gastric ulcers, colitis and various other such disturbances, are very often psychosomatic. Various exercises and breathing techniques are given in our book **"Self Healing"**, to help release the energy blocked in this center, so as to help restore the proper functioning of our digestive system. This center is also responsible for the body's heating needs. If one has poor circulation or feels cold easily, he may need to free this center with the various techniques given.

Emotionally this center has to do with personal power and self-affirmation. A person functioning basically from this center will seek to prove himself to those around him through his success or power in various areas; professionally, socially, sexually, politically, athletically, economically, verbally, or intellectually, etc. He will be always comparing himself to others and competing so as to prove that he is right, or superior or the most successful. This, of course, is tiring for his body, his nerves and his mind. Deep breathing, with a short period (5 seconds) of holding the breath, will help to release the excess built up energy in this center. Relaxation techniques will also help.

The fourth center has to do with our heart, lungs and Thymus gland. When there is a blockage here, we may have problems with our breathing such as asthma, bronchitis or frequent colds. Or, on the other hand, we may have heart problems. This is not to say that these energy blockages are the only causes for such problems, but that they can be a factor. In our spiritual growth process as this "love" center starts to open, we may feel pain in the chest area. **If in fact** this pain is an energy phenomenon (which is seldom the case), then it has nothing to do with our heart. As the energy rises and centers open (like buds opening to become flowers) then temporary problems, or symptoms, can sometimes appear in the area of the energy activity. This may mean pains or various sensations in the chest, neck, forehead or top of the head. We will not be giving techniques for raising that energy upward in this book, however, because they require very specific guidance and purification, without which this process can sometimes be dangerous.

A person who functions from this heart center, acts out of unconditional love for others and himself. He likes to serve and help people. It is only at this stage that we begin to feel real love. Until then we feel love with conditions. We love people because they offer us security, pleasure or affirmation. When they stop offering us these or start obstructing us from having what we want, our love turns into hurt, disappointment, anger and sometimes hate. The process of evolving from this kind of love into the unconditional love of the fourth center is often a painful process, because we pass through many trials which test whether our love is really unconditional or not.

The fifth center is found in the area of the neck and regulates the energy flow to the neck processes, i.e. swallowing, speaking, singing etc. Its close vicinity to the thyroid and parathyroid make it responsible for the energy flow to those glands. This center has to do with the power of creation, which is very much connected with the throat, and the **logos.** It is the higher creative center. The lower creative center is the second center, through which we create children. Through the higher creative center we create music, art, poetry, drama and ideas. This center is directly related to the subconscious and to psychic abilities. We are not interested, however, in cultivating psychic powers and are cautioned not to play with them!

The sixth center is in the center of the forehead and it regulates the energy flow to all the muscles of the face and the brain. It is identified especially with the pituitary gland. It is the center of higher knowledge of the inner witness, the higher self. It is the seat of the conscience and of spiritual discrimination between the real and the temporary. Relaxing this center and concentrating on it, help us to withdraw our attention from the physical body. It is an excellent way to overcome pain. No matter where we are having pain in our body, if we can isolate our awareness in the center of the forehead, we will not feel the pain. A person who functions from this center is detached from what he does. He is the eternal witness. He realizes that he is not the body and mind which are acting, but actually an immortal soul which is temporarily occupying and using the body and mind.

The seventh center is not actually considered to be a center. The corresponding organ in the body is considered to be the pineal gland in the brain. We still do not know much about this gland, probably because it is not yet functioning as it will after some thousands of years of more evolution. This center is beyond the body. A person centered here is in blissful union with God, nature and all beings. He is in a state of continual bliss, which is unaffected by the changing conditions around him. He is in a continual state of meditation.

The various techniques suggested to the spiritual aspirant; physical exercises, breathing techniques, cleansing techniques, deep relaxations, dietary guidelines, prayer and meditation - are all designed to establish harmony in these centers and gradually liberate the energy from the lower centers and let it rise up into the higher centers of higher consciousness. Especially important in bringing about harmony in these centers and in the general flow of the bioenergy throughout our bodies are the various breathing techniques and especially the rhythmic breathing through alternate nostrils.

HUMAN EVOLUTION

Let us take a brief look at what role these energy centers play in the overall evolution of mankind. Consciousness existed before the creation of the Sun and Earth and the eventual creation of physical life here. This consciousness began to express itself first as tiny one-celled organisms (that is if we exclude its expression as the elements of nature such as minerals, water, air and heat, light). Evolution took place and this consciousness became more and more capable of expressing its unlimited, latent powers in more and more advanced ways. In this way it became able to create increasingly more capable vehicles for expression of its innate nature, such as plants, animals and then man. In each stage of this evolution this consciousness obtained greater freedom from the limitations of matter.

The Art of Meditation

Along with this freedom of expression man also gradually began to experience consciousness of himself as something separate from the rest of creation, and the freedom to choose to live in accordance with natural laws or not. These two discoveries were to become his great undoing and possibly his destruction. He can also now learn to choose to **live in harmony with the universal laws and rediscover his oneness with all of nature.** There are indications that more and more people are doing this today.

Until now this evolutionary process has been an unconscious one. Few have participated consciously, seeking to improve themselves and evolve. What this book is all about is participating consciously and willfully in this process of evolution. That is the purpose of life. One's evolutionary progress is accompanied by the gradual awakening of the higher centers of consciousness. Thus, as we meditate and employ other techniques for increasing spiritual awareness, we will begin to experience the awakening of these centers. Some will experience phenomena at the sites of these centers. But, most will simply see the results of these openings as changes in their mental and emotional states, and predominately in their character. We become more peaceful, more loving, more universal, in our perspective, more creative and, in general, happier and more in balance.

But the road is not always without obstacles or difficulties. We have already mentioned to some degree in chapter five about the phenomenon of un-stressing. Let us look into this in a little more detail.

The energy flow between these centers is obstructed by the following factors:

1. Toxins obstructing the free flow of nerve impulses.

2. Weakness in the organs, limbs and spine.

3. Muscular **tensions**.

4. Poor posture.

5. Emotional blockages - especially insecurity and fear.

6. Attachments, habits, addictions.

7. Identification with the body and mind.

8. Tendencies, habits or karma from before our birth.

As the energy seeks to move upward into the higher centers it will encounter these obstructions. Just as water passing through a pipe, through which there has not been any flow for a long time, will begin to dislocate and carry with it sediment which has accumulated, this energy will do the same with these obstacles. As these are pushed to the surface of our body or mind, we may begin to experience various "healing crises" or "growing crises", as they are called, because although they may be unpleasant and temporarily disorienting, they are actually a beneficial process of healing and growth. Many seekers will not experience any of this because the "pieces" are dislodged and released in small regular doses and everything proceeds smoothly.

If serious problems occur it is usually because the person already had a high degree of imbalance physically or mentally (regardless as to whether it showed to himself or others), or because he overdid some techniques.

THE SYMPTOMS

What symptoms might one encounter in such a case? What usually happens is that a person experiences one or both poles or extremes of the various physical and mental opposites. For example one might feel intense inner heat regardless of the temperature around him. Or he may feel so cold that no amount of clothing can warm him. He may experience a tremendous appetite that knows no satisfaction, or have no appetite at all. He may feel intense sexual impulses or none at all. There may be moments of ecstasy with the simplest things, or depression, which nullifies everything. He may have unlimited energy or no energy at all. He may need very little sleep or need to sleep continuously. He may have visions - pleasant or unpleasant. There may be pains in various parts of the body where the energy is trying to flow more abundantly but is receiving resistance.

Such symptoms are also experienced when one employs methods of natural healing, such as Homeopathy or fasting. Meditation is in fact a "fasting" from thought forms. I repeat that very few will experience these symptoms. If they do let them employ the guidelines given in Chapter 5.

PREPARING THE BODY AND MIND

We can, however, help this energy to flow more freely by employing various techniques which purify the body and mind and make the spiritual growth process much safer, quicker and more pleasant.

1. FASTING once a week will help us to clean out our bodies of various toxins that accumulate there and gradually destroy our health. This fasting can also be an excellent way to increase our spiritual discrimination and will power. You can fast on water, or juices or herb teas, or, if you cannot go without food for some serious reason, then eat only fruit. This can be done for twenty-four hours. For example we eat Thursday afternoon, fast Thursday evening and Friday morning and eat again Friday afternoon. Or we can fast longer. For example from Thursday evening all day Friday until Saturday morning. (Anyone who has anemia, very low blood pressure, heart illness, or is under heavy medication, should check with his doctor before fasting).

2. A PURE DIET is the greatest insurance for a healthy body and mind. The vibration of the food we eat has an effect on the quality of our body and mind. If we eat food that is dead, over-processed, over cooked without life, we will create a body and mind that are similar - without life, without vitality. If we eat foods that are stimulating, corrosive, agitating, we will have a similar nervous system - uneasy, nervous, anxious, perhaps even aggressive.

In both cases it will be difficult to meditate. We want our food to be harmonious, life-giving but calm.

Thus we will want our diet to be basically:

1. Fresh vegetables and fruits.

2. Whole grains and beans.

3. Fresh un-roasted, unsalted nuts and dried fruits.

4. Various dairy products.

These should be the basis of our diet, if we want spiritual growth and health. We should avoid as much as possible eating meat, fish, poultry, overcooked foods, sugar, polished grains and chemical preservatives. Meat is recognized by all religious traditions as **non-spiritual food.** For this reason all peoples of all religions abstain from meat before the major spiritual events such as Easter and Christmas. According to the official church calendar, a Greek Orthodox who followed all of the days of fasting from meat, would eat meat approximately 50 days a year. (It varies from year to year). Thus even Christianity, the religion that supposedly condones the eating of flesh, suggests that we abstain from it about 300 of the 365 days of the year. It is an obstacle in our spiritual growth.

I would suggest, however, that one not force himself to stop eating meat. Let him think about it. Let him ask himself if he really wants to eat it or whether he is simply in the habit of eating it or believes that he must eat it in order to be healthy or have energy. This last belief is one of the greatest misconceptions of our times. So many millions of people in the East have lived all of their lives without ever eating meat of any kind, and they have evinced all of the physical and mental capabilities that we see in those who eat meat. They work hard physically and are as mentally astute as any meat eater. How is this explained?

There is a simple test that you can employ to determine whether meat, or any other food, is suitable for your psychosynthesis. A code for determining what is suitable for you to eat is to eat whatever you feel that you can procure with your own hands. If you feel comfortable in plucking an apple off a tree, or pulling a carrot out of the ground, then these are suitable for you. If you feel comfortable in cutting the throat of a cow, lamb, pig or chicken or fish and then cutting them up into pieces, then these too are suitable for you. One may say, "I feel comfortable about the fish and chicken but not about the cow and the lamb". This is your choice. Eat what your conscience and feelings allow you to procure with your own hands without feeling badly. This does not mean that you have to do it and feel comfortable about it. In this way our inherent sensitivity is the best guide as to what we should eat. Those who are less sensitive do not harm themselves spiritually by eating other animals. When one is more sensitive his feelings tell him when something is not good for him anymore. It is best, however, to make any changes in your diet gradually and if you have serious health problems to discuss them with your doctor.

3. DAILY EXERCISES help to remove the toxins accumulating in the body. They strengthen and relax the muscles so that one can sit for longer periods of time in meditation without being bothered by pains or discomfort. They also strengthen and attune our nervous system, endocrine system and immune system for a more harmoniously functioning, healthy and vital body and mind. But, most important of all, they release the energy blockages that exist in the energy body and especially between the energy centers.

The exercises ,which each should do in order to maintain his health and proceed spiritually, will differ according to his type of body, specific needs and how much he has worked with his body. But there are some general guidelines, which will help you use exercises to improve your meditation.

a. Do your **exercises before** your meditation. Energy flow will be freer, your spine straighter and concentration easier.

b. Do exercises which **free the spine from its tension;** stretching upward and exercises in any position which create backward stretching, forward stretching, sideward stretching and twisting of the spine in both directions.

c. Do exercises that **free the neck** from its built up tension.

d. Perform positions with the **head down** so as to increase the blood flow to the brain.

e. Free the **abdominal area** of tension with exercises that work for you.

f. Work on any parts of the body which are **weak or need help.**

g. Move on to **breathing techniques** and then onto your meditation.

For those who have cultivated their body through yoga exercises and have moved on to the essential static poses, we can suggest the following series as an excellent preparation for meditation. The spinal twist (lying or sitting), the shoulder stand, plough, fish, forward stretch (sitting), cobra, bow, locust and then the prayer position (or yoga mudra, for those who can without harming their knees) and then assume a sitting position for breathing techniques and meditation. (Those who have not been trained in these techniques should not try to do them without guidance).

The above series is easier to do in the evening. One may have difficulty with such static positions in the morning upon first waking when the body is stiff. Of course the body can get used to any routine given time and practice. Some, however, prefer dynamic exercises in the morning. The salutation to the sun is an excellent way to prepare the body for meditation in the morning. Those who have not been initiated in these techniques can do any exercises, which make their bodies, feel lighter, less rigid and more alive.

This progressive movement from exercise to breathing and then to meditation is like driving a car. When we start out, we have it in first gear, we need plenty of gas to get going. First gear is our exercises. Then we move into second gear after having already achieved some momentum. That is our breathing techniques. Having achieved even more momentum, we move into third gear (prayer or invocation) and finally we slip into fourth gear (meditation) and cruise along with very little effort. If we had tried to start the car in fourth gear, it would have been much more difficult (or impossible).

Do not, however, get the idea that one cannot meditate if he does not make all of these preparations. There are many schools of meditation which do not refer to them at all. Our experience, is, however, that these preparations offer one a much deeper meditation and help one absorb these spiritual changes into his body and mind much more effectively. If one is, however, unable to employ these techniques he can meditate anyway.

4. BREATHING TECHNIQUES as we have already mentioned in Chapter 5, are very important for the balancing of energy and for the increased energy, which is necessary for one to transcend his mind.

5. SELF-OBSERVATION and **SELF-ANALYSIS** are important aspects of the purification process that will facilitate the rising of our bioenergy into the higher centers of consciousness. Our feelings and habits, which result from our basic beliefs, are the major obstacles to our spiritual growth. Observing, analyzing and then changing those mistaken beliefs is an essential part of our growth process.

6. DEEP RELAXATION TECHNIQUES are also useful for this purification and attunement process. In relaxation we can remove the various psychosomatic tensions, which obstruct the energy flow in the body and in the mind. Also, as relaxation is very similar to meditation in many ways, we can sometimes have meditative experiences (especially of total surrender) in our deep relaxation. This then helps us with our meditation.

7. PRAYER AND CHANTING are also very important methods of emotional purification. They release emotional energies and awaken higher spiritual emotions of love, gratitude and ecstasy, helping to open the higher centers. They develop faith and a feeling of connectedness with God which facilitate our inner peace.

8. ETHICAL BEHAVIOR is perhaps the most basic preparation for any spiritual effort. As we will discuss in much more detail later, ethical behavior is the foundation of spiritual life. Without a solid foundation all of our spiritual "structure" is likely to collapse at some point.

As you can see, there are a number of ways in which we can facilitate the flow of energy into the higher centers of consciousness. These methods are a very important preparation for, and supplement to, our meditation and should be incorporated as much as possible into our daily life.

CHAPTER 11

UNDERSTANDING, INCREASING AND HARMONIZING OUR BIOENERGY

Until recently, scientists believed that **atoms** were the building blocks of the material world. Recently they realized that these "building blocks" are simply dense manifestations of **energy**.

This energy is the basic creative "essence" behind this material universe. In the future they will realize that the creative source of this energy is **consciousness** and that consciousness is the causal factor of all that exists in all planes.

Energy, however, plays an extremely important role as the connecting link between consciousness, thought and action in our material reality. Energy is the connecting link between the spirit, the mind and the body.

When there is insufficient energy in the soul-mind-body system, then there will not be health, peace, clarity, happiness, love or effective functioning on any level.

UNDERSTANDING THE ROLE OF ENERGY

Let us examine the hierarchy of bodies as it is explained by the great minds, who have penetrated deeply into man's inner being. The following diagram will help us to understand this relationship between the various levels of man's existence.

SPIRIT
I
CAUSAL BODY
I
HIGHER INTELLECT - MIND
I
ENERGY BODY
I
PHYSICAL BODY
I
NERVOUS SYSTEM - ENDOCRINE SYSTEM
I
ALL OTHER SYSTEMS

1. The **spirit** is eternal consciousness without beginning or end. Without birth or death. It undergoes no changes. It is Divine Consciousness - Existence - Bliss.

2. The **causal body** is the "subconscious of the soul" in which are imprinted all of the soul's memories and tendencies from the beginning of its evolutionary journey through the material planes.

3. The **higher intellect** is the part of the mind that has greater clarity, spiritual discrimination, and detachment from the illusions of the common mind.

4. The **common mind** is a programmed system of beliefs and reactions. When one functions from his common mind, he is under the influence of past experiences which have programmed him to react and think mechanically towards situations without the freedom to act from his highest possible potential. He reacts like a robot as he has learned to.

5. The **energy body** is an energy system, which supplies all of these other bodies (including the physical body that is next in line) with the power upon which they function. If this energy system is depleted, or if the energy is not flowing harmoniously, then these bodies and their respective functions will suffer (while the soul is incarnated).

6. The **physical body** is the one we all know and to which we all are attached and give so much importance. We are obsessed with its health, its appearance and its pleasures. These attachments are the cause of most of our problems.

EVIDENCE OF THE ENERGY BODY'S EXISTENCE

Some scientific experiments will help us to understand the importance of this energy body. One experiment was with fertilized chicken eggs. These eggs were photographed daily in an electromagnetic field so that, through Kirlian photography, the scientists would be able to see the energy field of the egg. After a few days an embryo appeared on the Kirlian photography of the egg. This surprised the researchers, because it was much too early for the development of the embryo. They opened the egg and there was no embryo. The most likely conclusion then would be that the energy field of the embryo exists before the actual development of the physical embryo in the egg.

We can understand from this that the energy body of each person exists before the formation of the physical body in the mother's womb. The cells then form around this energy field, guided by its "energy structure", which eventually becomes a material structure. Thus the energy body is the creative force - structure for the creation of the physical body. Of course this energy field has its own cause in the higher bodies.

A second experiment concerns sea sponges, which were taken from the sea, cut up into small pieces and passed through a silk screen so that they were broken up into individual cells and placed into a large laboratory beaker. The next day the very same sponge had reformed itself into the exact same structure. A logical conclusion would be that the energy field of the sponge remained intact, although the physical structure was completely dissolved. The remaining energy field was then able to guide the cells into the particular positions so that the sponge could continue its life and functions.

We can see, from these two experiments, that the energy body is an energy field, which both guides the **creation** of the physical body and **maintains** its structure and vitality throughout its life. Few of you will need proof that, when our energy is low our emotional, mental and creative functions are all diminished and frequently negative and unpleasant. Neither do we need proof that our physical and psychological health is much more vulnerable when our energy is run down.

THIS ONE ENERGY HAS MANY FUNCTIONS

This bioenergy is to our body as electrical energy is to our house. Our electrical energy can be used and expressed in a variety of ways such as to provide heat, cold, music, vacuum, or movement, according to the machine or instrument through which it is expressed. In the same way, our one bioenergy is used for heating the body, for walking, running, working, creating babies, thinking, creating new cells, removing unwanted guests in our body, digesting our food and, of course, the functioning of all our senses and limbs.

What can we expect when this energy is flowing abundantly and harmoniously through our body-mind system? On the physical level we can expect health, vitality, agility and freedom from pain or illness. On the emotional level we will experience peace, contentment and love. Mentally we will experience inner peace, clarity, effective functioning and creativity. Socially we live in love, mutual respect, openness, cooperation and unity. And eventually we will be the recipients of the spiritual qualities of universal love, wisdom, inner peace, unity with all beings and transcendence of our personal self and the realization of our Universal Self.

Thus, we can see from our discussion until now that this one universal bioenergy is a creative force in the development of the body. It is the sustaining power, which keeps the body alive. It is essential for proper physical and mental functioning. It is also the vital energy through which our being will evolve and develop higher spiritual qualities. It is, in addition, the connecting link between ourselves and all beings and objects around us. We connect with these beings and objects through our invisible energy fields. We even connect with other dimensions of reality, of which we are not even aware, through these energy channels.

As shown on our original diagram, this energy field is the connecting link between our body and our mind. When there is a disturbance in the mind, such as anxiety, fear, depression or anger, there results a corresponding contraction and distortion of the energy field. This then has a direct effect on the pituitary, pineal and hypothalamus glands, which transfer these emotional states into physical conditions in the nervous and endocrine systems. These changes in these two master systems are then manifested in all the systems, including the immune system, the digestive, respiratory, skeletal, circulatory, muscular, lymphatic and eliminative systems.

On the other hand, when there is some disturbance in the physical body, such as in the digestive system, due to poor eating habits, or in the spinal column, due to poor posture, these physical factors inhibit and distort the energy flow and this creates negative emotional and mental states. Thus we can see the extreme importance of keeping this energy in a harmonious flow.

THE KEY TO HARMONY

Just as there are laws that govern the harmony of the universe, such as the law of gravity and laws governing electromagnetic fields, and just as there are guidelines that contribute to the creation of harmonious music, there are laws that govern the harmonious functioning of the individual and society. These laws have to do with the natural ways in which man was made to eat, breathe, move, think and interact with others and his environment. When man functions in harmony with these laws, he experiences an abundant and harmonious flow of energy. When he does not live and act in harmony with these laws, his energy field, health and thoughts and social behavior become discordant.

Only man has the **choice not to live in harmony** with these laws. All other beings on the earth are bound to live according to their inner nature. Only man has the free will to ignore his inner nature. This is his blessing and his curse, depending on whether or not he uses this opportunity to consciously participate in his divine nature. This offers him the opportunity of evolution or of losing his balance altogether (at least temporarily).

Let us now consider the factors we need to take into consideration in creating an abundant and harmonious energy supply. We are interested in both quantity and quality. We are not interested in having large quantities of nervous energy, which we cannot express harmoniously or creatively. Such energy often causes emotional outbursts and can be harmful to our relationships and clarity of mind. We are interested in a steady flow of energy, which does not have abrupt changes such as exhaustion or aggressiveness.

Take a piece of wood as an example. By itself it does not emit large quantities of energy. You might say that it is in a state of inertia exhibiting a low energy flow. If we set it on fire, then there is a large amount of energy being released but it is not easily controlled or utilized effectively. This is like the nervous energy that flows out of some individuals in an uncreative and often destructive way. Eventually we have the glowing coal, which emits a steady flow of intense energy, which can easily be used effectively for our needs. This is the type of energy we are seeking. We are neither interested in being dead wood, nor in being a raging fire.

THE HUMAN ENERGY SYSTEM

Let us now refer to the accompanying diagram, which will help us understand the human energy system. The rectangle with four holes on the sides and one hole on the top and one on the bottom represent the individual. The circle above represents the universal source of energy, which most of us call God, or Universal Being, or Universal Energy Field. Imagine this circle as a sphere and around it as many rectangles as there are humans or beings of all kinds. Each being takes its energy from this one source. It is the only source.

Each being receives this energy from the hole at the top of the rectangle.

The Art of Meditation

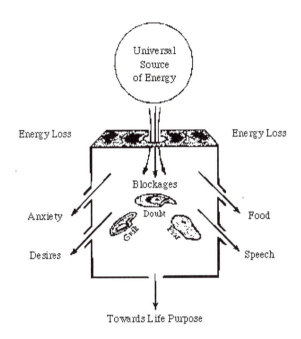

Towards Life Purpose

Some naturally receive more than others do as their upper aperture is more open. They have greater contact with the higher levels of their being and more abundant flow of energy. Everyone has this contact with this universal source during the hours of sleep. Without sleep we would become totally exhausted and disoriented. The purpose of spiritual life, however, is to learn to open up to this energy consciously and to eventually be constantly open to it so that even sleep would become unnecessary.

The ultimate function of this energy is to flow towards the purpose of each individual's life. Each soul has come to this earth for a specific purpose. Each has come to learn, to serve and to create. We need to learn what we have come to learn, and how we have come to create and serve. Few, however, are aware of their life purpose, and thus they do not direct their energies towards that purpose. Their energies are lost in seeking after temporary pleasures, security or self-affirmation. We become drained, disillusioned and unhappy because we spend much energy without the corresponding feeling of satisfaction we are seeking. This satisfaction can be had only by those who have discovered their life purpose, and are directing their energy towards it.

The aperture at the bottom of the rectangle represents the energy flowing towards our life purpose. The four holes on the sides represent the energy being lost in other directions. One major loss of valuable energy is **superficial talking.** Most of us talk much more than we need to. Our goal is usually to affirm ourselves in the other's eyes, or to fill in the silence with which we feel uncomfortable. We not only lose a tremendous amount of spiritual energy but also fill our minds (and others' too) with a large quantity of useless information or negative impressions which then disturb our mental and emotional state. Inner silence is then even more difficult and we need other forms of tension release in order to balance ourselves. Thus, even more energy is lost and thus fails to be directed towards our life purpose.

A second hole, through which we lose energy is **overeating**. We eat in order to get energy. But through over eating and through eating difficult combinations of foods we actually lose energy and lower our spirituality. This is why all religions encourage fasting before the major spiritual events. In this way people's senses are more spiritually attuned.

A third hole through which we lose valuable spiritual energy is through our **chasing after temporary sources of pleasure, happiness, security and self-affirmation.** Our attention and energy are continuously focused outwardly as we try to obtain and hold onto whatever we believe will make us happy or secure. We may chase after relationships, money, possessions, professional or social positions, drugs, food, vacations, recreation or anything else which we hope will make us happy.

There is nothing wrong with having any of these. The problem occurs when we waste large quantities of energy trying to **obtain** them, and then trying to **keep** them. We also lose energy **fearing** losing them and then feeling **depressed** when we have lost them. In reality they offer very little happiness and much unhappiness.

The fourth hole, through which we lose energy, is through our **anxiety** and **worry** about what will happen. Most people lose large quantities of energy because of their lack of faith and fear which causes them to worry about the very little details in their lives. They often imagine the worst in every situation, as their minds conjure up the worst possible outcomes for whatever problem may concern them. They have little faith in themselves, in others and in God.

INNER BLOCKAGES

In the center of the rectangle we see various blockages which obstruct the free flow of the individual's energy towards his life purpose. What might these blockages be? One main blockage is the **lack of self-confidence**. When one is not sure of his abilities and, especially, when one is afraid of failure in the eye's of others, he is not likely to allow his energy to flow freely towards what his inner self guides him to do. Out of fear he will suppress his creativity and fall into a state of inertia.

Another basic energy blockage is created by the feeling of **guilt,** or the **lack of self-acceptance**. When someone does not accept himself, or feels shame or guilt, he does not feel that he has the right to express his inner energies or to create a more beautiful life for himself. He withholds his energies, and often becomes caught up in self-destructive mechanisms with food, alcohol, drugs or relationships, thus undermining his own happiness, creativity and success. Obviously it will be difficult to direct his energy towards his life purpose.

Fear is another major obstacle towards the fulfillment of one's life purpose. Fear is an imaginary wall, which prohibits him, who fears it, to pass through it. Each of us has limited himself in a self-created prison that limits our freedom. The walls of this prison are made up of his fears. When we overcome fear, we will be free to move creatively and effectively towards our life purpose. The main fears we will have to overcome are our fears of death and of what other people think about us. When we have overcome these two we will be considerably freer.

OPENING UP TO THE SOURCE

How then can we proceed towards increasing our energy level and directing it towards our life purpose? The first step is to search for our life purpose and get free from any obstacles preventing us from realizing it to our fullest potential. We do not have space in this book to go into this matter deeply. This subject is covered in detail in our book "**Universal Philosophy**".

The importance of connecting to one's life purpose can be understood by the example of an electrical cable, which needs to be plugged in at both ends, on one end to the wall source and on the other to a cassette player, or an iron, or a vacuum cleaner. If the cable is plugged into the machine and not into the wall source, then no energy will flow, This is like someone being connected to his life purpose but not to the universal source. Thus there is a lack of energy with which to act. On the other hand if the cable is connected to the wall source but not to the machine or instrument, again no energy will flow. In order for the energy to flow from its source, it must be connected to a purpose, otherwise it will remain stagnant. The same is true of the human being. If he is not connected to some purpose, his energy will stagnate. At first the purpose which stimulates him has to do with his physical and emotional needs and his energy is stimulated by these needs and desires. Eventually he realizes the temporary and superficial nature of these goals, and seeks for something deeper - a meaning in life.

Another reason why it is necessary to first connect, at least to some degree, with one's life purpose is that if one increases significantly one's energy level without having an outlet for that energy, then one may encounter various physical and emotional problems. This "outlet" may not be the highest spiritual purpose for which one has incarnated but it can be something constructive and beneficial for the person and those around him.

The second step in this process is to begin **removing the energy blockages** within the system such as fear, and the lack of self-confidence and self-acceptance. These can be done through self-analysis and various reprogramming techniques as described in our

The Art of Meditation

book "**The Psychology of Happiness**". Understanding the spiritual truths, which are at the basis of our own existence, will also be beneficial.

The third step is to begin to **reduce the amount of energy being lost through the holes** on the side of our rectangular energy system. This means a change in life style, with less superficial talking and less overeating. Gradually, with the help of the various spiritual techniques such as exercises, breathing techniques, deep relaxation, positive thought projection, prayer, analysis, meditation and selfless service towards others, one will begin to free himself from the illusion that happiness can be found through external factors and thus will spend less energy seeking outward for satisfaction. In the same way, as we develop greater faith in ourselves, in others and in God, we will lose less energy through worry and anxiety.

The fourth step is to **open up the upper aperture through which we receive this spiritual energy** from the one universal source. This will be done as we increase our hours of prayer and meditation and, gradually, transform our belief system, so that we feel an ever more steady opening of the heart and feelings of unity towards others and our environment. When all this has been done, we will experience a steady and harmonious flow of energy in all aspects of our lives. The techniques that will help us with this process have been discussed both in this and our other books. Let us simply enumerate them here:

1. Daily contact with water in the form of a shower and frequent washing of the face, arms and hands renews and harmonizes the energy flow.

2. A pure **healthy diet** of fresh vegetables and fruits, whole grains and beans, un-roasted and unsalted nuts, dried fruits and dairy products, will create a healthy and vital body.

3. Physical exercises, both dynamic and static, are essential for the release of energy blockages and the free flow of bioenergy.

4. Breathing techniques with emphasis on deep rhythmic breathing, according to various specific breathing ratios, increases and harmonizes the bioenergy. When this breathing is done through alternate nostrils the harmonizing effect is even greater.

5. Deep relaxation techniques allow us to become mentally aware of these blockages and to release them through inner mental processes of surrender and letting go, as well as positive imagery and conscious guidance of the energy flow.

6. Self-analysis enables us to discover the psychological mechanisms that impede and distort our energy flow. Gradually we are able to free ourselves from these mechanisms and liberate our energy flow from these emotional mechanisms.

7. Prayer opens our minds to the higher sources of spiritual energy, which gradually transform our inner vibration and bring peace.

8. Positive thought projection develops positive flow patterns in our energy field, allowing our energy to flow towards the creation of positive realities for ourselves and others.

9. Creative activities allow our inner creative energy to flow outward, releasing blocked energies and offering us a sense of inner satisfaction and self esteem.

10. Connecting to our life purpose is essential for the reasons we have mentioned earlier.

11. Meditation frees the mind temporarily at first and, gradually, more and more permanently from the various thought forms, which limit our flow of energy, love and creative power throughout our life activities and contacts.

12. Love is the state in which our energy is open towards all of those around us. This opening ensures a steady flow to us from the divine source and from us to others. We become like channels of love energy flowing through us into our environment.

13. Wisdom of the spiritual truth that all is God and that we are not these bodies or minds but, actually, divine consciousness in a body, which allows us to overcome all obstacles toward harmony, love, evolution and the manifestation of our inner divine potential here on Earth.

CONCLUSION

We can understand now what an important role energy plays in our search for health, harmony and evolution. The understanding of energy is then an essential for any attempt towards meditation. The quality of any meditation is clearly dependent on the quality of energy, which we have at that moment. If we are lacking energy, our meditation is likely to be filled with images and feelings from the dream state. If we are nervous and upset, we will think throughout the meditation about what is bothering us. Any one who wants to succeed in meditation and in the process of spiritual evolution, or who simply wants to live a healthy and happy life, would be wise to attend consciously to his energy system through the techniques mentioned.

CHAPTER 12

UNDERSTANDING MEDITATION THROUGH MODELS

Models, examples and parables are often more effective than word descriptions in enabling us to understand new concepts. You have heard the saying that a picture is worth a 1000 words. Well, the same holds true for a mental picture. It facilitates our comprehension of a new subject by using an example with which we are already familiar. It helps to understand mental or spiritual concepts in terms of material examples.

We have already used a number of examples in the previous chapters, such as the example of the river grasses, the boat on the sea, the fire in the bedroom, the pressure cooker and others. Here we will offer a few more examples, which we have found useful in understanding the various aspects of meditation and its benefits. Be aware, however, that no model or example can ever be perfect. There will always be flaws or possible contradictions. Their usefulness, however, is not diminished by that fact.

THE MAGNET AND THE IRON

An interesting phenomenon has been discovered by scientists studying magnets and pieces of iron. A magnet is simply a piece of iron in which all of the molecules are oriented in the same direction, which means that they all have their positive pole in the same direction and their negative pole in the opposite. The molecules are ordered. In the common piece of iron this is not so. The molecules are randomly oriented and not organized.

You will have noticed that when we put an ordinary piece of iron in contact with a magnet, it temporarily obtains the qualities of the magnet and can attract other pieces of iron. While in contact it obtains magnetic powers. When it is removed from the magnet, it loses those powers. But what scientists discovered was that the ordinary iron was not exactly the same after this contact. Some subtle changes had taken place. Some molecules had, under the power of the magnetic field, actually changed position and more of them were oriented in the same direction. This slight change after each contact between the magnet and the iron is called "the hysteresis effect". If this contact occurs for a long enough period of time, or for sufficient number of repetitions, then the ordinary piece of iron undergoes enough of a change in its molecular orientation, so that it permanently becomes a magnet. After such a transformation, it maintains its magnetic powers even when it is not in contact with the magnet. This is because its molecules are now all organized and oriented in one direction.

This is an excellent example of what happens to the mind after years of meditation. The magnet is the inner self, soul, spirit, higher self or higher intellect, or even God, depending on the way in which you have learned to view the spiritual self. The ordinary piece of iron is our mind. During meditation we bring the mind into contact with this higher aspect of our being. Temporarily, for the duration of this contact, the mind obtains the qualities of peace, clarity, freedom, bliss and wisdom. It is under the influence of the power of the spirit. When we come out of meditation, we return to our ordinary way of thinking and reacting. But a small, imperceptible change has taken place like the "hysteresis effect" in the piece of iron. Our mind has been slightly altered by this contact. Our mental energies are slightly more organized, more focused in a spiritual direction, less scattered, more centered.

When this goes on for years, then we begin to experience those

The Art of Meditation

spiritual qualities throughout the day more and more. These feelings are no longer limited to the duration of the meditation. Just as the piece of iron, through repeated contact with the magnet, obtained magnetic powers, the mind, through regular daily contact with the spirit, obtains spiritual qualities and our energies are more spiritually oriented.

THE LIGHT BULB AND THE LASER

The difference between an ordinary light bulb, say of 60 watts of power, and a laser, is not in the power available. The difference is that in the ordinary light bulb the rays of light vibrate at various frequencies and go out in all directions, whereas in the laser all the rays have the same frequency of vibration and the same direction. Thus, while the light from the light bulb can simply light up a room and cannot penetrate through any surfaces, the laser, with the same available power, can penetrate through surfaces as it burns through them. It has penetrating power. This is because its energies are organized, synchronized and unidirectional. There is no loss of energy to other directions or other frequencies.

The same difference exists between the ordinary mind and the mind intensified by meditation. After years of meditation, our mental energies scatter less and become more focused. We eventually see that many pursuits, which were previously so important to us, are in reality superficial and not worthy of spending energy on. We begin to have greater faith and lose less energy in fear, anxiety and worry. We accept ourselves and need to expend less energy on seeking self-affirmation. Thus our mind, like the laser, begins to function on the basic frequency of spiritual evolution and its energies flow all the more comprehensively in this one basic direction.

The mind gradually becomes like a laser, which is able to penetrate into problems and situations and see them as they really are, and not as our programmings and mechanisms make them out to be. We are able to solve problems more effectively and create and produce with greater freedom of thought. The mind is more effective.

THE WAVES AND THE SEA BED

The mind is like the sea. It is in a constant state of movement. Underneath the sea is the seabed, which is stable, unmoving, and permanent. This stable, unchanging structure, upon which the mind is moving, is the spirit. Regardless of whatever may be happening in the mind, deep in ourselves, our spiritual being is steady, peaceful, unchanging bliss. Here there is no fear, no doubt, no effort, and no anxiety. This is the eternal peaceful witness who is unaffected by the ups and downs of our emotional life.

When the water is disturbed by waves we cannot see the bottom. Its appearance is distorted by these movements, particles, and objects. These movements are our thoughts and feelings which continuously disturb the peace in the sea of our mind. As long as there are these thoughts and feelings, we cannot even sense the existence of this inner spiritual self. When the waves calm down and there is no movement at all, then we can see the bottom clearly. In the same way when there are no thoughts or feelings we can then experience that deep inner peace of our spiritual self. Meditation is the process through which we calm the waves and bring the thoughts to total silence, so that we can experience our real self, which is usually covered by the incessant waves of thoughts and feelings.

THE MIND IS LIKE A PIECE OF CLOTH

The mind is like a piece of cloth in which the threads are our thoughts, emotions, expectations, habits, needs and desires. Each thread adds its own reality to the mind. If all threads were removed, the mind would be empty. It has no reality of its own. Like any cloth, our personal reality is created by the type of "threads" (thoughts) which make it up.

Meditation and all efforts on the spiritual path are the process by which we remove, one by one, these various threads from the weave of the mind. Gradually, as the years pass the density of the threads is diminished and in this way the cloth becomes more transparent, more porous. This is important, because when this cloth is densely

The Art of Meditation

woven, very few experiences can pass through it without getting caught up in it. This means that very few things that happen to us are able to pass through our mind without triggering off some belief or emotion, which causes that experience to remain in the mind and occupy it to some degree. When one is totally secure, he does not need to hold on to experiences, but can let them pass, so that the next moment he may again be in the present.

We can understand this difference by moving temporarily to another example. If we drag a knife across a piece of metal or stone, which are inflexible, then it will leave a mark, which is, for all practical purposes, permanent.

If we drag the same knife with the same strength over a body of water, the water will react momentarily in the form of outflowing waves. It will then return to its natural state as if nothing had happened. Because of its flexibility, it does not retain the past but returns to its responsiveness to the present stimuli.

Returning to our original example of the cloth, the denser the cloth, the greater the weave of the past, because the threads are basically the imprint of the past onto the mind. Through meditation we gradually remove these threads and the programming of the past. Eventually the weave is quite lose, which means that we are more open to the moment because there are less threads of the past to hide and distort the present. Gradually, after many years of spiritual practice, the mind becomes an open channel and very few experiences can disturb our flowing peace, our inner security, which is now based on our contact with our inner spiritual SELF.

Since few events can now annoy us, we become more open, more loving and experience more unity with all. When the mind has become totally freed from all threads, then we experience the state of enlightenment and become open channels for all the qualities of the divine.

THE MIND IS LIKE A PLASTIC BAG

As in the previous example, the mind has no reality of its own. Its reality is formed by its contents. It is like a plastic bag or cellophane that takes the shape of whatever you put into it. If you wrap up something long and slim then it takes that shape. If you wrap up something round, it assumes that shape. It obtains the shape of its contents.

Thus the mind takes the shape of the thoughts, feelings, desires, needs, habits, expectations which occupy it. When specific thoughts, emotions or desires occupy the mind frequently, or for long periods of time or, in some cases, incessantly, the mind begins to crystallize around those thought forms. It loses its flexibility and becomes almost permanently obsessed, or associated, with a particular subject or concept. In such a case the mind is not free to experience the present. It is not free to think of subjects other than the one with which it is obsessed. It cannot derive joy from what is offered to it because it is stuck in that particular thought-form, which limits its ability to connect with other realities from which it could learn and receive joy.

In many cases, these thought forms around which the mind has crystallized, are negative thoughts and beliefs, such as that we are weak, that we need someone else or something else for our happiness, or fear for ourselves or loved ones. In such cases, these negative thought forms often actually create the negative realities upon which our mind is dwelling.

Meditation is the process through which we temporarily (and, eventually over the years, more permanently) empty the mind of these various thought-forms, which have crystallized, and give this inflexible form to the mind. The mind becomes softer but stronger, more responsive to the present moment, experiencing greater unity with all.

CLIMBING FOR THE COCONUT

We can imagine that a coconut, which is high in the palm tree, is like our spiritual reality, and that its shadow on the ground is the physical reality. Our physical reality with all of its physical objects is actually simply a shadow of the spiritual reality from which this material reality is manifested.

We see the shadow on the ground and seek to grab it, just as we seek to accumulate riches, objects, relationships etc. But the shadow passes through our hands and we are left with the sand on which it was projected. In the same way we are left with nothing after all our efforts to find happiness through the material world.

After a number of years of vainly trying to find happiness, seeking after shadows of these coconuts on the sand, one day it occurs to us to look upward and we notice perhaps for the first time the coconut high up in the tree. We begin to realize that the shadow is the result of the coconut and that, if we can get the coconut, we will also have its shadow. It is not so easy, however, to climb the palm tree. It takes strength, stamina, perseverance and much practice until we are able to reach that height. This is the process of meditation and all spiritual effort. Once we realize that we will have both worlds - spiritual and material - when we obtain the spiritual, then we begin to direct our energies in that direction, withdraw our attention from the shadows and start directing it towards the spiritual realities from which those shadows are created.

MOVING UP THE INNER STAIR CASE

Our mind, with its various centers of consciousness, is like an apartment building with seven stories. The view from each story is different. The higher up you are, the more you see, and the clearer you see. You can see the same events and external realities but you see them completely differently, because you have a higher viewpoint. The higher up you are, the more objectively and with better perspective do you see things.

Meditation is the process of moving up that inner staircase to the higher stories, where all is much clearer and more in perspective. At first you can only temporarily visit these higher stories. Eventually, after many years of meditation, and other spiritual practices, you can begin to reside there permanently.

CHAPTER 13

PREPARING THE MIND

Traditionally in most cultures (India, China, Greece, Egypt, North America, South America, Africa, Australia and Europe), intensive spiritual experiences, or techniques such as meditation, require preparation. Three basic forms of preparation are traditionally suggested for the spiritual aspirant who seeks success on the path of meditation. They are:

1. Self discipline, self-control or self-mastery. "TAPAS"

2. Self study.

3. Devotion and surrender to God.

 In one sense these are a preliminary preparation through which an individual can see if he is ready for this committed type of life. Thus he will see if he is ready for a spiritual path.

 These are the beginning of self-discipline, through which the individual begins to purify himself in preparation for more advanced techniques and knowledge.

In addition they reduce the amount of ego-centeredness, and break down the emphasis on the personal self. Thus egoism, the cause of all suffering, is attenuated and the individual moves toward self-realization.

Before discussing in detail these three techniques of discipline, self-study and surrender to God, it is interesting to note that Patanjali (300 BC) has seen fit to mention them more than once in his **Yoga Sutras**. Those familiar with Patanjali's sutras will know that it is the epitome of conciseness. Only the bare skeleton of facts is given. The student must add the meat of the matter through his own meditation practice. It is significant that Patanjali saw these three techniques so important as to mention them twice. The individual who seeks to improve himself, to transcend the suffering of life, to grow spiritually, or to have union with the divine, will give special attention to these three purifying attitudes and techniques.

These three subjects are covered in detail in our book "**Universal Philosophy**", and thus will be discussed only briefly here.

TAPAS - DISCIPLINE

Every effort made to improve oneself, or to control the body or mind in any way can be considered a form of "Tapas" or discipline. The word discipline does not really encompass the meaning of the word Tapas. Tapas is any act of the body, mind or speech which develops the will or serves to control unconscious robot-type activity. Tapas is the controlling of the desires and impulses of the body and mind so as to bring them under control of the higher self. Tapas is any vow which might be taken for spiritual purposes, as is any form of self control, such as control of the body, breath, senses or thoughts, in addition to meditation, prayer, fasting, observing silence, celibacy or taking vows abstaining from various self-weakening activities. Or tapas can be taking vows to perform certain actions regularly such as lighting candles, reading the Bible, regularly giving some of your money each month to the poor, or any other type of act which serves to reduce the power of the lower selfish nature and increase the power of the higher universal nature of the individual.

The many types of tapas serve to purify and strengthen the body and mind. We are soft and weak from living lives of comfort. We have no inner strength. We have many fears. Our luxuries have made us weak and sickly, without self control .

We need to return to a more simple way of life, trading our comforts for inner physical and mental strength and virtue. Regular fasting and silence will help us develop inner virtues. We need to do away with superficially oriented tendencies, which weaken our health and character. We need to increase our inner moral strength and will power so that we can be the masters of our lives. Now we are like puppets being pushed around by every fad, advertisement and fashion of society. We have little basis within ourselves to discriminate between what will help us and what will destroy us. In the name of social obligations, we damage our bodies with unhealthy foods, alcoholic beverages and smoke. Is this what we want as a society? Is this what we want for ourselves and our children?

Television is one of the great contributing factors to this sad situation. Children and adults sit for hours hypnotized by the frequently degrading flow of images on the screen. Our creative impulses are suppressed more and more deeply within us, and we become programmed with thousands of unnecessary, and often detrimental, desires through the programs and advertising.

We all need more "tapas", more self-control in our lives. Only then can we develop the concentration and will-power necessary to achieve our material and spiritual goals in life. Tapas develops greater concentration, magnetism and power within an individual. Eventually he gains spiritual powers. Miracles begin to take place around him as in the case of all great saints. You will remember the case in which Jesus' disciples tried unsuccessfully to exorcise a demon from the boy in the temple. When Jesus came and threw out the demon, they asked him why they were unable to do it themselves. He answered that this kind of power can be obtained only through "fasting and prayer".

The spiritual aspirant is cautioned, however, not to use the powers he may develop through his tapas for his own needs, for this will only perpetuate the power of the ego and subsequent problems.

The types of Tapas are divided into three categories:

1) "Harmonious Tapas" are those which are performed without desire for benefit, recognition or result. One is simply interested in bringing the lower nature under the control of the higher nature. One offers the lower nature to the higher nature.

2) "Egotistical Tapas" is done in order to attract attention or affirmation, or to gain powers or fame.

3) "Mechanical Tapas" is done in order to harm one's self or others, or out of fear, or mechanically without really understanding consciously why we are doing this discipline.

The types of "Harmonious Tapas" can also be divided into three categories:

a) Reverence for God, and the saints and sages; straight forwardness, harmlessness, physical cleanliness and sexual purity.

b) Tapas of speech, is to speak without ever causing pain to another, to be truthful, to say always what is kind and beneficial, and to study the scriptures regularly.

c) Mental Tapas is the practice of serenity, sympathy, meditation upon the Spirit within, withdrawal of the mind from the sense objects, and integrity of motive.

Sathya Sai Baba, living today in India encourages us to begin with the control of the tongue.

"Without the control of the senses, sadhana (spiritual effort) is ineffective; it is like keeping water in a leaky pot. Patanjali has said that when the tongue is conquered, victory is yours. When the tongue craves for some delicacy, assert that you will not cater to its whims. If you persist in giving yourself simple food that is not savoury or hot, but amply sustaining, the tongue may squirm for a few days, but, it will soon welcome it. That is the way to subdue and overcome the evil consequences of it being your master.
"The tongue is equally insistent of scandal and lascivious talk. You have to curb that tendency also. Talk little; talk sweetly; talk only

when there is pressing need; talk only to those to whom you must, do not shout or raise the voice, in anger or excitement. Such control will improve health and mental peace, it will lead to better relationships and less involvement in contacts and conflicts with others. You may be laughed at as a boring person but there are compensations enough for you. It will conserve your time and energy; you can put your inner energy to better use. My message for you is Control your taste, Control your talk".

We must be very careful, however, not to perform Tapas in an egotistical way. This kind of tapas which seeks to be recognized was warned against by Christ, when he told His disciples not to wear long faces when they are fasting, so that others would know that they were fasting. He told them to pray in secret so that their intent would be sincere. Praying in public can sometimes be tainted by the desire for others to see us and admire us. Some people have a habit of letting the whole world know when they are fasting. This develops what we call "spiritual pride", in which the individual begins to feel better than the others because he is able to fast or pray. This is a very subtle and dangerous trap for the spiritual aspirant. The less we talk about our spiritual efforts and practices, the better. We teach much better through transformation of our character, rather than through our exhibitionism and sermons.

Three basic disciplines with which we can begin are fasting, silence and meditation.

SELF STUDY

Although in the highest level of reality there is only One Being which encompasses all the visible and invisible world, for the purpose of understanding the world of duality we can consider that each individual has two selves. One is the personality - body combination that is temporary, mortal and always changing. This is the self with a name and form, which we usually identify with. We signify this self with a small

"s". It is not our real Self in the ultimate sense. The Real Self with a capital **"S"** is the immortal, unchanging witness of all the drama of our Life. It is called Spirit, Soul, Higher Self, Inner Self, The Witness, God etc., according to the system which one finds most suitable.

The personal self has a temporary reality similar to that of the dream self, which disappears upon waking. In our dreams we may have been rich, or poor, or in danger or in ecstasy, but when we wake up, we realize that this was only a dream and that none of that which seemed very real in the dream was actually true.

In this dream called life we will also wake up to our true Self some day and realize the impermanence of all this which we take so seriously now. This may happen at the point of death, as the soul leaves the body, thus realizing that it is not the body. Or this realization may occur during the incarnated state through a transcendental spiritual experience.

Self-study, then, is the study of the two selves and of the relationship between them. The personal self is the body-mind, and the higher Self, the knower of the body-mind. We need to discriminate between the changing temporary self and the eternally witnessing Self, which is pure unlimited consciousness.

As we study the personality through self-observation, we will realize that it is conditioned to behave in certain ways. We will see its weaknesses and strengths. We can work with the personality, chipping away as does a sculptor who seeks to improve his creation. We are creators of our minds and bodies and thus have the power to alter our creation. We create our realities and thus have the power to change our reality if we are not satisfied with it. This continuous observation of the personality, as separate from ourselves, frees us from identifying so strongly with the body and mind and all their attachments, fears, problems and sufferings.

Gradually the personality can be seen objectively as a vehicle through which the higher Self is expressing it-Self. When this attitude is taken, we can accept our self regardless of whatever weakness or imperfections may exist in it, because we then realize that we are not that acting self but rather the witnessing Self.

The higher Self may be studied through reading the various religious scriptures, which describe the Spirit and the higher spiritual realms. The many sages, saints, gurus and God -men, who have had the experience of the true Self, have tried in various ways to describe it to us. Of course words fail to describe something which is beyond the mind. The parables and descriptions they have given us can become subjects for meditation, through which we can penetrate their mystery, and experience the higher Self directly. What greater way to study something than to experience it directly? Meditation offers us that possibility.

SURRENDER TO GOD

We may also have this direct experience of the higher Self through God's Grace. This grace can come only when we have surrendered up to God (the Universal Spirit) all desires, and personal attachments.

Surrendering to the will of God means having faith that life offers us exactly what we need at each moment. It means directing all of our mental and emotional energies toward the worship of some form of God. The form of God you choose to focus on will depend on your religion and psychosynthesis. Most Christians will choose Christ. Hindus will have a choice between their various deities. All forms, even yours and mine are expressions of the one Divine Universal Consciousness. Only those who misunderstand, can argue, or fight, about what form God has. He cannot be limited by any particular form and yet all forms are His, even the forms of your family members.

Surrender to God is like the surrendering of the cell to the will of the body. A cell is a part of the body. The body is comprised of cells and all bodily functions take place through the interaction of those cells. Each cell receives all of its basic needs from the unified functioning of all cells. It is then only natural for each cell to see the wisdom of surrendering its own individual will to the body of cells. Only in this way can there be harmony and health. The consciousness in the body is God. This consciousness can exist without the body, but it cannot express itself on the material plane without that body.

Thus, the form of God that we worship is a symbol for the whole of all beings. God is the Universal Consciousness expressing itself through all beings. It cannot be limited to one particular form, but it can express itself more intensely and completely through a Divine Incarnation, so that we may be awakened to our real identity and the true purpose of life. Surrendering to God then is surrendering to a higher part of our own being, which we cannot perceive yet, because of our lack of spiritual sensitivity.

We are cells in the body of Christ, the Universal Spirit. Jesus was an incarnation of that Universal Spirit. We are each incarnations of the individual spirits which, when unified, make up the totality of that Universal spirit called Christ.

The ways in which people surrender to God are various and often completely personal. Some may go to church regularly, others may not go at all, but worship God within the shrine of their hearts. Others chant or sing hymns of praise to God. Others pray unceasingly. Others take vows of self-sacrifice. Others serve God's children in the form of the poor, handicapped and suffering. Others repeat God's name inwardly throughout the day.

Sincerity and selflessness are the main requisites. Silent prayers are more effective than loud public prayers. Acts of service to the unfortunate in life are more egoless than large donations of money, with name and fame attached. The more recognition we seek in the outer world, the less we can become aware of the inner world.

Surrendering to God means giving up all personal needs and desires and serving God in the form of Humanity. It means working hard at improving the quality of life for all human beings, without being attached to any particular results. It means having no fear, knowing God will take care of us and all our needs. It means giving our lives completely to the service of Light and Love on earth, as did Jesus the Christ who sacrificed His body for our sake here on Earth.

In the highest sense, however, there is no one to surrender to. We are simply surrendering to our own Higher self, which is one with God. Does a cell surrender anything when it succumbs to the will of

The Art of Meditation

the whole body? Of course not, it is surrendering to itself. Here is how Sai Baba expresses this fact:

"It is not a question of surrendering or giving to some other one. One surrenders to himself. Recognition that the Spirit is one's Self is surrender. Surrender really means the realization that all is God, that there is nobody who surrenders, that there is nothing to be surrendered, nor is there anyone to accept the surrender. All is God. There is only God".

This realization is the final goal of all the various religions and spiritual systems. Austerity, Self-study, and surrender to God offer us ways in which to get started on this long road back to our Selves.

These three preliminary steps are methods for the development of will power, emotional purity and mental clarity, three qualities absolutely essential for spiritual growth. They are simultaneously, however, methods of growth which will aid us **throughout** the long journey towards self-realization. They are not something we do in the beginning and then give up.

CHAPTER 14

THE FIRST STEPS
TO FREEDOM

Everyone desires freedom. Many revolutions have been fought and many people have died fighting for freedom. Few people, however, have discovered the real meaning of freedom. External freedom is important and should never be denied to any person, for all have the same rights to be free. Some may, however, lose that right by not respecting the rights of others or the golden rule to do to others what they would like others to do to them.

Here, however, we are not talking about this external freedom, but rather a much more important type of freedom - freedom from our ego and its beliefs, fears, needs, desires, expectations and emotional mechanisms. Freedom to be happy no matter what happens to us. Freedom to be able to love regardless of others' behavior. Freedom to feel secure and peaceful in every situation. Freedom to think clearly regardless of our environment. Are you free to be continuously happy, loving, peaceful, secure, clear and creative independently of what is happening in your life? Unless you are an enlightened, liberated soul, it is unlikely. We are all imprisoned in our beliefs, attachments, needs, desires and fears. These are what really prevent our freedom; not other people or governments.

We are prisoners of our social programming, of our fear about what others think about us, of our fear of death, of our ignorance concerning our real spiritual nature. We are prisoners of our senses, which control our mental and emotional functioning, causing us often to do what we have sworn many times to ourselves that we would not do because we have realized that we harm ourselves in that way. But our senses seduce our mind into repeating these mechanical thoughts or actions.

We can imagine that our body is like the body of a car, and that the engine is our energy body. The steering wheel is the mind, and the driver is the higher intellect, or the soul. The spirit is the owner of the car and sits in the back seat witnessing what happens, without participating.

When the driver has control over the steering wheel, all goes well. But this is not true in most cases. **The higher intellect in almost all of us is asleep.** It has not yet been awakened by intense spiritual practice. Consequently, our car is moving through life **without someone at the wheel.** Thus it moves in the direction of least resistance, which means "down hill". It follows the senses wherever they drag it. It is clear that this car will soon meet with some unfortunate fate.

The process of becoming really free is like waking up the higher intellect - the driver of our car, so that, with discrimination and will power, it can see where we are going, and steer our lives intelligently so that we move along safely and effectively towards our goals.

THE EIGHT STEPS

The ancient system of spiritual growth called Yoga is perhaps the system which has developed the technique of meditation to its greatest degree. The great sage Patanjali, who lived 300 years before Christ, combined these various techniques into a very clear and effective system called the eight-fold path.

This system has been proven effective by millions of spiritual aspirants over the last four thousand years. (The system existed before Patanjali wrote it down). It is a simple and effective system designed for setting ourselves free from the real source of our unhappiness - our ignorance of our real nature. It is really a Divine blessing.

Let us examine this system which eventually culminates in the technique of meditation.

According to Patanjali, spiritual realization will take place when there is a **cessation of the modifications of the mind**. The spirit is pure consciousness without any disturbance whatsoever. It is like the absolutely still sea that is so clear that one can see completely through it to its base. The mind, however, is full of waves and disturbances of all kinds caused by internal and external impulses. Because of these disturbances we are unable to experience the center of our being.

Spiritual growth is the process of gradually diminishing the quantity and amplitude of these waves so that we can realize in that stillness, our true Self. In the Bible, God commands, "Be still and know that I am God". Only when the mind is completely still without any internal or external object occupying its consciousness, can it realize its true Self as God.

This, of course, is not an easy task. In fact it is, without doubt, the most difficult of all human endeavors. However, Self-realization is the ultimate purpose of life on this earth. There is no greater task for man than to "know himself".

The soul's expression is limited by the various bodies through which it expresses itself during its incarnation on the earth. These bodies must be progressively purified so that the pure light of the soul may shine through into the world. The eight steps we are about to discuss are methods for the progressive purification of these bodies. Patanjali explains that when "The impurities are destroyed by the sustained practice of Yogic techniques; then the light of knowledge reaches up to the highest discrimination".

These techniques are broken down into steps in which one learns how to control the various vehicles or bodies through which he expresses himself.
They are as follows:

1. Control of behavior (YAMA).

2. Practice of disciplines (NIYAMA).

3. Control of the Body (ASANA).

4. Control of the breath and bioenergy (PRANAYAMA).

5. Control of the senses (PRATYAHARA).

----

6. Concentration (DHARANA).

7. Meditation (DHYANA).

8. Ecstasy - Union with God (SAMADHI).

One can see that the first five constitute the control of factors outside of the mind, while the last three constitute the control of the mind itself.

Let us consider each step individually.

YAMA - CONTROL OF BEHAVIOR

Unfortunately, very little attention is given to this extremely essential prerequisite to all other spiritual techniques. To allow an individual to practice more advanced techniques without first requiring him to control his behavior to some degree, is similar to giving him a license to drive a car without making sure that he knows how, that he can see and that he is not crazy. Otherwise he might be dangerous to himself and to others.

In the West, we are interested in quick results and exciting experiences. We want to do the most advanced exercises and meditations without having established the proper emotional stability required to support those techniques. It is similar to trying to build the seventh floor of an apartment building before the cement has hardened on the first. Obviously the building will crumble sooner or later.

Today many are concerned about freedom. Freedom of speech is important. An individual should be allowed to act freely according to his inner inclinations. Only through such freedom can a man mature and become a really conscious being, with his own center of action. This freedom is a necessary step in our evolutionary process. But what happens to the individual and to society when the person, who is given this freedom, is not connected internally to his own conscience?

What happens when a whole society of individuals, who have not yet developed the spiritual maturity to hear and abide by their own inner conscience, are given such freedom? The result is what you see around you today. Let me give you some facts about the American society which is the epitome of such external freedom in today's world. (The following passage is taken from Leo Buscaglia's book on "**Living, Loving and Learning**").

"I have learned some very interesting things that I believe are a result of people getting trapped in the concept of "I" and "me". This is from a book called, "**On An Average Day In America**". Get this: On an average day in America, 9,077 babies are born, and that's wonderful; 1,282 are illegitimate and not wanted. About 2,740 kids run away from home on an average day in America. About 1,986 couples divorce on an average day in America. An estimated 69 beautiful, incredible people will commit suicide on an average day in America. Someone is raped every 8 minutes, murdered every 27 minutes and robbed every 76 seconds. A burglar strikes every 10 seconds, a car is stolen every 33 seconds, and the average relationship in America today lasts three months. Now if that doesn't freak you out! And that's the world we are creating for ourselves! That's the world of I and me. Well, I don't want to be a part of that world, I want to create a different kind of world - and we can do it together. That's the wondrous thing".

This is an extremely sad state of affairs which our lack of inner development has gotten us into. Before we were given this freedom, we were just as immature, but we were less dangerous. For example, in countries where there is less personal freedom, there are less of the problems listed above. But that does not mean that they are more spiritually evolved or more mature than we are. They simply do not have the choice to follow their conscience or not. They are forced to behave in a certain way by the laws and strict governmental control.

Thus, to remove these freedoms would in my opinion be a step backwards in most cases. In some cases, however, it may be advisable, as an emergency measure, where people have lost control of themselves, and disharmony and chaos prevails, and there is danger of serious harm being done to the society.

At some point, however, we are going to have to learn to deal maturely and harmoniously with the powerful tool of freedom. We will have to grow up from being little children, who are well behaved only when our parents or teachers (or now a police force or judge) is standing over our heads. And when they are not looking, or when we know we can get away with it, we do what ever comes into our minds without thinking of the consequences to ourselves and society.

CELLS IN THE BODY OF SOCIETY

As we have already mentioned, we are cells in the body of society. Whatever we do and whatever happens to us affects society as a whole. Our thoughts, words and actions radiate out and affect the others' thinking and behavior. Our love generates love, our selfishness stimulates the selfishness in the others. Our anger provokes their anger. Our fears catch on like a contagious disease. Our peace calms the other. Our kind words stimulate feelings of kindness in others. Our violent actions come back to us through the others' aggressiveness. Our lies create in others the need to lie to protect themselves. Our ability to steal or cheat makes them equally able to do so, in the name of self-protection. And in some countries, where the actual system of law enforcement also becomes corrupt, there is a total disintegration of any semblance of morality.

Morality is the basis of all personal and social harmony. Morality is the expression of the highest spiritual truths, the highest natural laws of this universe on the physical, emotional, mental and social

The Art of Meditation

levels.

The basic truth of the universe is that there is only ONE SPIRIT and thus, in reality, ONLY ONE BEING which expresses itself as all the beings which inhabit the earth. The truth of our spiritual unity has been taught by ALL RELIGIONS. "There is only one religion - the religion of LOVE". This basic truth becomes then the basic law of all creation, which is that whatever we do to any other being, we are actually doing to our own selves, as the other being is simply another cell in the same universal body in which we are living.

Thus every thought, word and action is actually coming back to us, through its effect on this universal body, which is our only source of life. This law then becomes expressed as the law of Karma which says that whatever we do, think or say, will always come back to us in equal measure. Christ expressed this message many times in his teachings. He explained that we will be judged as we judge, that we will reap as we sow, and that he who lives by the sword, will die by the sword. He also healed people from their illness, paralysis or blindness by saying, "your sins are forgiven", meaning that this physical problem was the result of some previous sin.

A sin is nothing more than a selfish act which harms someone else or ourselves in the long run. The basic sin is believing that we are separate beings and that we can benefit by looking after our own needs only, often at the expense of others.

The word sin, however, is a word heavy with connotations of being unworthy and unloved by God. I would prefer the word ignorance or mistake. Our egoism, and resulting negative actions, are based on our ignorance of our spiritual unity and our mistaken identification with the body and mind which cause us to fear others and life and try to protect ourselves. We may resort to devious ways such as violence, lying, cheating or stealing. Thus, all "sin" and misbehavior in society, is a function of ignorance, mistaken identity and fear. This is the basis of immorality and resulting social and personal disharmony, illness, tension, broken families and unhappy people.

PUNISHMENT IS NOT THE SOLUTION

The permanent solution to this problem is not limiting people's freedom, nor punishing them; but rather **educating** them on a spiritual level. The awakening of every individual to his inner self-the conscience- is the only real therapy. The conscience, or higher intellect, of each individual is that part of his mind which is connected to the higher spiritual levels of his being.

The higher intellect is aware of that spiritual unity which binds us all and has the same advice for all of us - "DO TO OTHERS AS YOU WOULD LIKE OTHERS TO DO TO YOU". Sometimes it is expressed in the negative, "Do not do anything to anyone else that you would not like them to do to you".

Everyone's conscience is saying the same thing from deep inside them. Despite different cultural, religious and political traditions, all the inner voices of all the people in the world express in unison this one piece of universal advice. But few people on the earth are tuned in enough to their inner voice to hear this message. There are too many other voices which are produced by desires, attachments, aversions, fears and insecurities. The result is the individual's need to have his mental attention continually focused on the outside world.

Thus the problems of our world are not the product of evil, sin or bad people. They are the product of the **lack of wisdom** and lack of understanding at our present state of evolution.

One who is in a process of evolution must necessarily be in an imperfect state. An imperfect state in the process of becoming perfect means change and, thus, conflict between the old and the new. Birth, growth, decay and death are all a part of this process.

We are not evil because we have made some mistakes based on our fears, insecurities or need for affirmation. We simply are not evolved enough to not make these mistakes. But what can we do? We can start learning from our mistakes and stop repeating them.

The Art of Meditation

WHAT IS THE SOLUTION?

The only solution is for all of us to become inherently and voluntarily moral. We spoke of freedom at first. But does the average man have the freedom to be moral? Does he have the inner strength to be moral?

He would like to be moral. He would like to be good. But he feels weak, alone, unprotected and vulnerable, and thus resorts to lying, cheating, stealing, hoarding, and even violence and indifference toward his neighbors out of a desire to protect himself and his family. A weak man, a man without faith in himself or in some divine power, without the knowledge of his immortal invulnerability is not free to be moral, and thus is destined to disharmony with himself and society. The solution is **spiritual education.**

Moral laws are like the laws of nature. They cannot be bypassed. They are absolute (like gravity). If we lie, we will be told lies. If we steal, we will be stolen from. There is no way of avoiding it. This law requires no policemen, lawyers or judges to uphold it. The powers of nature and life will see that each gets what he deserves. These powers are absolute. When an individual goes against these laws, he goes against his own higher nature, which has established these laws for the harmonious functioning of the universe, the individual and society.

All spiritual systems require that an individual at least **try** to observe certain behavioral guidelines, before he is allowed to practice more advanced techniques, which have the ability to release the latent powerful energies which lie within him. This is for the safety of the individual and the society. The individual must first become pure and egoless before he handles greater amounts of mental and spiritual power.

Thus behavior in harmony with the laws of nature is the first and basic foundation of spiritual life. No matter how much power one has, no matter how many exercises one can perform perfectly, no matter how many hours one can sit in meditation, there can be no spiritual progress until the behavior is modified. Until egoism is overcome, all spiritual exercises simply lead to spiritual ego, which is the most difficult type of ego to deal with. The control of behavior suggested by Yoga is very similar to the Ten Commandments put forth in the Bible.

There are five basic guidelines for control of behavior. They are:

1. Non violence.

2. Truth.

3. Non stealing.

4. Non jealousy.

5. Moderation in desires (especially sexual).

Let us now examine each one separately.

NON VIOLENCE

We all want peace. We all want to feel safe and secure. No one likes to encounter violence. No one likes to be hated, to be harmed physically, be shouted at, be gossiped about, or to be thought of in a negative way. We all desire a world in which there is peace and love; where all beings sing and dance with happiness, and all are friends. This is an archetype in every human mind, even though it may be buried so deeply in some minds that it may never become conscious.

And yet we live in a world of anger, hatred, competition, aggressiveness and violence. Why are we unable to create the world we desire? The answer is **FEAR**. Why do we fear? The answer is ignorance. Ignorance of what? Of basic higher truths about the nature of reality. Ignorance of the fact that there is enough food, clothing, shelter and other resources - necessary for human survival and fulfillment - for all beings on earth to enjoy. There is no lack of anything upon the earth. **There is no lack of**

resources. There is, however, a lack of proper distribution of resources.

Our lack of understanding of this fact, causes those who have the power and the opportunity, to hoard whatever they can. Thus many others are left without. Those who are left without their basic needs of food, shelter, clothing, freedom and dignity react with violence towards the more subtle "violence" of greed, manipulation and suppression which they have experienced from those who hoard.

We are also ignorant of the fact that **real satisfaction lies within,** that we are whole inside. Because we seldom look within, we have not discovered that wonderful fact. Because we have not yet learned to experience that treasure which is within us, we are overtaken with desires, which eventually develop into attachments, addictions and lust. These become strong emotional and mental forces, which may eventually cause us to come into intense conflict with those who consciously, or unconsciously, obstruct our fulfillment of these intense desires. We also may be driven to ignore the needs of others, and even harm others (and ourselves), out of our strong attachments towards some form of pleasure or need.

ACTION AND REACTION

A third truth of which we are ignorant is that **we are all in fact one spiritual being.** Although we seem to be separate, and feel like isolated beings, the truth is that at the spiritual level we are all united into one universal consciousness. Thus Christ's law of doing to others what we would like others to do to us, actually stems from the truth that whatever we do to others we are actually doing to ourselves.

Through this natural law, whatever we do to anyone, at any time, will be reflected back to us by the mirror of life. It does not mean that we will receive the same act from the same person that we have acted toward. We may give love to one person and receive love from another. We may harm one person and be harmed by another. But the act must return.

The reaction to an act does not have to return in the same lifetime. As souls which incarnate over and over, we can receive the results of our actions many lifetimes from now. Or we may now be receiving the results of acts we have committed thousands of years ago.

This is one of the reasons why the concept of an eye for an eye, and the concept of revenge, are primitive forms of behavior unsuitable to man in this present stage of evolution. Christ tried, two thousand years ago, to teach us the lesson of forgiveness and turning the other cheek and loving our enemy. We have progressed little on this path.

It is difficult for people to forgive others or even themselves. Whatever anyone has ever done to us, was exactly what we deserved and what was useful for our evolution. It was always the perfect return of our previous thoughts, words and actions, even if we are not consciously aware of what those acts may have been or what the lesson might be.

BASIS OF PERSONAL AND SOCIAL HARMONY

NONVIOLENCE is the basis of personal and interpersonal harmony. Only by perfecting nonviolence will we be able to personally experience higher levels of consciousness of undisturbed inner peace and unconditional love. Only through nonviolence can society survive and thrive. Only through nonviolence can nature (including man) maintain its ecological harmony, which is essential for the harmony of the planet.

Let us investigate nonviolence in all its forms, including words and thoughts. Nonviolence needs to be exercised towards all beings including animals, plants and insects to whatever degree is possible, while maintaining our survival needs. Without doubt we have to kill something in order to eat. We either have to kill, for example, an animal or a carrot or an apple. However, few people will **feel** that it is the same to kill an animal or a carrot or an apple.

Imagine that you get up and go out and find a cow or a sheep and take a knife and cut its throat, and watch its reaction to your intentions, and watch its blood flowing all over the ground, and the life go out of the animal as it is overcome with spasmodic reactions. Do you feel the same about that as you do when you go out into the garden and uproot a carrot or pluck an apple off the tree? Whoever feels the same about these three acts, can comfortably eat these three types of food. Whoever would feel horror at killing the animal is at a state of evolution where this food is no longer suitable to him at that level. He should not fool himself by ignoring the fact that the meat that he buys in a plastic bag has come from an animal (with eyes, a brain, feelings and senses) which has been murdered by someone else for its meat.

THE RESULTS OF VIOLENCE

We are not concerned only about obvious acts of violence, but also about sarcasm, lying, stealing, cheating, hoarding, indifference towards the needs of others, gossiping, hating, wishing something evil for someone, speaking harshly, rejecting, and not forgiving others, etc. What are the results of this type of functioning?

1. There will be a **lack of INNER PEACE**. Even those who have buried deep their conscience, are not able to make it disappear completely. It is immortal. We may not hear it consciously, but, at some level of our subconscious mind, there will be a conflict between what we think, say and do and this inner voice which says, "do not do to others anything that you would not like them to do to you". Thus there will be an inner conflict, which will not allow deep inner peace.

2. The **INNER DOOR to the subconscious mind** and, thus, to higher states of consciousness which lie beyond it, is closed. Since we cannot bear to hear our inner voice, we close the door to our inner self. Thus we close the door to higher parts of our own being.

3. The **LINE OF RETURN to the higher parts** of our being is closed. Meditation is difficult. Emptying the mind becomes impossible. It wants to be constantly distracted towards the outside world, so that it doesn't become aware of the inner conflicts.

4. The personal will is disconnected from the UNIVERSAL WILL. Most individuals have decided to live for themselves ignoring the needs of the whole. Such a being becomes like a cancer cell in the body that does not only not care for the needs of the other cells, but eventually becomes destructive towards them. He is out of harmony with the universal flow of life. He is capable of harming another or ignoring the other's needs.

He is not connected to the universal will which seeks to provide for the good of all beings. This creates even greater feelings of separation and isolation, and thus leads to the development of even more egotistical "self protection" mechanisms. In the end, he becomes a fearful and defensive individual.

5. At some level of his being he will feel **guilt** and, thus, will consciously, or unconsciously, reject himself or even try to punish himself in subconscious ways.

6. There can be **little spiritual evolution**. Spiritual progress is a movement towards greater feelings of unity with all beings, the realization that we are all expressions of one spiritual essence or power. This realization cannot be experienced by one who is capable of harming someone else or even of thinking negatively about another.

7. Violence is a communicable disease. When one individual acts in a violent way, this stimulates the same tendency in others, who have this potential within them. In moments of fear, almost all individuals are capable of reacting with violence. The more violence there is around us, the more our center of violence is activated, and the more ready we are to "protect" ourselves with the same behavior.

The news media, TV and movie productions present a barrage of scenes of sex, violence and fear which do much to program man's mind and disturb his feelings of security. How many dead people have you seen on TV and in the movies? How many acts of violence, how many robberies, how many lies, how many evil intentions, how many scenes of sexual desire and of emotional pain have been

The Art of Meditation

presented to you on the screen? And how frequently do you witness these acts in your daily life? The ratio of violence in the media in relationship to our daily lives is at least 10,000 to 1.They have created in our minds a distorted view of reality.

8. Insecurity leads to attachment, and attachment to fear. We are faced with a vicious circle of fear, which gives birth to indifference towards the others and, eventually, violence, which then creates a more intense feeling of separateness, isolation and fear, which leads to increased violence.

Someone has to break this cycle by having faith in divine protection and in the reality that nothing can ever happen to us that is not in the interest of our spiritual growth. We can be surrounded by thieves and killers, but if being stolen from or harmed, is not a part of our growth progress, then we will not be affected in the least. And if our spiritual evolution requires that we experience being robbed or harmed in some way, then all the attempts to protect ourselves will not succeed in averting those experiences which are for the good of our evolution.

We must, of course, take measures to protect ourselves, but those measures should never include violence towards others unless we are actually at this moment being faced with someone who wants to harm us or someone else in our presence.

It must be remembered, however, that in fighting violence when it is before us, we can fight the **act** and **not the being.** Once the act has been averted (perhaps with aggressive means if necessary), then the individual must be forgiven, and attempts should be made to help rehabilitate him, so that he may find a new way of living and acting.

Thus we can see that the commandments of the Judeo-Christian heritage and the basic behavioral code established by the system of Yoga, emphasize this basic first step on the spiritual path, not because they want to "control the masses" (as some believe) but, rather, because these are practical effective codes of behavior which allow the individual to come into harmony with his own higher energies, and with his environment, so that he can proceed more efficiently, and with less difficulties and accidents, along the road to higher consciousness.

Most will agree with what is said here. Few, however, feel that they have the strength to take the first step, **to become really ethical beings in an unethical society.** There is a fear that others will "laugh" at us, they will cheat us, will use us, they will think that we are stupid and walk all over us. "We will not succeed". "We will not be safe". "We will not be able to support and protect our families if we do our job ethically".

We do not have faith in Christ's promise, that we will be cared for if we live in harmony with His basic laws. The **greatest safety is in purity.** Purity will put us in harmony with the COSMIC WILL. No force in the universe is greater than that. There is no insurance company or insurance plan greater than that.

Life is peaceful and happy to one who has chosen purity over slyness, surrender over resistance, love over fear, and forgiveness over bitterness and revenge. It is worth giving it a try.

We are going to die anyway, whatever we do. We and everyone we know is going to die. Isn't it better to live each moment with a sense of inner peace and harmony with ourselves and the universe around us; with peace of mind and a clean conscience? Then, at the moment of leaving the physical body, we will feel that same inner peace and harmony. For in life and in death we simply experience our own mental states which are governed, to a great degree, by our conscience.

It is important, however, to understand that **only an individual who is enlightened can perfectly observe nonviolence or any of the other Yamas**. As long as there is any ego and body identification, there will be fear, attachment and the tendency towards selfish behavior. The most we can do is try, to the best of our ability, to improve our behavior every day, while at the same time accepting ourselves as we are.

Feelings of guilt about the past will not help us very much to improve. We must accept that we are in a process of evolution; that the vehicles, through which we are expressing our Selves, are far from perfect, and resolve to gradually and persistently improve them.

When we find ourselves becoming closed, self centered, talking or thinking negatively about others, or actually abusing some other being, let us remember that this behavior does nothing to improve our relationship with ourselves or the world around us. Let us understand that all our anger is a result of our fears, attachments and aversions, which are in turn the results of our inherent ignorance of what we really are.

Violence can also be done to one's self, in the form of overeating, or harmful habits such as not giving the body what it needs in order to be healthy. Some people have negative self-images and create much suffering for themselves.

As we open up to love for ourselves and others we will be liberated from all forms of violence.

TRUTH

Everyone wants to be told the truth. It is important for us to feel and believe that the other person is telling us the truth. Otherwise we feel insecure. When we are looking to form relationships with people, regardless of whether they are personal, social, or business relationships, we expect, if not demand, that the other person be truthful in his interactions with us.

In spite of this very common feeling among all people, there is a growing lack of truth in the world today. This lack of truthfulness is one of the main causes of the decline of trust and cooperation among people. This is in turn leading to increased feelings of separateness, isolation, vulnerability, competition, aggressiveness and, eventually, violence. Other results of this vicious circle are social unrest, strikes, economic instability and general social disharmony.

TYPES OF DISHONESTY

Let us investigate some of the gross and subtle manifestations of the absence of truth.

1. The first and most obvious manifestation is the "**gross lie**" , which has nothing to do with reality as it is. These might be the lies which business partners tell to each other in order to make some illicit gains, or lies to the tax department, or lies to one's spouse to cover up an extra-marital relationship. Included here are the lies we make about ourselves, when we brag about what we have done in order to make a better impression on others.

2. Then there are the "**white lies**", which seem harmless but camouflage the truth, such as lies about our real age or about our real feelings about something or someone.

3. Not being true to who we are is another form of lie. When we change our appearance, our beliefs, our opinions, our feelings and attitudes and behavior depending on whom we are with, then we are creating a different lie for each person or group, hoping to be accepted by them. We do not stand up for what we really believe. There is no consistency in our behavior, there is no stable self. We are constantly lying, in a way, about what we think and how we feel and how we live. This is not being true to our self.

4. We also **lie to ourselves**, or **rationalize** our actions. We say, "Oh, I can stop smoking any time I want. I just don't want to now". Or, "I have no time to help out; I 'm too busy". We lie to ourselves and others, and actually believe that we are telling the truth, that we don't want to stop smoking, or that we really do not have time. The truth is elsewhere, but we do not want to admit it. These are the most difficult lies to discover, because we actually believe them ourselves.

5. When we **say we will do something and actually do not do it,** it then becomes a lie. When the words come out of our mouth, they are not yet a lie. They will become truth, or a lie, depending on whether our body and personality executes the promise or statement we have made. When we say "I will be there at 5 p.m. and we show up at 5.30 p.m., then our words have become a lie. When we say the work will be ready on Monday and it is not, then our words become a lie. When we promise some type of help or participation in some type of activity and do not fulfill those promises, then our actions are not in harmony with our words and thus they are not truth.

Thus, we must be very careful concerning what we say we will do. This is absolutely essential both for our personal evolution into higher states of consciousness and for the harmonious functioning of society on all levels.

Truth is the complete harmony and consistency between beliefs, values, thoughts, words and deeds. When any one of these five levels is out of alignment, then there is no truth, and contact with the universal source of life is obstructed.

The practice of absolute truth, which means making all of one's words come true (and being very careful about what one promises) eventually gives the power or ability to manifest one's every wish. One's will becomes connected to the universal will, and whatever is thought or spoken by that individual, can immediately become manifest. It is as if the mind is a film, or a slide, in front of the light of a projector.

Whatever is on that film or slide gets projected onto the screen of life. But there are few, if any, people today who have the courage, the strength, the self confidence and the self mastery to always keep their promises, and make their words become a reality.

Most of us have too little control over our bodies and minds to be able to overcome attachments, programmings, beliefs, habits and fears which prevent us from living up to our word in all cases. There is also a lack of discrimination on the part of many persons when they are making some promise. If they thought clearly about what they are saying, then they would realize that what they are saying is not possible, or that they really have no intention of doing it.

People today in general take their words lightly. Which means they take their promises lightly, and thus themselves lightly. Thus their words have no meaning, no power. Eventually no one takes them seriously, since they do not take themselves seriously.

WHAT PREVENTS US FROM BEING ALWAYS TRUTHFUL

Let us consider some of the reasons why we distort the truth:

1. Feelings of **separateness, vulnerability** and thus **mistrust** can cause an individual to "protect" himself by not being totally honest to others about his real feelings, thoughts or life situation.

2. A feeling of **not being good enough to be accepted as he is** may push a person towards magnifying himself in front of others in an attempt to gain their esteem or their approval.

3. A lack of **self-acceptance or self-esteem** may cause some to withhold information, which they fear will cause others to reject them. This is rather common, since we learned, at a very young age, that it was best to withhold any information from our parents which might not be acceptable to them so as to avoid rejection and perhaps even punishment or personal harm.

4. The **fear of punishment** may lead one to tell lies.

5. The **fear of losing something** such as money, possessions, acceptance, a job position or the others' love or esteem, may also be a cause to tell lies.

6. On the other hand, the **desire to gain something** important to us, such as some pleasure, a job, money or some other material or emotional gain (affirmation) may cause us to lie, or distort the truth.

7. We may hide the truth in order to **avoid conflict** with another.

8. We may hide the truth in order **not to hurt** someone else.

The Art of Meditation

Thus the need to lie is, in most cases, based on feelings of weakness, lack of self-acceptance, inferiority, fear and attachment. **Lying, then, is a sign of weakness**. It requires an individual of great inner strength, self-acceptance, self-love, self-confidence and self-mastery to be able to live by the truth in every situation. And if he wants to avoid conflict with others around him, he will have to learn to speak that truth with plenty of love. The truth is less likely to hurt the other when it is really expressed with heartfelt love.

Lying is a waste of time, because the truth will always prevail. It cannot be any other way. We cannot live in continual conflict with ourselves. This suppression of our real feelings, this rejection of who we really are and what we really believe, this constant tension of being something different from what we are, will destroy us physically, emotionally, mentally and spiritually. We cannot protect anything with lies. Whatever is gained through lies, will be uncovered sooner or later. All that which is gained in this way will turn sour. It is an universal law.

Truth brings peace to the mind, power to the spirit, health to the body. Sai Baba says, "He who protects the Truth will be protected by the Truth". Few people today believe that. They believe that they must lie in order to protect themselves. Being in harmony with the Universal Will is our ultimate protection. Man's power is small and temporary. It is like a small wave on the vast oceans: ephemeral and insignificant. We lie in order to protect ourselves from these small waves when we could have the protection of the whole ocean. When we lie, we cut ourselves off from the ocean and we are in a very vulnerable position.

THE HIGHEST TRUTH

This brings us to the highest form of truth. The truth of our **real being.** The practice of truth means the remembrance of who or what we really are. Here we are referring to Christ's words that the **"Truth will set you free"**. That truth is that we are immortal spirits who are invulnerable and always safe. That there is never any need to fear anything. That we are a part of that universal ocean. That we are in fact that ocean itself. That we are wonderful, beautiful beings, the truth of whom is always acceptable and lovable, if we let it flow out undistorted and uninhibited. The truth is that we are not these bodies, nor these personalities, but that they are temporary vehicles, which we are using here on earth for our expression and evolution. We shall give them up one day and we shall then realize the **TRUTH OF OUR SPIRITUAL BEING.** It is possible to realize that truth before leaving the physical body. That is the purpose of life. When we have done that, we will have the inner strength to be always truthful.

NON STEALING

Few of those who are reading this book are capable of outright stealing from others. Few of you would have robbed a bank or have broken into some house to steal jewelry or money. Some may have had some rebellious moments as young adults in which they may have stolen something from a department store, an airplane, hotel or some other large organization. But it is unlikely that many of us have made this a habit in our lives. However, there are some more subtle forms of thievery which may go unnoticed in our lives. Let us discuss some of these subtle forms of thievery.

Everything upon the Earth belongs to the Earth and its creator and owner. We are all visitors or guests on the Earth and whatever we "have" is really on loan from the earth. Nothing reality belongs to us. We arrived here naked, without anything at all, and we will leave with absolutely nothing.

Thus the concept of possession is, in reality, a false and misleading concept. Nothing really "belongs" to anyone. Everything is on loan from the Earth for our use in the process of our spiritual evolution. When we become preoccupied with "Having" and "Owning", with "me" and "mine", then we create the stage for stealing on all levels.

When one man hoards for himself large portions of the Earth's resources while others have none, then he is in a very real way creating a need in the other to steal. Hoarding is one form of stealing which creates another form of stealing. Let us analyze this unusual idea.

There are two factors which determine the morality and purity of what we own and our relationships with our possessions. One is **how we obtain what we have** and the second is **how we use what we have** or what we do with what we have. Let us examine the first.

HOW WE OBTAIN WHAT WE HAVE

There are two ways of right earning. One is through work based on right action. The other is through inheritance. Whatever we inherit is ours rightfully to use (right use will be discussed later). We are talking about what we inherit in actuality, not in theory. For some obstacles may come between what we are "supposed" to inherit and what we actually do inherit. Such cases are not injustices in the eternal sense of justice.

Often such cases are a matter of old unpaid debts from previous lives. In other cases we need to learn some lesson through not receiving "what is rightfully ours". We can never know before hand. We must **do everything we can,** within the guidelines of lawful and correct conduct and the truth to receive what belongs to us. But, if the powers of life prevent it, despite our best effort, then it is best to get on with our lives, forget the past, forgive those who have "wronged" us and assume that this, in some way, which it may be difficult for us to perceive, actually was the "just " result.

Whatever we receive through our parents in a lawful way is given to us to use properly in this life. However, because one has chosen to be born into a poor family which leaves him no inheritance does not mean that he is less blessed. There are much more valuable things to inherit from one's parents than money or houses or land. There is love, self-confidence, intelligence, compassion, integrity, and a wide variety of talents and abilities. These are the real gifts which make life easy and beautiful. Without these a fortune can be consumed in a few years. Without these a fortune cannot bring happiness and is worthless.

Now let us look at **earning through right action.** The basis of earning through right action is that every exchange that we make is based on the principle "Do to others that which you would like others to do to you". What are some aspects of this golden rule?

1. No lies are used to earn what we receive.

2. The product we are selling is of the quality which we would like to buy. We would gladly pay what we are asking for our product or service.

3. Our product, service or work is exactly what we say it is, and we do not distort it in any way.

4. The work that we do for someone is of the quality we would like someone to do for us. If we allow ourselves to be paid for half-hearted work with only 50% effort then in a way we are stealing from the one who is paying us.

5. On the other hand, he who is paying for a certain job should feel that he is willing to do the same job for that pay, or else he is stealing from the one whom he is paying.

6. In building a home or making a product, one puts the care and proper materials into it which he would put into his own home or his own product.

7. Also included here would be not taking an office or a position in any government or private organization which we are not rightfully qualified for, or is not rightfully ours in line with laws of longevity and experience. Thus we do not give or accept jobs which have to do with family or other relationships, rather on the basis of a person's ability to perform that job better than the other candidates who do not have those "contacts".

Thus, the key to right earning is that **we should always be ready to be on the other side of the bargain or exchange.** If the sides were instantly switched and we were receiving what we were just previously giving, we would be equally happy. If it is not so, then we are in a way "stealing" in that interaction.

RIGHT USE OF WHAT WE HAVE

There is a beautiful ancient Sanskrit saying "**Ardha - Dharma, Kama - Moksha**". Ardha means wealth in the broadest sense of the word including our money, land, houses, objects, energy, ideas, talents and thoughts. The word Dharma has many meanings and is difficult to translate easily into western terms. It means right action. It means all acts which contribute to the physical, emotional, mental and spiritual welfare of the individual and society. It means transcending the personal ego and selfish needs and living for the good of the whole. It means doing the right thing at all times. It means using whatever "wealth" we have as we would like others to use it, for the good of humanity. It means being in harmony with the flow of Life, with the flow of evolutionary forces within and around us. It means doing what we were born to do, creating what we were born to create, and living as we were born to live.

Thus all that we have received from this life is really a test to see how capable we are of **using it all correctly, which means unselfishly**. There is in the Bible the parable of the "Talents" which a master gave to each of his three servants. The first two who doubled their talents by using them, were deemed capable and put in charge of higher sums. The third servant, who went and hid his talent, was deemed incapable of handling money, and it was taken from him and given to the others. In another parable, when Christ passed the fig tree which was not producing fruit, he cursed it and it died.

We are here to produce, to create, and to offer. Not to hide what we have in fear of losing it. Thus the "Dharmic" use of all our wealth would be to provide for the basic needs of our family and those who are dependent on us. This means food, clothing, shelter and education. Beyond this there should be limits on what is spent on various temporary whims and desires, which are created by our consumer-oriented society. Care should be made not to waste the various resources of the earth such as water, food, electricity, petroleum etc. Wasting is like stealing from others. We make ourselves ill with too much food while others are ill because they do not have enough to eat. We would all be healthier if we made attempts to help those others find ways to procure their own food.

Another great waste is hoarding and collecting. We are creating a bottleneck in the flow of energy in society when our closets are full of extra clothing and shoes, our walls are decorated with expensive pictures and our bathrooms stocked with expensive cosmetics, while 40.000 children die **every day** of hunger. That money could go towards various programs in education, well digging and the creation of small industries, which would help those people raise their standard of living.

We create our wealth and they create their poverty. That is the result of the past. But it is also the test for the future. We are being tested to see what we are going to do with our wealth and what they are going to do with their poverty. The lesson is that we are all one. Our indifference to their plight is another type of stealing.

We have been given what we have to be tested as to whether our maturity, compassion, love and wisdom are great enough to withstand the glamour and comfort of material possessions. It is not easy. That is why Christ said it is very difficult for a rich man to enter the Kingdom of Heaven. He gets enamored by his objects and in the end **they own him.** He cannot bring himself to use them for the Dharma, for the good of all. That wealth, in the end, is a curse and obstacle towards his spiritual progress. It is likely that he will have to experience, at some point in the future, starvation and poverty so as to awaken a feeling of compassion towards his fellow man.

We have been given our wealth by the one source of all wealth. What we have is not so much a function of our personal effort as it is of Divine Grace. So many others have worked much harder than we and have nothing to show for it. Others have worked so little, or not at all, and have so much more. It is all a theater, a test, an opportunity for spiritual growth. But most of us are failing the test. All that we have is on loan from the earth to use properly for the good of life on this planet. It is as if are in charge of the investments of a bank and we started to take the money for ourselves, rather than to use it for the benefit of the bank. We are **in charge** of what we have. It is not ours.

WHY DO WE HOARD?

Thus there are many subtle forms of stealing. What causes us to do this?

1. Our **insecurity** causes us to take and accumulate more than we need (often at the expense of others) just in case things may get difficult in the future. This is logical to a reasonable extent. But how much does one have to put away to be safe? Is one ever safe from earthquake, fire, violence, war, illness or the loss of loved ones because he has plenty of money? In such situations the greatest security is the love and cooperation among friends which can overcome any difficulty. This overemphasis on money often leaves us with few friends, and the few that we have are probably our friends because we have money. Will they be so in difficult times?

2. Greed for objects and pleasures also pushes a man to accumulate money and objects so that he may ensure the satisfaction of his desires.

3. The **need for affirmation** from society through an image of success measured by how much money, houses or objects one has is another motive for keeping one's wealth to one's self. It may also lead one to unethical ways to accumulate that wealth. Accompanied with this may be a need for power over others, which may cause one to use money to manipulate others to affirm himself; that he is great, that he is strong, that he is worth more than others.

Thus the blockage towards using our wealth towards dharma comes from basic inner doubts about ourselves and a lack of inner fulfillment. A man who has inner security, inner satisfaction, inner affirmation and self-acceptance has no need to accumulate money and objects. He will get free from those traps and will use all his material, emotional, mental and spiritual resources for the healing of humanity. He will dedicate his house, his money, his abilities, his mind, his energies, and his life towards the transformation of society.

At each moment of our lives we have a choice between moving towards security (external) or towards growth. The second part of the Sanskrit phrase is applicable here. "Kama" means desire and "Moksha" means liberation. Just as all wealth must be channeled towards the dharma (the well being of all), thus all desires must be channeled towards liberation or enlightenment. Thus we must constantly be aware to choose growth and liberation over the various insecurities which cause us to run after flimsy temporary comforts and pleasures while our brother souls are dying of starvation

NON ENVY

We have heard the commandment not to be jealous of our neighbor many times since our childhood. We usually hear it expressed with the condemnation that we are committing some great crime to the person we are jealous of. It is true that extreme jealousy may cause us to react extremely egotistically and negatively towards others. But, in most cases, our envy and jealousy harm our own selves most.

ENVY IS A LACK OF SELF ACCEPTANCE

When we envy others for what they are or what they have, then we are not accepting the beauty of our own lives. We are ignoring the perfect uniqueness of our life and how different our life is from those around us. No two beings ever born on this earth have lived the same lives with the same thoughts, abilities, belongings, talents, interests, and roles to play. Each of us is a unique expression of that one universal consciousness. To envy another person, for what he has or what he does, is to reject our own selves and all that we have been given. It is to reject the Divine Plan.

What we have been given may seem less than what others have been given in their lives, but what we must understand is that each person has **exactly what he needs to proceed in his evolution and to learn the lessons and play the roles he came to earth to play in this incarnation.** If we have less of something, it means that it would not be useful for us to have more, at least at this moment. It means that having more at the present time would be an obstacle to our growth. We, however, may need to have less in order to **activate** ourselves, so as to **work** toward having more. Our goal may be more money, objects, knowledge, abilities, or spiritual awareness. In each case, we will learn something as we try to better our condition.

When we feel jealousy towards others, **we lose much energy** in desiring what others have, rather than seeing how we can use what we have been given in order to fulfill our purpose in life (however we may perceive that purpose at the present moment). When we are envious, we cannot relax and be at peace. We feel a need to have what the others have, to be like the others; not because doing so will make us more content or happy, but because we do not **accept our selves as we are.**

A person who accepts himself as he is does not feel jealousy or envy. He is satisfied with what **he has** and with what **he is**, while at the same time realizing that he is in a state of evolution. He spends time and energy improving the quality of his body, mind, personality and even his material life, without doing so in order to be like others or to have what others have. He follows an inner voice, which guides him forward towards self-improvement, regardless of what others are doing around him. A person who does not accept himself necessarily follows the voices, needs and desires of those around him. He has no stability.

Envy and jealousy are obvious signs of a lack of self-acceptance and a lack of self-affirmation. A person who is victimized by these emotions has not yet felt his own inner self worth. When he eventually becomes aware that his life is a perfect part of the perfect divine plan, which is gradually unraveling, he will cease to envy others. Then he will rejoice in all that he has been given from life, even if what he has seems outwardly negative, such as illness or poverty. He will realize that those conditions are exactly what he needs in order to continue his evolution. His lesson may be to accept these states or to make an effort to overcome or change them. In both cases, he will be the winner.

It is time then to understand that the ten commandments were not created in order to control people, or to keep us from sinning. They were constructed as guidelines which help us to raise our consciousness and realize our true spiritual nature. It is impossible for someone to be aware of his true spiritual nature and simultaneously feel envy, lie, steal or act violently. He will feel so powerful, so large, so fearless, so complete, so satisfied, that he would never need to act in those ways. He will be all love and service.

CHAPTER 15

SEX, EROS AND LOVE ON THE SPIRITUAL PATH

Sex, Eros and love are our most powerful drives. They are simultaneously the sources of our **greatest happiness** and our **deepest pain**. How can we balance these energies in our lives, put them into perspective and experience their benefits without their disadvantages?

Man is body, personality and soul. **When one body is attracted to another body, that is sex. When one personality is attracted to another personality, this is eros. And love is the attraction between two spirits.**

There is much confusion today about these three subjects. We receive different and conflicting messages from the church, our parents, our friends, psychologists, doctors, TV, the cinema, and the various magazines. Who can we believe? How can we construct a personal belief? Some of the various opinions which we hear floating around are:

1. Sex is a sin except for the purpose of creating children.

2. Sex is made pure by the sacrament of marriage.

3. Sex outside marriage is a mortal sin.

4. Sex is okay with anyone as long as there is a feeling of «love».

5. Sex is a sacred act of union between two conscious beings.

6. Sexual activity is good for one's health and should be carried on as late as possible in life.

7. The sexual act wastes precious vital energy which could have been transmuted into higher forms of creative activity or self-knowledge.

8. Sexual activity should be freely expressed with anyone whom one feels - even with members of the same sex.

9. One should never suppress one's sexual urges - it could harm one physically and psychologically.

10. Men should be allowed extra-marital relationships, but not women.

11. Both men and women should be allowed extra-marital relationships.

12. Sexual attraction is a trap which causes a man to lose his clarity and reason.

13. Eros is a sacred joy in life and is worth chasing after no matter what it may cost one on other levels.

14. One's success and manhood is measured by one's sexual and erotic achievements. Otherwise there is something wrong with that person.

15. Real love does not exist.

16. Real love encompasses both sexual and erotic energies.

17. Spiritual growth is impossible as long as an individual is focused on his sexual and erotic energies.

18. Sexual energy can be transmuted into spiritual energy if one knows how.

The Art of Meditation

Which of these opinions do **you believe**? Perhaps you could add another ten beliefs, or so, which I have not thought of here. Who is right and who is wrong? What is the truth in all of this? How can one formulate a personal philosophy concerning this powerful, and yet confusing, aspect of one's life?

I cannot personally claim to have any answers for society in general. But after much experience and thought on the subject, I have come up with a personal philosophy which satisfies me at present and which may be useful to you in working out your own. The thoughts which I will express here are personal and do not represent any particular system or established philosophy, except for the fact that I have obviously been influenced by all the philosophies I have studied, teachers I have met, and relationships I have experienced.

IT IS NOT A MATTER OF RIGHT OR WRONG

First of all I do **not believe** that it is a question of Who is right and who is wrong. All these statements are **correct** and **incorrect** depending on the path on which an individual finds himself in his journey towards self-knowledge or spiritual enlightenment. We must try to let go of the pride and guilt which are associated with the concepts of right and wrong, good and sinful. That which is «right» and «good» is that which helps us to proceed on our path towards unity with others and with God. **That which is «bad» and «sinful» is that which creates a sense of distance between ourselves and others or between ourselves and the Divine which lives within us.**

Thus, sexual activity for one man may be a harmonizing, unifying factor in his physical and psychological life and yet for another a little further down the road, a drain on his spiritual energies and a distraction from his spiritual focus. One man is not any better than the other, just as the college student is not better than the elementary school child. Both are good and equally divine in their inner nature. One is simply older, more experienced, and ready for more difficult lessons and responsibilities.

We must be honest with ourselves, look deeply into our lives, our

Sex, Eros and Love on the Spiritual Path   215 goals, our desires, our habits, our attachments and motives, and determine clearly whether, at the present time, sex or eros has helped us move towards love or away from it. For the majority of the masses of society, sex and eros still play a basic part in resolving differences, harmonizing energies, and bringing people closer together. The basic problem is that the means have become the goals, not only the goals, but gods. Sex and eros have become the gods of modern media, of TV, of cinema, and magazines. Everywhere we look, whatever is advertised, is passed into our subconscious through our sexual center (obviously because the advertising companies have discovered that this is the most open center of focus in people today).

Sex and eros exist for the purpose of gradually learning to love. And for this reason it is necessary for most of us at some time in our lives, usually in our earlier years, to experience these forms of contact. But we have forgotten what love really means. We confuse it with attachment, affection ,desire, lust, identification, worry, anxiety, fear, pride, control and various other emotions. Thus **we must ask ourselves if our sexual activity, or feelings of eros, are bringing us closer to a feeling of pure love for our loved one**, and not only for our loved one, but also for all our fellow souls. Or are they simply manifestations of our personal physical needs, feelings of insecurity, or need for ego-affirmation or sensual pleasure?

BODY - PERSONALITY - SOUL

Where there is love, then eros and sex play a natural role of manifesting the already existing spiritual unity now at the level of the personality and the body. Whenever there is sex or eros without love, then there is little real unity and usually many drawbacks and eventual problems. **All three are attempts to erase a sense of separation, loneliness, or emptiness**. All three express the need of the soul to reunite with the others, who are simply parts of its own true being - the universal spirit. But sex and eros alone can seldom, if ever, bring about a total sense of unity, if there is not simultaneously that pure and lasting love to **unite the souls rather than only the bodies or the personalities.**

What we usually call love is really sexual attraction or eros; the attraction between two personalities. The proof of this is that if the other personality starts to change, or our interest changes, our love withers and becomes disappointment and sometimes anger, hurt, bitterness and resentment. Our love is not unconditional. Usually the attraction is on the level of our personality needs, sometimes purely on physical needs, and seldom, if ever, on our soul needs.

EXTRA-MARITAL RELATIONSHIPS

A wide section of society today advocates and practices free sexual activity with the claim that this is the modern and psychologically healthy way. They claim that all the church dogma is simply an attempt to suppress the masses.

My personal observation of both my own life and the lives of many others, however, has shown me that there are some practical reasons why this free sexual attitude does not bring real happiness, or harmony, which people are seeking.

One reason is that the **satisfaction of the sexual orgasm is short lived** and the sense of unity (which is the basic underlying motive; whether we know it or not), if it was ever achieved, soon disappears, leaving both partners in approximately the same state as before. Perhaps they have released a little physical or emotional tension and are temporarily more relaxed.

Unfortunately, in most cases, these moments are seldom used to further the spiritual contact between these two souls. Rather, most often, it is simply a mechanical process of **releasing accumulated tension**. Men are usually more guilty of this mechanical approach, lacking in affection or deep communication.

Moreover, this source of momentary pleasure starts to become an addictive habit for some, and rather than adding something meaningful to their lives, they become slaves to its power over them, just like any other addictive pleasure, such as cigarettes, drugs or tranquilizers. In many cases, when one becomes so addicted to this pleasure, he is often ready to sacrifice his principles and beliefs in order to fulfill it. He may cheat on his wife, or she on her husband, even though he or she would not like the other to cheat on them. Often relationships are developed with others who are already married. Although one would certainly not like others to have sexual relations with his own spouse, he is forced through the power of sexual urge, or eros, to do to others what he would not want others to do to him. He is creating a «karma»; the act will have to come back to him in some way.

Besides the «karmic» reaction, there is the problem of a **lack of consistency** in the individual's beliefs, values, thoughts, words and deeds. This creates a schism in his character and a **conscious, or subconscious, confusion** and scattering of energies which usually prevent him from finding the happiness and contentment which he is seeking. He is trying to find happiness and pleasure through the other relationship, but in the end he gets only confusion and inner conflict.

An individual who becomes addicted to the excitement of momentary pleasure of his sexual activity or eros with someone, often loses his clarity and is fully capable of lying to others in order not to lose his source of pleasure and, often more sadly, is **fully capable of lying to himself.** All the above, of course, can be a great obstacle to one's spiritual growth and can even create physical and mental problems.

THE SEA, THE WAVE, THE FOAM

When we are focused on the sexual level, we tend to see others around us as bodies. We see them as sources of pleasure or perhaps if they are contenders, as threats to our pleasure. Thus we cannot see the other as a soul and sometimes not even as a personality. How many young people have rushed into marriage, through their sexual adventures,   only to find out in the end that they have completely different personalities, goals, and interests in life? And how many have felt the powerful excitement of eros gradually subside, when time passes and life is full of responsibilities, bringing up children and making a living? It is usually at these moments that married people seek out new extra-marital relationships in order not to lose that feeling of excitement, of youth, of joy, or pleasure.

But the nature of eros is that it passes. It is like the big wave which grows bigger and bigger gaining momentum, creating an orgasmic flurry of foam and slowly disappears into the sea again. **It was nice, but it ended.** Love is like the sea: deep, steady, unchanging, uniting all. How many waves do we have to ride into the crash of disappointment, confusion and sometimes depression, in order to start preferring the sea itself. **The sea is love, the wave is eros, and sex is the foam on top.** The foam is short lived, the wave survives somewhat longer, and the sea is forever.

THE PROBLEM OF ENERGY DRAIN

Another problem which results from free sexual activity and multiple relationships is one of **energy drain.** Each individual has only so much energy with which to sustain his balance, and his health, and simultaneously cope with his responsibilities and problems. **When one person enters into sexual union with another, their auras or energy fields intermix.** There is momentary blending of their emotional and physical energies. If they are spiritually attuned, then there can also be a uniting of their spiritual energies which is a beautiful event. But this is, as yet, seldom the case.

When one engages in sexual contact with another person a few times, there starts to build up between them **linking emotional channels which make one very open emotionally to the other.** Identification and attachment result. Emotional dependencies and expectations start to develop. One becomes more vulnerable to the energies of the other. One can be easily hurt, disturbed, and can more easily lose one's calm and peace of mind, when things do not go well with the other person, which can occur quite frequently. This is draining enough on one emotionally, mentally and spiritually when one has one sexual relationship. Imagine what happens to one's emotional, mental and spiritual reserves when he has more than one relationship. He becomes torn, drained, depleted of clarity and cannot reasonably fulfill his responsibilities to any of these relationships.

We are continuously affected by the various psychological atmospheres of our various relationships, unless we cut ourselves off emotionally altogether, as some men do, but then the condition simply exists on the subconscious level and one soon has some serious physical or mental problems. I have seen this problem occur more frequently in men of about forty years of age ,who try to «regain» their youth by chasing after many women often much younger. Needless to say, neither happiness nor health nor spiritual growth are possible under such conditions.

Every attachment is another chain on our legs which limits our freedom. We become slaves, serving our desires. What we usually call love is often an attraction, which is based on our need for security, sensual pleasure or ego gratification. Consider how we would feel if our loved one died. Would we be sad? Why?

Our loved one is a soul who is very happy to be free from the limitations of his physical body. He would be in a much better state after leaving the body. Then why would we feel sad? Because **we have lost something important to us, something we need, or believe we need,** something which gave us a feeling of security, pleasure or a sense of affirmation. This is what we usually call love.

When we enter into relationships on the basis of needs, it means that we expect the other to create within us a feeling that we do not have, such as security, happiness, or self-acceptance or self-worth. But it is seldom, if ever, the case that someone else can create this feeling in us if we do not have it in our selves. These are inner feelings which are the result of experience and inner work, and not objects which can be transferred from one person to another.

The result is that we become disillusioned because the other is not giving us what we need, what we want. We fail to realize that he cannot. This creates tension between us and thus 50 per cent of all American marriages result in divorce.

The Art of Meditation

PERSONAL LOVE VS. UNIVERSAL LOVE

Another problem with sex and eros is that, because they are based on the physical and personality levels, they are necessarily limited to expression toward a few people, and not toward society as a whole. In our spiritual evolution, our love must expand to encompass a wider and wider circle of beings. Sexual attraction can be felt only for a few beings, usually of the opposite sex, who are physically attractive to us personally.

Eros in the same way can only be felt for a few beings who happen to match the personality traits which we value and which excite us. Thus our focus is naturally limited to a few people whose body or personality are attractive to us.

As we mentioned earlier, for someone who is feeling isolated or has not experienced a feeling of union with other beings, sex and eros may be stepping stones toward love. But for someone who has frequently tried the sweet and sour taste of sex and eros, to continue chasing after such experiences may simply retard his emotional, mental and spiritual evolution. And it will certainly limit his energy flow to a small group of people, when he should start to express his energy as love to hundreds and thousands of people through social service.

The sexual energy itself is perhaps the most powerful expression of the universal cosmic energy in man at this stage of his evolution. **Perhaps in a thousand years man will have evolved to the state where the value which he gives to sex and power today will eventually be given to love and service.** We would then get the same orgasmic pleasure in simply loving, or serving, or feeling unity with another person that we feel today with eros and sexual contact. And some thousands of years later - man will get the same orgasmic joy out of his feeling of oneness with God, the universal energy which resides in every being. He will feel total unity with all beings and thus there will be no «other» to be attracted to.

But we are not there yet. Each person must see where he stands on his evolutionary path and evaluate his needs and his goals. What does he want to do with his life? He must use his life energy for the achievement of that purpose. He does not have any other way of achieving it. If he uses all his energy in sexual activity, emotional games, all his time seeking security, pleasure and ego-affirmation through chasing after various relationships, he will, of course, have no energy left over to direct towards those goals, whatever they may be. Neither will he have the time, peace of mind and clarity to spend on techniques such as meditation and prayer which may help him find inner-security, happiness and self-affirmation.

OUR POLARITY

On the other hand, as long as we are in these physical bodies, our sexual polarity is a reality. We are like electrons and protons with opposite charges who cannot help but attract each other. This is something which no one can overlook. Yet man is more conscious (or should be) than the electron and proton. He has the ability, through conscious spiritual growth, to start to harmonize himself and reduce his charge, which means to develop the qualities that are missing from his being.

A man is attracted to a woman for the qualities which she has, which he has not. And a woman is attracted to a man for the qualities which are not yet incorporated in her conscious self. **But as souls we are neither male nor female. We are both,** and yet neither. Thus, as men develop more love, affection, tenderness, sensitivity, purity, peace and humility, and as women develop more strength, courage, self-confidence and philosophy, the two will feel more whole - their charge will not be so opposite and thus their love can be expressed towards all, without being limited by sexual needs or eros.

This wholeness and harmony of male-female characteristics has been exemplified in Christ, the Mother Mary, and many saints who embrace a beautiful and complete combination of love and peacefulness, combined with determination, strength, and the courage to fight.

THE TRANSMUTATION OF SEXUAL ENERGY

It is known in many circles of esoteric philosophy that the sexual energy can be transmuted into spiritual energy for greater creative power or for the purpose of enlightenment. It must be understood here that transmutation does not mean suppression. When we suppress something it just remains as it is, stored up, building pressure somewhere within us. If we learn to transform it, it becomes something more subtle and is eventually expressed in another way, such as writing, dancing, music, art, social service, meditative states, etc.

But the art of transmutation of sexual energy is often dangerous and requires a spiritual teacher, and, of course, a suitable consenting marriage partner. And even more important, it requires great self-control and discipline, years of vegetarianism, meditation, abstention from drugs of any kind and impeccable control over the movements of the mind. Otherwise the mind will be overcome by the surge of sexual energy and it will be lost, or worse, may travel in dangerous directions, creating physical or mental problems.

ONE UNIVERSAL SPIRIT

The key to the process of transmutation of sexual energy is the transmutation of the way we see the world. When we manage to see our loved one as an incarnation of God, when we manage to experience everyone as a manifestation of the same one universal consciousness, of which we are a part, when this ceases to be a thought and becomes an **experience**, then all our energies will be transmuted and everything we do will be divine. Thus, what is really necessary is a transformation of our way of seeing the world - a purification of our mind, beliefs, thoughts, desires and motives, so that we may see the world more clearly and not be overcome by the illusion of temporary forms.

It should be clear in our minds that that body or personality which we desire so much and believe we «need», is simply a temporary formation of earth which will some day again become earth. The spirit within there, however, is eternal - but it has no sex or personality.

THE ROLE OF AFFECTION

Let me close with a bit of practical advice, which I have found very useful. What we are really looking for is love. We all want to be loved, to feel it, to give it. The showing of affection between relationship partners is a very important balancing mechanism in this exchange of love and vital energies. If there were more innocent hugging and kissing as the children do, there would be much less need for sexual contact. The energy would be transmitted and our sexual potential charge reduced.

If we can again become **like children** and have more innocent affection, touching, holding, embracing and hugging, then there would be much less feeling of separation, doubt concerning the love of the other, and much less need for sexual contact, which may waste precious spiritual energies. Often the need for verification of love, of unity, or caring creates in us the need for sexual contact. When there is no doubt, there is less need for verification.

SEX AND OLD AGE

Let us close with the question of sex and the aging person. I have met many people who try to keep up their sexual activity as far into their later years as possible, often in conflict with their failing body energies. They keep up their energies psychologically out of the need for affirmation from others, or out of a belief that it is healthy, or that it keeps them younger. It is sad to waste those later years of life in this way. These later years are a great opportunity for inner work, i.e. to satisfy that psychological need from within through inner work, **to start to identify with one's soul and not with one's body and personality.** The body and personality have only some more years to live, say 20 or 30 at the most. Why chase after such temporary solutions to problems?

When one's children have grown up and one is also able to retire, it is such a wonderful opportunity to let go of all those activities,

The Art of Meditation

which draw one towards identification with the body and personality. **One is free to start a life of intense spiritual activity, meditation, prayer, reading, social service, and thus end one's life in dignity, with a sense of fulfillment of purpose and peace of mind.**

In summary, each will have to make his own decision concerning this aspect of his life. It is not a matter of right or wrong, but a matter of what is effective in bringing him the happiness which he seeks and what is likely, in the long run, to leave him empty and still seeking it. This decision should be made consciously and with objectivity. One should be sure that he is not suppressing an important part of himself but at the same time that he is not being blinded by habits, desires, and social conditioning. One needs to very clearly decide what he wants out of life and see how he can best achieve it.

CHAPTER 16

CONTINUING OUR STEPS TOWARDS FREEDOM

We can see from our discussion so far that the Yamas, or codes of moral behavior, are not simply moral restrictions blindly accepted by the spiritual aspirant, but rather a scientifically established code of behavior, which guide the individual from the confinement of ego-identification to his freedom as a spiritual being.

This is true of an alternative view of "good and evil". Good is whatever helps us to expand out of our ego-centeredness toward identifying with the universal. Good is what helps us to overcome our identification with the body, our feelings of separateness, fear and competition with the others. Good is what moves us in the direction of selflessness, love and unity with all beings. Good is doing to others as we would like them to do to us.

Evil is whatever keeps us bound in our illusion of separateness and isolation from the world. Evil is what causes us to fear, hate and feel rage towards the world around us. Evil is what increases our selfishness and ego-centeredness. Evil is not treating others as we would like them to treat us. Evil is Live spelled backwards.

We can see that in some cases, the same action may be good for one individual and evil for another. For example, for the average individual, romantic love may be a movement towards more unity and selflessness. Whereas for the advanced spiritual aspirant, who has already passed through that stage, to become infatuated in romantic personal love could possibly prevent him from taking the next step toward universal love. Thus, what is useful for one is useless for the other. Perhaps these words "useful" and "useless" should replace good and evil. What is "Good" is what is "useful" for our fulfilling our purpose on the earth. What is "bad" or "evil" is simply what is "useless"; what will prevent us from realizing our real nature.

If we begin to use the words useful and useless, we will be able to see this problem of morality in a cleaner light. Now it is confused with feelings of guilt and also resentment towards the church and society who impose these concepts upon us.

But from the objective point of view we see that they are quite practical guidelines, without which we will never be able to achieve any personal or social peace or fulfillment. Thus, actions are not good or bad in themselves, but they either help us or hinder us from finding peace and happiness, and fulfilling the good of our life.

We can imagine that we are on a voyage from one shore of the sea of life to the other. It begins with the individual ego and ends with the universal spirit.

These "Yamas": non-violence, truthfulness, non-stealing, sexual purity and non-envy, are five plugs with which we can prevent the water from coming in through holes in our boat and sinking us along the way.

Let us remember, however, that only a realized being can, in actuality, perfectly practice the Yamas in all circumstances. Let us not be hard on ourselves, but simply, try to the best of our abilities, to observe these very wise guidelines in our daily life.

We will now proceed to discuss the second step towards freedom, which is called "Niyama". These are five guidelines, which have the purpose to help us develop discipline, fortitude and clarity which are required for one to proceed safely along the spiritual path.

NIYAMA - OBSERVANCES

Whereas the Yamas explain to us what we must **not** do, the Niyamas suggest to us what we must **do** if we want to succeed in fulfilling the purpose of our lives. As in any endeavor, the degree of our success in our spiritual search will depend on our effort and sincerity.

There are five Niyamas. They are Discipline, Self-study, Surrender to God, Physical and mental Purity and Contentment. You will recognize the first three from Chapter 14. There will be no need to discuss them in detail here in that they have already been discussed. We will simply mention them briefly.

1) "Tapas" or discipline, is obviously essentially important to anyone who is seeking to overcome his identification with the body. The desires and habits of the body can be overcome mainly through learning to do without them. Thus desire is transformed into will-power. Will-power is essential to the success of any endeavor, but most especially in the spiritual endeavor. It is said that when one masters discipline, the impurities of the body and mind are removed, and the individual gains special supernatural powers, such as clairvoyance and telepathy.

As we have mentioned before, the spiritual aspirant is warned not to use these powers until his ego is under full control by the higher vehicle, the 'buddhi'. Otherwise there might be unwise use of these powers, which would result in harm to himself and others.

All of us will benefit from practicing such disciplines as fasting one day a week, speaking less, making a vow to speak only sweet words, and to never speak about anyone in a demeaning way. Those who indulge in smoking or drinking, too much food, or drugs of any kind would do well to practice austerity from these health and character weakening activities.

2) Self- study is essential to anyone who wants to achieve even the smallest degree of peace of mind, let alone self-realization. Because we are the creators of our reality, we can change our reality only when we can objectively understand the ways in which we are creating the reality, which we presently experience. Until we can objectively observe our personality, and see it as a vehicle through which we are operating, rather than as the totality of our being, there is no possibility of change or growth. Until we can get out of, and above, the ego to see its functioning, we cannot "see the forest through the trees". Until we can begin to identify with the higher Self, the spiritual nature, we cannot make much progress.

3) Surrender to God is mentioned in Patanjali's Yoga Sutras as a separate and independent path to union with God. The individual who practices perfect surrender of the ego, and its attachments and desires, up to the higher Self, merges with the Universal. There is no need for any other types of techniques. This is the path of love or Devotion. It is the path emphasized by Christianity, especially by St. Paul in his letters. An individual who follows this path of love for God (towards whichever form of God he may prefer) will find that God union perhaps more quickly and safely than any other.

4) Purity is a quality that we all enjoy. That purity may be the beauty of nature or the simple spontaneity of a young child. Purity attracts our attention and makes us feel relaxed. It is an essential quality for spiritual development.

In order to obtain the clarity of mind needed to experience higher states of consciousness, it is necessary to be pure physically, emotionally and mentally.

a. Physical Purity

There are various aspects to physical purity. First there is the outside of the body, the skin and the hair. These must be kept clean in order that we may be free from microbes and various forms of illnesses. Washing the body every day is extremely important for many reasons. When we wash the body we do not only remove microbes and dirt, but we also purify our aura or energy field. The nervous system and energy field of the body are relaxed and revitalized by the application of water to the body. We have all witnessed this effect when a shower has removed our tiredness or

The Art of Meditation

nervous tension. We feel relieved and rejuvenated.

Besides the full body shower, which is necessary each day, one would do well to take a number of "half baths" in which he washes his hands and arms up to the elbows, as well as the face and neck. This helps to rejuvenate the body and relax the nerves. It is especially important for people who are low in energy or who are subject to nervous tension. The custom is to take these half baths upon waking, before eating, before praying or meditating, and before sleeping. In this way, one's energy is kept in harmony throughout the day. It is very useful before meditation in that it removes the "vibrations" of the previous activities and enhances our concentration. It also prevents sleepiness in meditation.

The inside of the body must also be pure. When it is not, toxins of various types clog up the functioning of the body and eventually of the mind. It is well known that people who have constipation, have a tendency towards headaches.

The body is a machine, and like any other machine it gets clogged up when we put the wrong fuel into it, or overstuff it with various impure substances. All machines need a specific type of fuel to function. If we put in something else, it will not only not function well, but it will most likely also break down. The human body is made to function on natural organic substances, which come from nature. When we fill our body with various chemicals in the form of fertilizers, colorings, preservatives and flavorings or drugs of various types, it does not have the capacity to break down and eliminate these substances, and the liver and other organs get clogged up. These toxins then affect the clarity and purity of the mind.

Also, when we put processed substances, like white sugar and white flour or meat, which has hormones and antibiotics in it, the body becomes very impure inside. This weakens our healthy immune system and clarity of thinking.

All machines require occasional cleansing. The human body can be cleansed through fasting and other techniques. All religions and spiritual systems use fasting as a way to prepare the body and mind to be capable of higher emotions and higher thoughts. This is why fasts are done before the major spiritual celebrations, which in the past were initiations of various types.

Along with fasting, there are various cleansing techniques which one can use to clean out the inside of the body such as enemas and stomach washes.

b. Emotional Purity

In chemistry, when we speak about a pure solution we mean that the solution has only one substance in it. There is no impurity in it. There is no other substance in it.

The same is true of emotional purity. It means that we have one basic emotion or feeling. It means that we basically feel love, understanding, and compassion for the people around us. Consider the openness, honesty and purity of a little child. That is emotional purity. He is direct, honest, not harboring hidden thoughts or feelings. His emotions are basically those of love and caring for others. He does not have sly thoughts.

The importance of emotional purity is evinced by Christ's comment that only when we become like children will we be able to enter into the Kingdom of Heaven.

Emotional purity can be achieved by keeping company with simple, pure people, by chanting, praying, meditating and through self-analysis, in which we remove gradually negative emotional states from our basic programming.

c. Mental Purity

Mental purity, like emotional, is a matter of having the mind filled with one type of thoughts, with one goal or principle. If we have conflicting thoughts, goals, or desires there can be no progress in any direction. We must analyze what we want from life, what we believe is important, what our goals are, how we want to live. We must choose between the various conflicting thoughts, goals and desires which now create confusion in our minds.

Through self-analysis, meditation, prayer and the study of spiritual truths, we can eventually get free from this confusion and focus on the basic truth that we are all immortal souls in the process of evolution. Then we will dedicate our lives towards the basic goal of enhancing this evolutionary process for ourselves and others.

When we have physical, emotional and mental purity, we will obtain an internal harmony and peace, something like what you may have experienced after a shower, after a fast or after receiving Holy Communion. When we are pure, we want to remain pure and thus we feel less attraction towards actions which might impede our ascension into higher levels of consciousness, where we will experience inner peace, satisfaction and unity with the world around us.

5) Contentment is a very scarce state of mind in our present society. Very few people are content with what they have, or with what they have achieved in life. They feel that if they can just get one more thing or achieve one more goal, they will be content.

But it simply does not work that way. Either we are content or we are not. No external object, position, relationship or event can give us lasting contentment. Contentment comes with the realization that we already have, and always will have, exactly what we need in each moment for our fulfillment. If contentment is contingent upon any external factor, then it cannot be lasting contentment, because it will have to change as the external factors change.

There are actually two methods of developing contentment. One is by learning to be content with what one has, and with what life give us. The second is to become more and more able to obtain what we want in order to feel content. The East has mastered the first way. They have learned to be content with little. The West has focused on the second method of becoming ever more able to manifest what we want and desire.

I suspect that the real solution is to be found in a marriage of both methods. We can seek to continuously improve the quality of life for ourselves and others, while accepting and being content with the actual results that we have at each stage of this process of improvement.

This brings to mind the wisdom in St. Francis' prayer, "Lord, give me the strength to change whatever I can, the ability to accept what I cannot change, and the wisdom to know the difference".

Thus we make every effort to find contentment by improving the conditions of our life, but are ever ready to feel contentment with what we cannot actually change. We accept the present moment, and all its conditions, as perfect.

This holds true for the wide variety of needs which we have such as survival needs, pleasure needs, needs for affirmation, love and even the need for spiritual evolution or union with God.

In the beginning, the spiritual aspirant is overcome with anxiety as to whether he will succeed in this tremendous adventure of self-transformation. He has little patience and wants results immediately. He is discouraged and depressed by every setback, and often feels that he is not making much progress. He feels discontent. This discontentment is perhaps useful to drive him on, to inspire him to make more effort.

But as the years pass by, when the aspirant realizes that progress is very slowly being made, he learns **patience** and **faith.** But most important of all, he gradually learns to identify less with the personality, which is experiencing the cycles of discontentment and contentment, and begins to develop a permanent inner contentment, in spite of the drama which is going on outside.

He is then able to watch the ups and downs, the successes and failures of his life with an equal eye. It is said that the perfection of contentment brings supreme undisturbed happiness or bliss.

The Art of Meditation

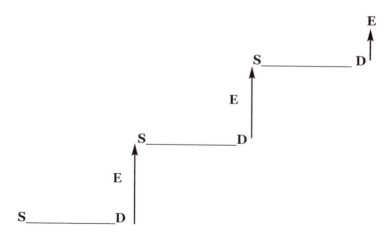

S = Satisfaction, contentment
E = Effort for change
D = Dissatisfaction

We can understand this with the help of the accompanying diagram. At a particular point we feel **dissatisfied** with our selves or with our life condition. We want to change our character, get free from some negative trait or overcome some habit. We are not happy with ourselves. We may reject or even hate ourselves.

As a result of this discontentment, at some point we make an **effort** to change that which we cannot accept. After some period of time (short or long, in some cases many years) we manage to succeed. Now we feel **contentment-satisfaction** that we have succeeded.

But this satisfaction does not last very long. We soon discover something else that we want to change about ourselves. We feel discontent again. After a period of discontent, we at some point make another effort. While making efforts towards change we often have anxiety, doubts and fear that we will not succeed. This is often accompanied by feelings of self-rejection until we actually succeed. And thus, this circle goes on. The unhappiness of discontentment. The anxiety of effort and the pride and elation of success. But again discontentment.

After many years, the spiritual aspirant begins to realize that the process of change and growth is slow and difficult and requires patience. Gradually he becomes detached from the whole process. He becomes detached from the effort and result. He continues to make efforts towards change but does not doubt so much any more. He goes through all of this without the self-rejection, anxiety and pride usually associated with such a process.

It is important to keep in mind that spiritual traits must be allowed to develop naturally in an organic way. Plants grow and develop naturally and patiently. We must grow in the same way. It is **not** useful to pretend to have certain spiritual qualities that we read about in books. This will be false to our character. Let us practice the suggested techniques and simultaneously be true to what we really feel, and allow these changes to take place naturally, from within.

ASANA - PHYSICAL POSTURES

Let us now move on to the third step toward freedom; the control, mastery and transcendence of the physical body.

The ancient sages sat for many hours each day in meditative postures. In order to prepare the body for this difficult physical and mental task, they developed a series of postures for strengthening the body. These postures also kept the body vital and healthy with the least expenditure of effort, time and energy. They developed a science of physical culture for keeping the body in perfect harmony.

These postures are basically static postures, which are taken and held for long periods of time, while keeping the body still and completely relaxed. The mind is also relaxed, even to the point of deep relaxation or meditation in each position. Such postures, in combination with breathing regulation and proper diet, powerfully affect the nervous and endocrine system in a positive way. This is the great secret of yoga exercises, that they are able to harmonize the nervous and endocrine systems, which in turn harmonize all the other bodily systems. This is done through the function of the energy system of the body. These postures release blocked energy in the form of tensions. This frees the nervous system and mind of the various blockages and creates an energized and relaxed body and mind.

Tension is released from the muscles, nerves and the mind itself. All those who have practiced yoga exercises will realize the truth of their powerful effect on the body and mind. In the West today, Yoga exercises have been made an end in themselves. They have become another form of gymnastics and even a competitive sport in some cases. This is not in accordance with the intentions for which the yogis developed this system of exercise.

These exercises are a means to an end, which is beyond the body. They are performed simply to keep the body in optimum functioning condition, so that it is not an obstacle along the path to self-realization. Whatever we want to do in life - whether it be a material or spiritual goal, we need a healthy body in order to succeed. The slightest disharmony of the body will be reflected in the mind and vice-versa. Thus, before the spiritual aspirant can try to control his mind, he must remove the tensions and weaknesses of the body.

It is said that whoever perfects these postures becomes free from the opposites of sense experience such as heat and cold, dampness and dryness, hunger and thirst. The body is then strong and able to support all types of difficulties and stresses. Thus the mind is less easily disturbed and more adaptable.

PRANAYAMA - CONTROL OF BIOENERGY

We have already mentioned in detail the subject of bioenergy and the centers of energy along the spinal column. The fourth step towards freedom is to bring this energy under control, so that we can have an abundant and harmonious flow.

Breath control techniques are used in conjunction with concentration in order to ensure an optimum supply of this 'prana' as well as its harmonious flow through the body. One might have enough energy, but it might not be flowing properly to all parts of the body or mind. Certain areas of the body or mind could be lacking in energy supply due to physical tension or blocked emotional or mental patterns.

Through deep, slow, rhythmic breathing one is able to harmonize the quantity and flow of this energy, so as to create not only a state of perfect health, but also a feeling of peaceful vitality. The prana is the connecting link between the body and the mind. As we mentioned earlier the prana acts upon the body through the endocrine system and nervous system. The mind communicates with body through the prana, and vice-versa. For this reason the prana is the key to health, vitality and peace of mind.

Many psychological problems are locked up in the breathing apparatus, and can be worked through once an individual learns to breathe properly using his lungs to their full capacity, in a rhythmic way. Eventually the student or spiritual aspirant learns to control the amount of air passing through each nostril individually. This technique of alternate breathing is extremely effective in relaxing the mind and purifying the nervous system. It balances the passivity and aggressiveness in an individual.

All these disturbances must be dealt with before an individual can progress on to the more advanced stages of control of the senses and the mind. It is said that through perfection of pranayama techniques the mind gains great power of concentration.

We will not give more details here as such a subject requires that one study with an experienced teacher.

PRATYAHARA - DISCONNECTING THE MIND FROM THE SENSES

The five senses are continuously sending a barrage of impulses to the mind, informing it of external factors. The mind spends a great amount of energy, time and effort each day interpreting and reacting in various ways to these sense inputs. While on the one hand, this is absolutely necessary for an effective and harmonious interaction with the world around us, on the other hand, unless one

The Art of Meditation

has control over this process, it can disrupt the mind and prevent it from concentrating.

There is a humorous story concerning a king who had five wives and could not control any of them. He was very unhappy because they controlled him from the morning when he woke up until the evening when he fell asleep. They even bothered him in his sleep.

He decided to get help and find a solution by calling a conference of all the men in the kingdom. He had two large tents constructed. The one had a sign which said "MEN WHO ARE CONTROLLED BY THEIR WIVES", and the other had a sign which said "MEN WHO CAN CONTROL THEIR WIVES".

To the king's surprise the tent for those who are controlled by their wives was completely full and there was only one single man in the tent for those who can control their wives. The king ran with desperation up to this man, in hope of finding a solution for his problem.

He asked the man, "Tell me your secret, how do you control your wife?" The man looked at him in surprise, "Me, control my wife? I cannot control her; she controls all my life".

And the king asked, "Then why are you sitting in this tent and not in the other?"

The man answered sheepishly, "My wife told me to".

In this parable the king is the mind and the five wives are the five senses. The mind unfortunately cannot control the senses but is controlled by them.

Pratyahara is the step in this process by which we learn to disconnect the mind from the sense inputs.
It is our natural experience that when we are deeply engrossed in some activity, we lose contact with the messages which are being received by the senses. We become unaware of sounds, sights and sensations of temperature. Someone may even speak to us and it

will not register in our conscious mind. We also have the experience of sleep in which the senses are functioning but are not registering in the conscious mind.

In some cases, the sense inputs go directly into the subconscious mind, so that the conscious mind may concentrate on more important matters. In most cases, if there is any danger perceived by the subconscious mind, it will in some way inform the conscious mind so that it may react properly.

It is easy to understand that this ability to disconnect the conscious mind from the senses is absolutely essential for one who wants to penetrate the mind with deep concentration. Concentration will not be possible if every sound or other sensation is creating streams of reactions and thought patterns within the mind.

The relationship between Pratyahara (the fifth step towards freedom) and concentration (the sixth step) is an extremely intimate one. It is rather difficult to see in some cases, which comes first. For one is obviously needed for the other. Withdrawal of the mind from the senses is both dependent upon and prerequisite to concentration. They work together, supporting each other.

There are some available techniques in which one learns to concentrate on the sense messages coming into the mind, without getting caught up in interpreting and reacting to them.

One such technique is "passive listening", where one assumes a relaxed position and allows all the sounds in the environment to pass through the mind. He learns not to identify the sounds as this or that, or interpret the sounds as pleasant or unpleasant. In this way, the sounds are experienced as pure energy impulses, which do not create thought patterns and reactions in the mind. One can practice this type of passive sense experience with all the senses, and even with pain. Through such techniques, the senses lose their power to influence the mind so easily.

The mind is freer to concentrate.

The Art of Meditation

CHAPTER 17

THE LAST STEPS TOWARDS FREEDOM

We have now discussed the first five steps towards freedom.

1. YAMA - Guidelines for moral behavior.

2. NIYAMA - Spiritual disciplines.

3. ASANA - Control of the body.

4. PRANAYAMA - Control of the bioenergy.

5. PRATYAHARA - Control of the senses.

These first five steps have to do with controlling all factors external to the mind; the behavior, the body, the bioenergy, and the senses. The last three steps have to do with controlling and transcending the mind itself. The last three steps are concentration, meditation and ecstasy. They are three degrees of concentration, or absorption, each step more intense and complete than the previous.

DHARANA - CONCENTRATION

The sixth step towards freedom is learning to concentrate the mind.

According to Patanjali "Concentration is the confining of the mind within a limited mental area (object of concentration)". Actually no human act is possible without some degree of concentration. If one does not concentrate while cooking, the hand will be cut, or the food will be burned or taste horrible. If one does not concentrate while driving a car, there will be an accident. If one does not concentrate at work, mistakes will be made which may cost much money, and perhaps even lives. If we do not concentrate while walking down the street, we may trip or bump into some object. Obviously study and learning require even more concentration than the above mentioned tasks.

So we can imagine what degree of concentration is necessary to hold the mind in one area or on one point of focus for a long period of time. For most of us this is simply impossible at first. We have not been trained to do this. The ability to hold the mind on a subject, idea, image, sound, inner feeling, location of the body or any other object of concentration is developed through **practice**. There is no other way. If you want to learn to swim, you have to go into the sea and do it. If you want to learn to concentrate, you simply have to practice regularly.

All of the previously mentioned steps of this path will help to calm the mind so that concentration will come more easily. Concentration, mediation and samadhi are the "inner work", for here we are dealing with the mind itself.

Each individual will find varying degrees of success in attempting to concentrate. It is rather important not to force this effort. When we try to force the mind, we create more tension. The mind is often like a little child. When you try to force it, it rebels. We have no difficulty in concentrating on a movie or the television. Our interest holds our concentration. If we develop the same type of interest for inner and spiritual subjects, our concentration will come easily.

Concentration must be developed slowly and with much patience. It must be developed with regularity, practicing each and every day. The time of concentration can be increased gradually as it becomes easier. The practice of the yogic exercises and breathing just prior

The Art of Meditation

to sitting for concentration makes the process much more effortless.

Remember that while sitting for concentration it is important that we do not expect certain experiences or results. We simply sit contentedly keeping the mind in the area designated for concentration. When the mind becomes distracted, we patiently and persistently bring it back to the point of concentration. The object of concentration could be a philosophical idea, a virtue like love, or a sound, or the name of God like Jesus Christ; or a flame of a candle or any other elevating object.

External objects such as a candle flame or flower are easier for the beginner. As concentration is increased, it is better to move on to an inner object of concentration. The final goal of this concentration is to transcend the mind altogether.

Remember the example of the common light bulb and the laser. In the ordinary light bulb, the waves of light are sent out in all directions and at various frequencies. The light from the light bulb reflects off the walls and objects in the room. The same power of light is passed in a certain way, through a crystal and becomes concentrated, so that all the waves are going in the same direction and with the same frequency. The light source is generating the same amount of power, but now that power is concentrated and is able to penetrate through the wall. The unconcentrated mind is like the ordinary light bulb, which reflects off of everything it sees. The laser beam is the concentrated mind, which is able to send all its energies in one direction and penetrate each object, thus uncovering the ultimate Reality behind every object of concentration.

In concentration we work in three basic ways:

1) We work on having less unrelated thoughts.

2) We develop a more clear concentration on the object of concentraticn.

3) We keep bringing the mind back over and over to the object of concentration.

DHYANA - MEDITATION

Concentration and meditation are two stages of the same process. They are like the flower and the fruit. According to Patanjali, meditation is "the uninterrupted flow of the mind towards the object of concentration". Thus meditation is simply success at concentration. What most of us practice today is not meditation but rather concentration.

In meditation the mind flows consistently and freely towards the object of concentration in the same way that the mind flows freely toward an interesting movie. There is no effort and no distracting thoughts.

Obviously most of us can maintain such a state for only short periods of time. It must be understood that this is not a static process. Although the mind is fixed on the object of concentration, the object itself may be experienced in various ways. For example one may be concentrating on the breath. The breath will be always changing. It may be incoming, outgoing, rapid, slow, deep, shallow, or even non-existent for periods of time. But the mind is always there with the breath, however it may be changing.

The same may be true of a mantra, or internal sound, which one chooses to meditate on. It may change its vibration, feeling, or become more or less subtle. However the mind stays with it throughout all its changes and movements, just like two butterflies chasing each other in the wind. There is a growing unity of movement between the mind and the object. They grow intimate.

In such a state, the mind becomes intensely peaceful. It is revitalized and filled with inner wisdom. We could imagine that each meditation is like contact with the true inner self, which benefits the personality in numerous ways. The mind becomes gradually purified, and aware of the inner voice of guidance and motivation. The individual becomes slowly attuned to the forces of

The Art of Meditation

nature and life itself.

We have already discussed this seventh step towards freedom in great detail. It remains then to move on to the eighth step, which is simply the result of the seventh.

SAMADHI - ECSTASY OR TRANCE STATE

Patanjali explains that "the same meditation, when there is consciousness of the object of meditation and not of the mind itself, is Samadhi". Thus concentration, meditation and Samadhi are simply three stages of the same process. The following example taken from I.K. Taimni's **The Science of Yoga,** will help us to understand this.

1. A B C D A F G H J A A   > **CONCENTRATION**

2. A A A B A C D A A D A A

3. A A A A A A A A A A A A > **MEDITATION**

4. A (A) A (A) A A A (A) A A A A

5. (A)(A)(A)(A)(A)(A)(A)(A)(A)(A) > **SAMADHI**

The letter "A" has been chosen as the object of concentration. In line 1 we see that we are able to keep "A" in the mind only for very short periods of time, until a foreign thought like "B" or "D" will interfere. In line 2 our concentration is better. We can hold "A" for longer periods of time but there are still interruptions. Lines 1 and 2 represent concentration.

In line 3 we have achieved meditation in that the mind is flowing "uninterruptedly" towards "A". In line 4 we see that some letters are in brackets and others do not. This requires some explanation.

In meditation, as in every other act in the world of duality, there are three aspects to this process. There is the actor, the acted upon, and the process of acting. For example there is the eater, the eaten and the eating. There is the speaker, the spoken to and the speaking.

This is our natural experience in our illusion of separateness from the world, in which we feel separate from the objects and beings we act upon and which act upon us. Even in meditation this duality exists in which there is the meditator, the object of meditation and the process of meditating.

In "Samadhi", the mind of the meditator merges with the object of meditation and disappears. There remains only the object of meditation. Since there is no more meditator, there is no more process of meditation. The illusion of duality has been pierced and the meditator has merged with the ultimate reality in which he and all beings are one. He has transcended the mind and experiences his unity with all of life. The mind loses its own form and takes the form of the object of concentration. The (A) with brackets around it represents the awareness of A without awareness of self. Thus line number 5 represents the state of Samadhi.

There are various types of samadhi corresponding to various stages of development. They can be basically categorized as Sabija and Nirbija samadhi. "Sabija" means "with seed", referring to samadhi which is attained through concentration on a subtle object of some type. Nirbija samadhi is without seed. It is the merging with the space or void between two thoughts. It is merging with the unmanifest from which all creation springs forth in some mysterious way.

Thus the goal of life has been achieved. The individual has returned to his source, he has merged with the Universal being from which he has originally come. He has realized his true UNIVERSAL INFINITE REALITY.

This goal of reunion with God, the one Divine Being, is the goal of all religions and spiritual philosophies. This eight-step path of increasing control over the body and mind is an invaluable tool for achieving that goal.

We can imagine this path as an ascending stairway, which facilitates our ascension. Let us remember also that the first two steps, of moral guidelines and spiritual disciplines can never be perfectly employed until we are actually enlightened and have realized our true Self. Thus we can imagine them as banisters on the sides of that stairway which both help us to ascend and prevent us from falling.

This eight-step path, however, is not the only path. Let us remember that this is the path of will power and self control. There are three other basic paths that can be followed separately or in combination. Most find that a combination is more fulfilling, as man is a multi-dimensional being with various needs. As these paths are described in detail in Chapter 1, we will only remind you of them here.

One path is the path of **service** to our fellow man or even to animals and plants. This service is done in humility, without feelings of self-importance and without attachment to the results of our efforts. We weaken the sense of ego-identification by serving others' needs rather than our own.

The second path is that of love and devotion towards God. Through prayer, chanting and surrender of our personal will to the Divine Will we are gradually liberated from the web of egoism, selfishness and false pride.

The third path is the path of knowledge and discrimination between our true immortal spiritual Self and our temporary body and mind. This spiritual discrimination frees us from our spiritual ignorance, which is the cause of all of our problems.

Most of us find that a combination of these paths offers us a balanced mode of evolution. In this way we simultaneously develop:

1. Will power and self control.

2. Love and devotion towards God and Humanity.

3. Wisdom and detachment.

4. Unity with all through service.

I would like to take this opportunity to wish you, the reader, much success on your path. May you be blessed with health, happiness, harmony and evolution.

CHAPTER 18

OBSTACLES TOWARDS SPIRITUAL GROWTH

In the world of change, which encompasses all physical, energy and mental phenomena, there are three qualities constantly at play. These three qualities can be used to describe any object, being or event, including thoughts, emotions, perceptions and actions.

Once again we will need to adapt the Sanskrit terms for these qualities since we do not have single word translations for them. These three qualities are called "**Tamas**", "**Rajas**" and "**Sattwa**", and are called the three "**Gunas**".

THE THREE QUALITIES

Tamas represents the state of heaviness, immobility, darkness, dullness, ignorance, tiredness, lack of energy, delusion, depression, discontent, and other similar states.

For example a tamasic person is a person who has few interests, little energy, who misinterprets and misunderstands. A tamasic person lacks motivation and is often afflicted with illnesses. Tamasic food is food without energy, overcooked food, food left over for days, or food stored in cans. Such foods, when eaten regularly, create a tamasic state in the body and mind. Tamasic acts are acts done in an ignorant, unconscious way, without clarity or concentration. Tamasic impressions are those which bring about a state of delusion or depression such as certain movies or magazines with morbid themes. Tamas is a state in which the "materialistic" aspect of life overshadows the "energy" or "awareness" aspects of life.

Rajas describes a state of energy, activity, aggressiveness, non-harmonious action, uncontrolled energy, stimulation, agitation, nervous energy, being unable to relax, or a state of effort. It is a state in which the energy aspect of life is greater than the material and awareness aspects of life. Rajasic personalities are those who are running all day long after a series of goals and desires. The desire nature of the rajasic person is usually very strong. He is very active in life. He is often unable to relax when he needs to, and will usually prefer dynamic sports as a way of relaxing. The rajasic personality is competitive, and often can become aggressive and, in some cases, violent. Rajasic foods are fresh meat and spices, which stimulate and agitate the nervous system into even more activity. Rajasic impressions are those which stimulate the desires and aggressive nature, such as sex and violence oriented movies and magazines. The military, business and political world are comprised of a high percentage of Rajasic people.

Sattwa describes a state of harmony, equilibrium, balance, peace, contentment, and awareness. In this case the quality of "awareness" is greater than the "materialistic" and "energy" nature. A sattwic person has an abundant supply of calm and creative energy that he is able to use for the benefit of himself and others. There is a peaceful self-contentment, which pervades the atmosphere around such a person. He has found a balance of the passivity and stability of Tamas and the energy and creative force of rajas. Sattwa is the perfect harmonious balance of tamas and rajas.

Few individuals, if any, are completely tamasic, rajasic or sattwic. Although each has his particular tendency, each of us is constantly experiencing the changing flow of these three states through our being.

We all have moments of tamasic tiredness and depression. We all have moments of aggressive activity, or extreme effort, or restless

The Art of Meditation

nervous tension, or intense desire. We also have moments of peaceful contentment with ourselves and the world around us.

The individual who is seeking to work consciously on his self-improvement and spiritual evolution will try to cultivate a more and more sattwic state of body and mind. A sattwic state is much more conducive to success in spiritual life. Tamas keeps the individual from making the necessary effort, and rajas prevents the mind from being able to turn inward the goal of Self-realization.

Thus the spiritual aspirant seeks to ingest only sattwic foods such as pure and fresh vegetables and fruits, nuts, grains, beans and dairy products. He also tries to take in only Sattwic impressions such as spiritually oriented books, films, magazines and people.

The company we keep is also extremely important. We are very much affected by the quality of the people we associate with. This is especially important at the beginning of our spiritual effort, when we are still doubtful, unsure and easily influenced by others. As our faith increases, we can more safely associate with, and even help, people with tamasic or rajasic characters.

There is a state higher still than sattwa, in which we simply do not identify with the body or mind, through which these changing states are flowing. Tamas, rajas and sattwa will continue to do their dance through our bodies and minds, but we will not identify with them. The final goal of yoga is to transcend even the sattwic state. However, at our present state of evolution, most of us will benefit by seeking to cultivate a sattwic state of body and mind, as an essential step towards its transcendence.

Spiritual techniques and concepts are designed to help us gradually step upward from tamas, to rajas to sattwa, This is usually the way in which the progress must take place. It is difficult to go from Tamas directly to sattwa. One usually needs to pass through a stage of rajas, which eventually leads to sattwa. Eventually from the stage of sattwa all three gunas are transcended. But this transcendence would be difficult, if not impossible, from a state of tamas or rajas. Patanjali has pointed out for us some of the obstacles of spiritual life which prevent us from developing the necessary degree of sattwa and concentration, which lead to samadhi.

He states that, *"Disease, physical laziness, doubt, carelessness, mental laziness, craving for sensual pleasure, false perception, despair caused by failure and unsteadiness; These distract the mind and are obstacles to spiritual progress".*

Let us examine each of these obstacles separately, and reflect on how one might overcome them. In general Patanjali claims that they can be overcome by the constant practice of one truth or principle; that is, concentration. But they themselves are obstacles to concentration. Let us simultaneously consider what other techniques might help one eventually achieve that one-pointedness of concentration and effort necessary for success in spiritual life.

1) DISEASE

It is easy to understand that a "dis-eased" body will be unable to concentrate, for any length of time, without being distracted by pains or discomforts. Also there will likely be a state of tamas and lack of energy. When a body is diseased for long periods of time, the individual's mental outlook often becomes negative and depressed. If the individual tries to concentrate, he will likely be disturbed by the body, which will send messages of pain saying "look at me, I want attention". He will be unable to transcend body consciousness.

A healthy body is needed for whatever material or spiritual endeavor we may choose in life. Thus, it is important that we keep it healthy with the proper food, enough exercise and sufficient rest. The purpose of the physical exercises, breathing techniques, deep relaxation and dietary guidelines, is to prevent the mind from being disturbed by the weaknesses of the body.

2) PHYSICAL LAZINESS

Physical laziness is a symptom of tamas. When a person is afflicted with this problem, he will find every excuse not to perform his spiritual practices, He will not make the effort necessary to overcome the habits and desires of the body. Such a person will not succeed in any endeavor, material or spiritual. This laziness of the body must be overcome so that the body will not be an obstacle preventing one from finding fulfillment in life. Even the simple daily duties will not be properly performed if physical laziness is allowed to persist.

Through the use of yoga asanas, or other types of exercise, the bodily forces can gradually be awakened. Deep rhythmic breathing will be very helpful in revitalizing the body. A person suffering from physical laziness must also take care of his diet. He must avoid all tamasic foods such as canned food, food prepared some days ago, or overcooked foods. He must eat fresh fruits, vegetables, grains, beans, nuts and dairy products in order to have an abundant life force. He must also be careful not to overeat. Many people lack sufficient energy because they overeat and become heavy in body and mind.

In getting started, an individual will have to use his will power to overcome the state of inertia in the body. Gradually, as this inertia is overcome, and there is a flow of activity in the body he will not have to make so much effort.

This can be understood with the example of the car. When we start to move, we have to put the car in first gear and give plenty of gas. Gradually, as we gain momentum, we can gradually change to a less powerful gear. We arrive at fourth gear, where we need to give the car very little gas to keep it going at a high speed. The gas we need to keep it going at a high speed is less that that which we need to get started from a stationary position. The same is true of the physically lazy person. In the beginning, he will have to make a significant effort to overcome the tamas of the body. But once he is moving in a healthy routine, little effort will be needed to keep going.

3) DOUBT

We are full of doubts, especially about spiritual life. We have doubts about the existence of the soul, of God, about the value of all these spiritual practices, and about the truth of the spiritual teachings. There are doubts about one's ability to succeed in this effort. We doubt whether God really is aware of our actions and prayers. We doubt whether we will really continue to exist after death of the physical body. We doubt so many things.

This is quite understandable, for our social environment and conditioning do not in any way encourage faith in these matters. The goal of spiritual life is considered intangible and impractical; a path for madmen and mystics. Social values encourage faith in money, power and material possessions. Little value is given to spiritual qualities. There is a complete lack of spiritual examples in our present society. None of the public figures i.e. the politicians, movie stars, sports figures, businessmen, not even the clergy, present a proper example of a spiritual life. Few of them have inspired us towards a spiritual life by their living example. Many speak with beautiful words, but few live those words.

How may doubt be replaced by faith? One way is through experience. In the process of practicing the various spiritual disciplines, we often encounter experiences that increase our faith. Our increased faith opens our minds and hearts, which further increases the possibility of such experiences, which then again further increases our faith in an upward spiraling circle.

Contact with others who believe in the same goals and way of life, will help us to let go of various doubts. For this reason, we should each attempt to join in some group activity aimed toward self-improvement or spiritual development. Such a group will give us support, and we, in turn, will support others through our common belief and faith.

Study of the numerous books, available today on all aspects of human evolution, give us the confidence of knowing that other very wise beings who have traveled before us to light the way, affirm the truth of these spiritual concepts. They reaffirm the value of making a personal and social effort in this direction.

Perhaps the greatest doubt-removing experience is the opportunity

The Art of Meditation

to be in the presence of such beings such as Jesus the Christ, Krishna, Rama, Buddha or some of the great saints who have manifested spiritual powers.

You can imagine what a faith boosting experience it can be to be in the presence of such a being, and then to hear Him tell you that "God is in all beings - including you" and that if you practice spiritual disciplines you will manifest your divinity. Doubt is gradually erased.

4) CARELESSNESS

Obviously carelessness will undermine any endeavor. Carelessness, while driving, will result in an accident. Carelessness in preparing food will result in bad tasting or even poisonous food. Carelessness in spiritual practices will prevent success and can even cause harm to the body and mind.

In some cases, carelessness comes from being without "care" for, or simply not "caring" enough about, the activity being performed. If one does not sincerely care about what he is doing, he will obviously not give full attention or effort to that activity. If one is careless in one's spiritual discipline, then there is no possibility of success.

On the other hand a person may care about what he is doing, but by nature may not pay attention to details. Whatever the reason for the lack of careful attention, carelessness represents a great potential danger for the spiritual aspirant and those around him. If one does not follow carefully the guidelines given by the spiritual teachers while practicing these techniques, one can do serious harm to the body and mind. Disturbances can be created by the lack of regular harmonious practice of the disciplines.

At the same time, if the spiritual aspirant does not carefully observe the yamas and niyamas he may do great harm to himself and others. If he is careless about his emotions and expresses angry, violent feelings towards those around him, there will be much greater damage done than if he were an average person. The spiritual aspirant gradually acquires the trust and openness of those around him. Consequently, those around him are more susceptible to what he says and does. If he should carelessly lose control, he can seriously hurt the feelings of those nearby.

The student of yoga gradually learns the importance of paying attention to details. Through experience he realizes that he cannot make excuses for himself, and that he must be serious and extremely careful about how he lives his life and performs his spiritual practices. As his goal becomes more firmly established in his mind, he is able to give more one-pointed attention to what he is doing.

5) MENTAL LAZINESS

Lack of clarity and singularity of motive are often the causes of mental laziness. The mentally lazy person also tends to focus on comfort. Such a person lacks discipline and the inclination to make the necessary effort to succeed in any task.

Such a person needs a goal to stimulate him. He needs some interest to bring him out of his tamasic state. It is not necessary that the goal be spiritual at first. A material goal will do just as well, or even better, as an initial motivating force. Thus, the individual will have replaced tamas with rajas. Once the mental activity has been stimulated, it can then be directed toward the goal of self-improvement and self-discovery.

The role of work or activity that interests us is extremely important in overcoming both physical and mental laziness. The model of an electrical outlet may help us to understand this. Within the electrical outlet there is great potential energy capable of generating thousands of watts of power depending on the need. But if there is not work for the electricity to do, it remains static, where it is. Only when it is connected up to some work can it flow.

In the same way the physically, or mentally lazy person may have plenty of physical and mental energy waiting latent to be connected up to the right type of work or activity. If the work is not found, the energy remains latent, and the person is lazy.

The Art of Meditation

For this reason, work therapy and Karma yoga activities are a vital part of the life of every spiritual community. Many people who complain that they have no energy think that they need more rest. But in many cases, the opposite is true; they need some stimulating type of activity. They will also benefit from the various types of tapas, such as eating less, fasting, talking less, or taking cold showers.

6) CRAVING FOR SENSUAL PLEASURE   (WORLDLY MINDEDNESS)

This is perhaps the greatest obstacle created by our modern society. We have become addicted to all types of sensory inputs, such as variety of tastes, sexual pleasures, movies, magazines, comforts of all types and a barrage of involuntary visual, auditory and olfactory inputs which we cannot control. The average city dweller does not know how to tolerate silence. He must fill the silence with conversation or with the radio or television.

Few people can go for more than a few hours without putting something into their mouths; either food, coffee, an alcoholic beverage or a cigarette. The average urban eyes never see more than a distance of a 100 meters. Our vision is always bombarded by a barrage of various posters, advertisements, buildings, cars, people, etc. In other words, our senses have become accustomed to intense input. We have become addicted to this and feel uncomfortable when suddenly there is no sensory information coming into the mind.

When there is no sensory input, one is forced to face himself. This is very unpleasant for many people. How will we be able to meditate when the moment we enter into some type of silence we begin, out of habit, to crave for some sensory input? How can we concentrate on the spiritual goal of realizing the inner Self, if the mind is constantly pulled outward by the various sensory attractions?

This craving for sensual input (whether pleasant or unpleasant) causes us to expend a great amount of energy, effort, time, money and thought power which could be used for higher, more permanently satisfying goals. When the mind is so strongly pulled outward, it cannot possibly turn inward. These habits of sense craving will go on until we finally realize that they cannot ever possibly be satisfied; for the desire will always return again and again to disturb us.

The body and mind can be gradually purified of these cravings through the practice of tapas (austerity), through meditation and through contact with holy and pure people, who are not themselves so focused on sensual cravings.

Ultimately, time too is on our side, for gradually we will become tired of endlessly and unsuccessfully seeking lasting pleasure through the senses. We will turn our attention within to find the only real lasting contentment which is latent within.

7) FALSE PERCEPTION - DELUSION

Delusion means taking things for what they are not. Delusion means misinterpreting the external objective reality because of subjective distortions. Obviously this problem will cause us to make many wrong decisions and mistakes during our search for the truth. We are always full of misconceptions and wrong information because of our social conditioning. We are plagued by a superficial value system that prevents us from properly evaluating what we see in life.

Even in our spiritual practices we misinterpret and, thus, seek the wrong types of results. Many seek exciting psychic experiences in their meditation. When they eventually create these experiences from an astral level, they interpret them as divine in origin, when in fact, they emanate from the dream level.

This does not exclude the possibility of a vision of the Divine, but it is usually not the case with the average meditator.

We can be easily lead astray today by the many false prophets and greedy gurus who are parading around in the West. Many of them have started out with good intentions, but have fallen to the

The Art of Meditation

temptation of power and money. On the spiritual path, we have to develop razor sharp discrimination in order to travel this path called the "razor's edge".

We must analyze our own conditioning in order to see how we are distorting the world of people and events around us. Each of us interprets the same external reality in a completely different way depending on our unique conditionings.

Through self-study we will eventually be able to avoid this mistake of distorting and misperceiving reality. Joining with others in "satsang" (spiritual groups which discuss, meditate and chant together) or in psychology groups, we will gradually rectify our vision.

8) DESPAIR BECAUSE OF FAILURE TO ACHIEVE A STATE OR GOAL

This type of despair is quite common as we begin this immense task of mastering the body and mind. We often feel that we are making no progress. At other times we feel that we have gone forward, but then fallen further back than where we had started. We lose our faith, our patience and courage. Many become so despaired that they give up the effort altogether, deciding that they are not ready.

In order to overcome this obstacle, we need to develop understanding and patience; a more expanded concept of time. We need a new view of the life and death cycle, and a new view of the relationship between the personality and the soul. We must be patient through all the ups and downs in life. Life is cyclical by nature. The body, mind and emotions all exist within these rhythmic cycles, and we must be ready to accept that there will be days in which we are strong and vital and others in which we are weak and insecure. That is life.

If we reconstruct our concept of time, in order to see how small a period of time our effort has taken in comparison to our whole lifetime of about 80 to 100 years; and how small that one lifetime is in relationship to the whole series of lives we have had and will live;

and then realize how small that period is in comparison to our eternal existence before and after those series of lives, we will realize how ridiculous our impatience and despair are.

If too, we realize that we are not actually the entity which is undergoing all these efforts and changes, successes and failures; but rather the eternal and already perfect witness who is watching the whole drama, we will have more patience and compassion towards our personality's efforts. We will see that the body and mind are far from perfect, but that we can, with patience and regular effort, gradually purify and perfect them.

A spiritual guide is a great help in overcoming this obstacle, for he is an example of one who has traveled the path and can assure us of its value. When direct verbal contact with a spiritual guide is not possible, it is extremely beneficial to meet regularly with others who have the same goals.

We must learn to make the effort without becoming attached to the result of the effort, and realize that there is an endless series of steps that we must climb in order to reach perfection. You will remember this model, which again will help us to understand this point.

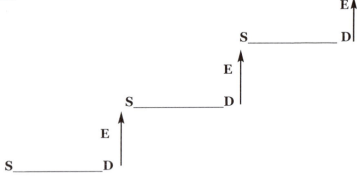

D = Dissatisfaction
E = Effort for change
S = Satisfaction, contentment

We see here a series of steps, representing the various tests, efforts

The Art of Meditation

and evolutionary quantum movements, which must be made in order to become a perfected being. Each step begins with **discontent** about some aspect of one's self. This stimulates an **effort** to improve, represented by the vertical line. When the effort is successful, we achieve the next level and feel **content** for some period of time. We may feel proud of our success and feel that it will be "easy sailing" from now on; that nothing will get in our way.

But what we soon realize is that the top of each vertical becomes the bottom of the next and we soon find ourselves in front of the next mountain we have to climb. We make the effort (rajas) and attain the contentment (sattwa) at the top of the mountain. But that contentment too turns into discontentment (tamas) upon realizing that we have new tests to face and changes to make.

When we eventually realize what is happening, we can step back and observe the process from a distance and take both the valleys and mountains in stride. We make our best effort and leave the results to God.

9) INSTABILITY

Instability is when we achieve a certain state and then fall backward. This often happens because of previous failure to establish the proper foundation of spiritual life, i.e. the Yamas and Niyamas. The way to avoid instability is to move slowly along the spiritual path, making sure of firmly constructing the previous level before moving on to the next.

The modern aspirant is plagued by impatience and a desire for quick and spectacular results. He wants to immediately practice the most advanced and powerful techniques so as to have the most exciting experiences. He wants to feel "high" and, at times, he may resort to chemical drugs to help him feel that way. When this is done, he does get high, but has no foundation to hold him where he is and soon finds himself flat on the ground again.

Patience, persistence and **practice** are the three "p's" which we need for a stable spiritual growth.

These **nine obstacles** are only some of the many which inhibit us in our effort. There are others. You may want to identify which ones are standing in your path now and make a program to get around them, go over them, go under them or go through them.

CHAPTER 19

REMOVING THE OBSTACLES
TO SPIRITUAL GROWTH

In the previous chapters we discussed nine of the various obstacles to concentration and spiritual evolution. You will remember that they are: disease, physical laziness, doubt, carelessness, mental laziness, craving for sensual pleasure, false perception, despair caused by failure to achieve a goal and instability in holding a state of achievement.

Patanjali suggests some ways to overcome these obstacles in his Yoga Sutras. You may also remember that, according to Patanjali, Raja Yoga is "the cessation or the inhibition of the modifications of the mind". The goal of spiritual life is to bring the mind to a completely peaceful state, so that it is no longer affected by either internal or external disturbances. Patanjali explains that these disturbances and modifications of the pure consciousness can be suppressed by "**persistent practice and non-attachment**".

Persistent practice and non-attachment are the basic tools of spiritual life. They are like the two co-operating pedals of a bicycle. One aids and furthers the other. The more we increase our ability to calm the disturbances of the mind through practice, the more we are able to be detached. The more detached from objects and people we become, the more we are able to calm the mind.

The following conversation takes place between Sri Krishna and

Arjuna in the Bhagavad Gita:

Arjuna: *Krishna, you describe this path as a life of union with God. But I do not see how this can be permanent. The mind is so very restless.*

Krishna: *Yes, Arjuna, the mind is restless no doubt, and hard to subdue. But it can be brought under control by constant practice and by the exercise of detachment. Certainly, if a man has no control over the ego, he will find this path difficult to master. But the self-controlled man can master it, if he struggles hard and uses the right means.*

Patanjali affirms that the result will be proportional to the effort, and suggests that the above mentioned obstacles can be removed by the practice of one truth or principle. This means bringing the mind to focus on a central point, and not letting it be disturbed by various distractions. It means learning to turn the mind inward, instead of letting it fly outward with every distraction. It means learning to concentrate and meditate.

This concentration can manifest as a formal sitting meditation or as a central goal or objective in one's life, which helps one to focus one's energies. A person with a goal in life is much more easily able to concentrate his energies and avoid distractions. An individual without a goal or central focus to his life tends easily towards distraction and negative states of body and mind. This can be witnessed in mothers who are passing through the stage in which their children are growing into adulthood and leaving home. Their previous goal and role in life is taken from them, and they have not yet found a new goal in life. Thus they often pass through a difficult period. The same is true for those who discontinue their work when time comes for their pension. They may go through a crisis of not having a purpose in life.

FOUR ATTITUDES

Patanjali suggests that the mind can be clarified for concentration and meditation by cultivating the following attitudes:

1) Friendliness towards people who are happy.

2) Compassion towards people who are miserable.

3) Gladness in the presence of virtuous people.

4) Indifference in the presence of evil people.

Although on the surface it would seem obvious that we would be happy because of someone else's happiness and compassionate towards their misery, it is not always the case. In our competitive society we are taught that we have to protect ourselves from the others and **compete** with them in every aspect of life.

We have learned to envy their success, and to rejoice in their failure and misery. We have also learned to ignore others' suffering as "their own problem". We are seldom indifferent in the presence of vice but rather are quick to judge others and enjoy feelings of self-righteousness.

In addition we are not always so glad to be in the presence of virtue. Sometimes we tend to feel uncomfortable or inferior in the presence of virtuous persons. Each of us will have to decide for himself whether he needs to spend time cultivating these four mind-purifying attitudes.

When the mind is purified, it will concentrate more easily. Let us now look at some of Sri Krishna's guidelines for meditation given in the Bhagavad Gita.

"Shutting off the senses from what is outward. Fixing the gaze at the root of the eyebrows. Checking the breath-stream ingoing and outgoing within the nostrils. Holding the senses. Holding the intellect. Thrusting fear aside. Thrusting anger aside and putting off desire; Truly that man is made free forever".

"As he sits there, he is to hold the senses and imagination in check, and keep the mind concentrated upon its object. If he practices meditation in this manner, his heart will become pure.

"His posture must be motionless, with the body, head and neck held erect, and the vision in-drawn, as if gazing at the tip of the nose. He must not look about him".

OBJECTS OF CONCENTRATION

Patanjali suggests the following objects for concentration:

1) We may concentrate on the movement of the **breath** in the nostrils. This is one of the basic meditation techniques, in which one watches the flow of breath, observing the breath as it changes in various ways. Whenever the mind is distracted, it is simply brought back to the breath. There is no need to control the breath in any way. We simply witness the flow of breath in and out at the point of the nostrils. This serves to increase concentration and purify the "nadis" and nervous system. (The nadis are nerve channels of the energy body).

2) One may become aware of, and concentrated on, the **inner** senses such as **sounds** and **visions** within. These are not to be misinterpreted as divine experiences, but simply they offer an inner object of concentration, which helps the mind to turn inward away from external distractions.

3) Inner experiences of light and deep serenity can be held in the mind for long periods of time as a way to increase concentration. Such concentration will relax all the systems of the body, bring inner peace to the personality and help one to develop a more relaxed and detached attitude towards life.

4) The mind can be fixed on the **image and name of a high spiritual being** who is free from attachment to the world. One may concentrate on an incarnation of God; such as Jesus the Christ. Through such meditation one begins to develop the divine qualities of the being upon whom one is focusing. At the same time, help in the form of Divine Grace comes to the individual from the being upon whom he is concentrating.

The average individual is more easily able to concentrate on a form such as that of Jesus, than on the abstract spiritual qualities such as divine love, inner peace, absolute truth and righteousness, which are embodied by such a being. Concentration on such a divine form is a stepping stone towards relating to the unmanifest Creative Force, which is without form.

5) One may also meditate on **information received in dreams and dreamless sleep**. We might imagine that occasionally we may get useful messages or feelings in our dream states that could be beneficial to meditate upon.

6) Then Patanjali goes on to add that we may meditate on **anything which suits us**, depending on our personal nature. The assumption here is that we will choose an object that will help us to expand our awareness out of our small ego identification and beyond the multitude of external and internal distractions.

The object of concentration may be experimented with in the early stages of one's spiritual search. However, an object should be kept for concentration for at least a period of 5 to 6 months before giving up for another. It is best to move from gross objects of concentration towards more subtle ones, as the concentration increases. There is a story which exemplifies this:

A student asked his guru for an object for meditation. The guru pointed to a star far away in the sky. The student concentrated on the star daily until he was able to see it quite clearly and hold it in his vision for long periods of time. Then he went back to his master and asked for a new object for meditation. The teacher pointed out a star much smaller and dimmer than the first. Through daily practice on the tiny dim star, he was soon able to see it as clearly as he had seen the previous one.

Upon returning to the master and asking for another object, he was given an even smaller and dimmer star that he could not see at all at first. But through repeated and persistent practice he was soon able to see the star as clearly as the previous two. This process went on and on as the student's vision became more and more penetrating into increasingly subtler realities.

It is not, however, necessary to change objects of meditation at all; for each and every object is itself a manifestation of the one Spirit which we are seeking to know. Through the penetration of the gross and subtle bodies of any object of being, we can realize the Spiritual Reality, which is simultaneously the causal force behind that object and our own selves. We are each unique expressions of the same One Universal Spirit whose body is the whole universe. By meditation on any aspect of creation we can discover the Creator.

However, "some nuts are easier to crack" than others. Some objects are more difficult to penetrate, in that their nature is very dense and gross. They are good for developing concentration in the early stages, but are too gross to be easily perceived as manifestations of the Divine.

For example, in one system we are encouraged to meditate on the physical body. Upon sufficient concentration on the physical body, we will become aware of the energy body. We may then meditate for some time on the energy body, following its movements and currents, until we become aware of the mental body, which is even subtler. As our concentration increases we can penetrate the mental body and become aware of the pure intellect. In the final stages, the causal body, which is subtler than the pure intellect (buddhi) is realized.

Finally, when concentration becomes intense enough, one enters into the samadhi of union with the Self - pure consciousness, which is beyond all these various bodies. Thus, through concentration on the physical body, our awareness penetrates into more and more subtle realities, until we reach the foundation of its existence, the Universal Spirit.

MANTRA

Another well-tested vehicle for traveling through the layers of the mind is the "Mantra". A mantra is an inner sound with a special spiritual vibration and meaning, which when repeated and concentrated on in the mind, purifies the mind and leads it into higher states of consciousness.

There are many mantras, representing the various attributes of Divinity. Some of them use the names of the various incarnations of God according to the various religions, such as "Lord Jesus Christ have mercy on us" or "Hare Krishna" or "Sri Ram, Jai Ram, Jai Jai Ram" or "Om Nama Shivaya" and others. Through repetition of and meditation upon the meaning of these mantras we gradually develop the qualities manifested by these great beings and attract to ourselves their Grace.

Other mantras relate to the unmanifest aspect of the Divine. "**So-Ham**" can be repeated with the breath concentrating on the sound "So" while inhaling and the "Ham" while exhaling. "So" means HE, the Universal Spirit who is in all beings, and "Ham" means I am. Thus with this mantra, used with or without the breath, one reaffirms one's identity with the Universal Spirit.

Perhaps the most celebrated and well known mantra is the "**AUM**" or "**OM**" which represents the Unmanifest God. It is said that meditation on the OM is sufficient for realizing the highest Reality. No other meditation need be used if one finds meditation on the OM comfortable and suitable to himself. OM is considered to be one with God and the sound through which God manifests Himself as the created world. OM is the word which St. John, the Evangelist, speaks of in the opening lines of his Gospel.

"Before the world was created, the Word already existed; He was with God, and He was the same as God. From the very beginning the Word was with God. Through Him God made all things, and not one thing in all creation was made without Him. The Word was the source of Life and this life brought light to mankind".

Sai Baba confirms St. John's words, explaining that God manifested Himself as the world through the sound OM.

"Every little movement or incident results in sound; only you may not be able to hear, because the range of your ear is limited. The falling of an eyelid over the eye makes a sound, the dropping of drop on a petal makes sound. Any little agitation disturbing the calm is bound to produce a sound. The sound caused by the primal

movement that resulted in the enveloping of God by self-evolved illusionary world is the sound OM".

Patanjali completely agrees with St. John and Sai Baba, and further claims that by concentration on this Universal Sound (OM), one can reenter into universal union. The steady internal concentration on the "OM" will purify the various bodies of a man, until he is pure enough to receive the Divine Grace of Self-realization.

For a more detailed explanation of this process one may refer to I. K. Taimni's **"The Science of Yoga"**, in which he explains that *"by producing a particular kind of vibration through a vehicle it is possible to draw down a particular kind of force through the vehicle or to produce a particular state of consciousness in the vehicle. Such vibrations can be produced by means of Mantras each of which represents a particular combination of sounds for bringing about certain specific results".*

Patanjali further mentions that through meditation on the OM the **obstacles to spiritual development disappear and the consciousness turns inward.**

Let us consider some of Sathya Sai Baba's teachings about meditation on the OM. The word "Pranava" refers to the OM.

"The best Upadesh is the Pranava, the sacred syllable OM which summarizes many principles of theology, philosophy and mysticism. Little children just learning to toddle about are given a three-wheeled contraption which they push forward, holding on the crossbar. The OM is such a "vehicle" for the spiritual child. The three wheels are "a", "u" and "m", the three components of the mantra. OM is the primal sound inherent in the life-breath. Every time we breathe, we say So-Ham; "So" when we inhale and "Ham" when we exhale, meaning "He - I" instilling into ourselves the conviction that He who is all this external world is I who is all this internal world, the conviction of Unity. During deep sleep, when the senses, the brain and the mind are dormant and de-functionalized, the "He" and the "I" are not cognized as separate; The So (He) and the Ham (I) both fade and the sound Soham is

transformed into OM, indicating the merger of the external with the internal into one Truth. OM has also many other significances and the meditation on the OM is a valuable Sadhana, for the seeker of reality. It is like the seven colors of the sun's ray merging into one colorless (white) brilliance".

"In the human body there are six nerve centers, all in the form of the lotus-flower. All the six lotus-forms have letters of sounds attached to each petal. Like the reeds in the harmonium, when the petals are moved, each one emanates a distinct sound. Those who follow this statement intelligently may get a doubt, if the petals are said to move, who or what is moving them? Yes, the Force that moves them is the Primeval Sound, the Undistinguished Indistinguishable Sound, emanating without Effort, irrespective of Conscious Will, That is the Pranava. As beads in the string, all letters and the sounds they represent are strung on the Pranava. That is the meaning of the statement that He is the "Pranava of the Vedas". Krishna's teaching is that you should merge your mind in the Pranava, which is the Universal Basis".

"There are many who argue that the Pranava can be repeated only by a few and that others are not entitled to it. This is wrong. This false conclusion has been arrived at since they do not know the truth. It springs from a mistaken belief.

The Githa does not mention this group or that group. Krishna declares "whoever" without any qualifying words limiting it to one class or sex. He has not even said, "who deserves or who does not deserve", "who is authorized or who is unauthorized". He has only said that for meditation on the Pranava, (mere "calling it to memory" is of no use) some preliminary disciplines have to be gone through, like the control of the senses, the concentration of the mind, etc.

For, when the mind is flitting from one fancy to another, how can the production of a sound Om, Om, by the vocal organs be of any benefit? The sound will not help the attainment of Liberation. The senses have to be curbed, thoughts have to be one-pointed, the Glory has to be apprehended. That is why the Lord advised that *from birth to death one must be engaged in the search for Truth. Instead, if you postpone your spiritual efforts until the last moment, you will be like the student who turns over the pages of his textbook for the first time, just before he enters the examination-hall! If the student feels that he has before him one full year and if he neglects to learn from the teacher and from lecture-notes and from books, how can anything enter his brain when he opens the pages of his book that very morning? It will only add to his despair. He can be pronounced proficient only in indolence.*

No tree will yield fruits the moment you plant the seedling in your backyard. To reach that stage, you have to follow carefully without break, the preparatory disciplines. No one can acquire the fruit without vigilance and steadfastness".

Thus concentration on the OM (or any other mantra or object of concentration) will be of invaluable use to those who want to overcome the obstacles and fulfill their spiritual purpose in life.

The Upanishads represent the highest truth of the Indian spiritual teachings and refer often with great praise to the use of "OM". Swami Sarvananda explains in his commentary on the Taittiriyopanisad that OM is considered to be the highest vibratory symbol for God.

"First it is laid down that one should meditate purely upon Om without thinking of any supervening factor. For Om is the manifesting word of God. In practice one should repeat the syllable Om with the mind fixed on its meaning, i.e. God. "Symbol", says Swami Vivekananda, "is the manifestor of the thing signified, and if the thing signified has already an existence, and if, by experience, we know the symbol has expressed the thing many times, then we are sure that there is a real relation between them...". The idea, God, is connected with hundreds of words and each one stands as a symbol for God. But there must be a generalization among all these words, some substratum, some common ground of all these symbols; and that which is the common symbol will be the best, and will really represent them

The Art of Meditation

all... Om (Aum) is such a sound, the basis of all sounds".

In conclusion, we may overcome the obstacles along the spiritual path through development of a pure one-pointed mind. This may be done through **practice** and **detachment.** There are various objects of concentration upon which one may practice. In the initial chapters of this book you were introduced to a wide variety of possible objects of concentration. Choose one suitable for your character.

Thus, the key to freedom from the various obstacles is concentration itself. This concentration has two forms. One is the method of meditation which we will employ daily. The second is to be focused on the truth throughout the day while being engaged in our daily activities. One way to do this is by praying internally such as with the Jesus prayer, "Lord Jesus Christ Have Mercy on Me". Another way is to continuously mentally repeat the name of God. Another is to concentrate on some spiritual value such as Love, Peace, Truth etc. or by contemplating on some spiritual truth such as "We are all immortal spirits", or "All is God", or "We are all one".

These types of mental exercises will gradually free us from the various obstacles to our spiritual growth process.

CHAPTER 20

BRINGING GOD
BACK INTO OUR LIVES

As we have now understood, each of us is an eternal spirit, we existed before our occupancy of these bodies and will continue to exist after these bodies decompose into the Earth. We were, are and always will be complete in our soul nature; in need of nothing and no one.

On the other hand, each of us has started this earthly incarnation as a single cell. Yes, there was a time when the body in which you are now residing was a tiny cell in your mother's womb. This cell began to divide, multiply and differentiate, gradually evolving into a complex human embryo.

As an embryo, your body was one with your mother's; sharing the same blood and life-force. You had no individuality. Through the agency of the umbilical cord all of your body's life needs were supplied.

Nine months passed and your body emerged. The umbilical cord was cut. The first breath ensued, and you became cut off from your source; your secure union. Now as a separate entity, you cling desperately to your mother's breast for life nourishment and security.

As a result of this traumatic separation, you must now, for the rest of your life, seek reunion. You will continually search throughout your life for that one thing or anything, which can reestablish that secure union from which you were cut off.

This need forms the motivating force behind all relationships, religion and science. This separation of the child from the mother is symbolic of the separation of the mind from the soul, the soul from the oversoul. Of man from God. The word religion is formed of two Latin roots; "re" (again) and "legere" (to link), meaning to re-link or reconnect. The purpose of religion is to reestablish the union between man and his Cosmic Mother; God.

Science is attempting to understand the laws which govern the relationships and functioning of all the beings and objects of the universe. Through science man is seeking to understand and reestablish his true relationship to the Universe. Universe comes from Latin "uni" (one) and "vertere" (turning into); **turning into one.** The Universe is something that is turning into one. That One is God, from which the Universe emanated (or turned out of).

In the past years, religion and science have found themselves converging to the same point through the different paths of the intuitive and the rational.

All relationships, in the same way, are attempts to connect with the beings and objects of the world around us in order to reestablish that secure union which was lost when individuality occurred through incarnation of the spirit.

Each of us is seeking to have union with other beings or objects in various ways in order to feel more secure. Some of us find security in food, others in money or material possessions. Others feel secure when they have power over others. Some feel secure in family ties or groups, or in organizations or professions. Still others in securing knowledge or abilities.

We gain union with these "external realities" one by one, and still remain feeling incomplete. Life is a process of securing union with, understanding of and mastery over each of those external objects in an evolutionary movement. We progressively eliminate each one, realizing that it will not give us the peace and happiness that we are seeking.

Finally, after searching long and hard outside of ourselves, it dawns on us to look within. Slowly the realization occurs that only a union with the ultimate source of our life will bring the eternal Peace and Love that will heal the wound of our separation.

If a baby wants milk, will it be satisfied with an empty bottle? All objects and people are empty bottles to the one who has not learned to see the milk essence within them. Only a union with God will bring the spiritual milk for which we thirst. God can be contacted in many ways, so let us consider some of the possibilities.

The bulk of humanity relates to God through the form and teachings of His saints, messengers and Avatars, who have come to show us the way. These are God-men, we are men-gods. The God in them dominated the man. With us the man overshadows the God-nature latent within.

So we worship those beings such as Christ, Krishna, Rama, or Buddha, as representatives of that Divine Potential that lies within each of us. By following their teachings and examples we come closer to that Divine essence within ourselves which brings peace and love into our lives.

GOD AS THE FORMLESS

Others worship God as a formless entity, as the Divine unmanifest source of all creation. We may relate to God as Primal Energy, Cosmic Consciousness, or as qualities such as Love, Truth, Peace or Righteousness. Some may feel God as the indefinable, or unknowable.

For many years I have sought for God in the solitude of retreats and nature; in breathing and meditation. I was looking for some type of "mind-blasting" experience, in which a being of light and glory would walk into my solitude and enlighten me. Well, it has not happened as yet. But something else, very beautiful is happening.

Instead of my having to escape into solitude to find God, He has started coming into my daily life. I feel somewhat like the lady who was looking all over the house for her necklace, which she was wearing all the time around her neck. The God I have been searching for, was right in front of me all of the time.

He is in every being I meet, in every tree, in every plant, animal, insect I see. I feel Him in the wind, see Him in the sun and the flame and hear Him in the sounds around me. I talk to Him within my own self. We feel so far from God and yet He is within us, around us, above and below us.

During the time period from 1964 to 1970 I believed that man had created the idea of God in order to calm his insecurity about life and death; and that science would soon explain God away through nuclear physics. Well, the opposite happened. Nuclear physics has penetrated through the wall of physical matter only to find a vast emptiness of uncertainty on the other side. They have found that there is really no such thing as matter, but only condensed energy. That energy is a manifestation of Mind or consciousness. That consciousness itself which pervades all animate and inanimate beings and objects, I call God.

THE PATH FOR HOUSEHOLDERS

Thus, we come to the most efficient spiritual path for householders; for people with families to provide for, and responsibilities to care for. The solution is simple. We must simply realize that, that pure universal consciousness which we call God, is the basic inner reality of our wife, husband, child, relative, friend, coworker, employer; and everyone we meet.

Through the paths of Love and Service we learn to see and serve God in everyone we meet. In this way, we treat them with the respect and love that they deserve. At first, this requires the use of imagination and memory. When we see the person opposite us as a body, a personality, a threat, a pleasure or a problem, we can remind ourselves that this being opposite us is, in reality, a physical manifestation of our own Universal Spirit. We use our imagination

The Art of Meditation

to recreate that feeling of oneness and overcome any separating feelings, or thoughts, that might be obstructing our love and acceptance of this person.

In this way, we bring God back into our lives on a very mundane and practical level. There are some practical ways to increase this feeling of being close to God. Every religion offers us such techniques. One is to hang pictures of our chosen form of God, such as Jesus Christ, Mother Mary or one of the great saints around the house so that our eyes and minds are constantly reminded of their love, strength, peace, example and teachings. What we see in our environment deeply affects the condition of our mind. It is out of fashion today to have religious pictures in the house. People prefer more "fashionable" exotic, and often erotic, images so as to impress the others that they are "modern" or intellectual.

Ultimately God is formless, unmanifest, indescribable, eternal, omnipresent and certainly cannot be limited to any one form, image, thought, idea, dogma or religion. But we can use all the above forms and concepts to raise our level of consciousness and purify our minds and emotions to the point where we can become ready to transcend the mind and experience that pure all pervading consciousness, we call God.

THE FORM AS A DOORWAY

Thus the form becomes a doorway to, or a means of constant reminder of, the purification by fire of the negativities and obstacles which prevent our spiritual growth. The flame reminds us of the Light (wisdom) of the Soul, or enlightenment, which removes the darkness of ignorance in which we live. The energy of the flame becomes a symbol of the One God from which can come forth an unlimited number of other flames without diminishing the original flame in the least.

The keeping up of the flame through remembering to add oil, and change the wick, gives us the opportunity to pause from our incessant concentration on our material pursuits and communicate our feelings, thoughts, needs and gratitude to God at that moment.

Placing flowers or lighting incense before the icon gives us a similar opportunity to express our thanks, or simply to have a moment of communication with that PRESENCE which is sustaining all this creation.

None of these external forms of worship are necessary or mandatory for a relationship with the Universal. They are helpful for those who enjoy them. It certainly would be more spiritually stimulating to spend our time on such activities than to spend time on movies, taverns and televisions.

The same holds true for spiritually oriented music and chanting. Sounds, melodies, and vibrations have been specifically developed to awaken higher feelings of peace and spiritual yearning in the individual. The same is, of course, true of all great classical music. In general we need more music and singing in our lives. Song is the language of the Soul...

Through the icons, flowers, candles, incense and music we offer the senses and, therefore, the mind with a spiritually stimulating atmosphere in which uplifting thoughts and feelings can grow and thrive. Thus, those sense inputs act as ritualistic mechanisms, which help the individual to feel somehow purer and closer to God. He then feels more content and secure within himself.

IMAGINATION

Some will consider this to be a type of self-delusion or imagination. Yes indeed, imagination is necessary in the beginning of this process. For we must fight fire with fire. We now **imagine** that we are these bodies and minds. This is the basic illusion of our lives. We live in an illusory ignorance that is based on our childhood conditioning. We falsely imagine that we are these separate bodies which will soon perish and be absorbed by the earth. We imagine that we are separate from God. We imagine ourselves helpless and unworthy. We feel separate and lonely, believing that we have to protect ourselves from the others and the world around us. Most of our actions are based on illusory fears and insecurities of material life. All this is an **imaginary,** temporary reality, somewhat like the dream reality we wake up from. When we leave these bodies, or when we become enlightened, we will wake up from this imaginary dream we are living.

Thus, we fight fire with fire. Imagination has caused the illusion and imagination can cure it. Imagining our relationship with God is the first step to "re-experiencing" it. Imagining that we are spirits in ONENESS with all other spirits is the first step in reawakening the mind to the reality. Gradually the reality, which we regularly imagine through the various rituals and techniques, becomes more and more established in the mind and emotions. The old false programming that we are these separate bodies and minds is erased and the new true program of our eternal spiritual nature is recorded and eventually experienced.

DAILY COMMUNICATION

When we want to develop a closer relationship with others, we seek them out and communicate with them. We think of them often. We think of what we can do to please them, to make them happy. We call them often on the telephone and ask how they are and share our feelings and thoughts with them. If we want a closer relationship with the Divine, then we must follow the same procedure. The telephone lines to the divine are always open, they are never busy (because there is a personal line for each individual, and the Divine has as many ears and mouths as there are individuals). So, if we want to develop this relationship, then we will naturally feel the desire often during the day to internally address that omnipresent, omniscient consciousness we call God and communicate to IT our deepest thoughts, feelings, needs, problems and gratitude.

Each may relate to the Divine in his own way. One may bring to his mind the image of JESUS the CHRIST, or Mother Mary, or one of the Saints. Another may prefer to think of God as the Sun, or as light. Another as IT, the unmanifest, nameless, formless reality from which all creation has come forth. Others may imagine God as Love or Truth or some high principle. It is not important what aspect of the infinite God one chooses to relate to. What is important is to **relate** as often and as sincerely as possible.

We spend so much time calling up friends who are as confused and misguided as we are, telling them our problems and asking their advice and help. This is fine, but wouldn't it be more useful to address all this to the ONE who has all the wisdom, love and power to solve absolutely any problem or question? We need more inner dialogue. That is what we mean by "intuition" - that is tuition from within. When we speak to the Divine within us, we get answers in the form of intuition or inner guidance.

We may also get messages from our outside environment. We may open a book to a random page and find the answer to our question or problem. A friend may suddenly call and inadvertently give us the answer that we are looking for. We may be walking in nature or stepping onto the bus and suddenly notice something which awakens the truth within us. The more we develop this inner conversation, the more we will be guided through the internal and external messages in our lives.

DIVINE GRACE

When we love someone, we want to do what makes him happy. When someone has selflessly helped us over and over in our lives we feel very grateful towards them and want to make them happy in the same way. Who has given us more than God has given us? It is a serious illusion to imagine that we have really obtained anything we have simply through our own effort. Our effort certainly plays an important role, but the result of every effort is up to the Divine. Two men can make the very same effort towards a business, or towards building a house or even towards spiritual growth. But the results each man achieves will be different. One will succeed more than the other. The result is a function of a number of factors:

1) The individual's effort.

2) The Karmic assets or debts from the past.

3) Our present beliefs, thought forms, expectations etc.

The Art of Meditation

4) The lessons which we have come to learn.

5) Divine Grace.

Serious thought will bring one to the realization that everything we have is due to the Divine Grace, i.e. the body, mind, food, the earth itself, the air, the water, fire, all the beings we know and relate to, all the objects, buildings, machines, all the plants and animals; everything that exists is a manifestation of the one divine consciousness.

When one realizes this, his ego is humbled and he lives with a constant feeling of gratitude, for all that he has been given. He learns to be grateful for both the pleasant and the unpleasant, for what he has and doesn't have. He learns to have faith that Life is giving him **exactly** what he needs in order to continue his spiritual growth here on the earth.

He lives with a feeling of security that as long as he does what is expected of him, all he needs will be provided for him. He works for the betterment of his self, his family and society, knowing that it is through his hands that all will be provided, but that the real source is far beyond the temporary material world.

OUR LIVES BECOME A MIRACLE

Our lives then become a continuous **miracle** in which we repeatedly see the manifestations of the Lord in our daily life. "Circumstances" occur too often and with too much regularity for them to be circumstances anymore. We begin to feel a Presence surrounding us, watching over us and guiding us, and begin to feel great joy, immeasurable gratitude and a desire to know and get closer to our invisible Friend.

We begin to sense inwardly what this Divine Presence expects of us; for it is written in all the great religious scriptures of the world:

1) LOVE OTHERS AS WE LOVE OURSELVES.

2) TREAT OTHERS AS WE WOULD LIKE OTHERS TO TREAT US.

It all seems so simple. We feel joy. We feel our love expanding towards a greater and greater circle of individuals regardless of who they are, where they are from or what they look like. We want to help, to serve, to see the others become as happy and secure as they can. We feel their problems as our own. We can't stand the idea of hurting anyone, because it would be like hurting our own brother, or like hurting ourselves.

We begin to see others as manifestations of that same Presence which we feel filling our life. We treat them with the same love and respect that we feel for that Presence. We worship God through our love for, and services towards, humanity.

We learn to act without attachment to the fruit of our action. We feel the inner urge to better ourselves and Society, but are not discouraged if our full hearted efforts do not bring the results we want.

We know that there is a reason for that result and we continue to do what we feel is right, without worrying about the result.

We may not be terribly intellectual. We may not know fancy words and complicated philosophies. But we have something much more precious; **love** and **peace** - the healing balms which are so rarely found in the world today. We may seem a little strange or even crazy at times. We may not fit in all the preconceived ideas of what a "spiritual" person is like. We may be full of weaknesses and problems, but all these fade into the background, because we have "brought God back into our life".

This type of relating to God as a dear, close one is an extremely important step in evolution from the philosophy of Dualism to Non-dualism. In dualism we feel separate and disconnected from the Divine. In Non-dualism we realize that God is the basis of everything which exists, and that we are in fact God himself. It is very difficult to go from not even believing God exists or feeling very

The Art of Meditation

separate from Him to believing that we as spirit are one with God. This intermediary step of relating to God through form and internal communication is a very useful (and joyful) step in this evolutionary process towards our Divine destiny.

The step can be accelerated by joining together with other like-minded individuals for spiritual stimulation through discussion, chanting, prayer and meditation. Through association with such a group, one's faith and sincerity are increased and negative tendencies are reduced. It is also extremely important to keep a specific time of the day set aside for communicating more deeply with the Divine through prayer, chanting, reading and contemplation or meditation. This discipline will enable us to keep up that contact with the Presence throughout all the activities of the day.

So let's all let go. Let's dare to talk to God; to ask Him for help, to sing a song to Him, (or Her or It) for all that we have received. Let's dare to believe that **He is here**, beside us, watching over us - actually **within us**. Thus He becomes our friend, our doctor, our priest, our psychiatrist, our guru, our lover; He becomes our own **self** ! In this way, it is no longer the blind leading the blind; but rather the light coming to remove the blindness.

VERTICAL AND HORIZONTAL RELATIONSHIPS

All of the above ways to relate to God and this creation which He sustains, can be considered vertical relationships. **Vertical relationships** are those interactions that pull us upward along the evolutionary path toward our Divine destiny. Each of us is a spirit which is evolving through matter from cells, to plants, through animal nature, to manhood; and now Godhood lies ahead. We are now at a point somewhere between animal nature and Godhood. We can move in either direction, depending on our thoughts, words and actions.

These vertical interactions pull us toward the universal, away from the individual; toward selflessness, away from selfishness. They create an upward spiral of progress in our human development toward more love, peace, harmony and fulfillment both as individuals and as a Society.

Horizontal relationships, on the other hand, can often generate a repetitive cyclical movement of either non-growth or backward movement. These are relationships in which we are seeking selfish pleasure, affirmation or security through other beings or objects.

There are many ways to transform the simplest repetitive acts into forms of spiritual upliftment. Each can constantly repeat his chosen name of God or mantra while working, sitting, waiting, traveling, falling asleep or at any other time when there are not "more important" uses for the mind. In this way the mind will take up the qualities associated with that word. For example, by repeating the name of Christ (or Christ Have Mercy), one will begin to acquire the qualities of Divine Love, Strength, Faith and Wisdom exemplified by Christ.

Each of our acts and duties can be offered up to God. While washing our bodies or the dishes, clothes or the floor we can ask that our emotions and mind will, in the same way, be cleaned by an inflow of Divine Grace. Each day every major task can be prefaced by a prayer offering up all thoughts, words and deeds, that they shall be in harmony with **Truth** and **Righteousness.**

Many of us have forgotten how to pray and may find all this a bit strange. Is it not more strange that so many children could forget their real father and even where they came from and **who they are?**

If we want to fulfill the purpose of our lives and reestablish that severed relationship with the Divine, we must begin to evaluate our relationships and activities. Are they vertical or horizontal? The answer is not in the act itself, but in the motive behind it. Conversation can be uplifting, idle gossip or simply a waste of time and energy. Work and even charity can be done for selfish purposes or for the good of others. The often-used example of the knife is a good one. It can be used to save a life through surgery, kill a man in anger or cut a piece of bread.

The Art of Meditation

Why not sit down with a piece of paper and list your daily activities? See which ones are vertically oriented and which are horizontal. Perhaps some are a mixture of both. See what you can do to progress more along the upward spiral, rather than revolving endlessly in the same circle.

One last point. Such changes in one's life are much more easily made with the support of others who are seeking the same transformation. Seek out the company of others on the spiritual path. Such a group is called "Satsang". "Sat" means truth and "Sang" company or group. You will derive much strength, comfort and support from such a **Truth** seeking group.

CHAPTER 21

CULTIVATING THE WITNESS

The supreme purpose of all spiritual efforts is the realization of our Real Self - the eternal divine witness which is the inner being of all beings. Without the gradual awakening of this witness, we will never experience the stable state of peace, fulfillment and happiness that we are all searching for.

Without the development of the witness, we lack clarity, objectivity and logic. We are more easily subject to negative emotions, conflicts and suffering. We are more likely to make wrong assumptions and decisions and thus more susceptible to various negative consequences.

There are a number of ways in which we can cultivate the ability to witness our personality with the same objectivity with which we would witness someone else. These techniques are described in detail in the book "**Psychology of Happiness** ". We will describe them only briefly here.

SELF OBSERVATION

Anyone who wants to see himself objectively will have to learn to observe himself objectively. There are a number of techniques that he can apply in order to achieve this goal.

1. We can keep a **diary,** written in the third person, in which we write a description of the day's major events and how we felt and thought in response to those events.

2. We can realize that **we are not our thoughts and feelings,** but that they are temporary states of mind which come and go depending on **a)** the various environmental stimuli and events, **b)** our own beliefs, and **c)** our state of mind and energy level. Thus we can watch our feelings and thoughts, and even physical reactions as if they are happening to someone else. This allows us to become witnesses of our various mental states.

3. The example of the river is helpful. Imagine that **you are the banks of a river** and that your thoughts and feelings are the objects flowing down the river. Just watch them. We are not attached to them. We don't try to stop them, neither do we chase after them. We accept them and are detached from them. We are the unconcerned witness.

4. We can also use our **body as a mirror** of what is happening within us. When we see that some part of the body is tensing, we can objectively ask why. We can try to search for the inner cause, most likely on the emotional level, which is causing this tension or contraction in our body.

5. We can also see **others' behavior and reactions in life events as a mirror** of the contents of our conscious and subconscious mind. This has many aspects.

a) People may mirror our own present or past behavior. If we are aggressive, competitive or egotistical, we may find ourselves confronting the same behavior in others. Thus, watching others and looking at ourselves to see if we have the same attitude will help us to become more objective witnesses of ourselves.

b) People and life itself may reflect our **own attitude towards ourselves.** If we do not accept ourselves and criticize or reject ourselves mentally, then we may find that we are receiving the same lack of respect or rejection from others. If we do not have confidence in ourselves, then we may find that others do not have confidence in us. If we believe that others want to use or manipulate us, we may find that we are attracting such behavior from others.

c) Others may also present us with situations and events that we have purposely come **to learn from and overcome.** They are most likely not aware of this. We are subconsciously using them to offer us opportunities for growth. In such cases we may find that **what annoys us in the other is what we cannot accept in our own selves.**

d) In some cases, people will mirror to us the **opposite of ourselves,** so that we can learn to come into balance by developing some missing quality. For example, if we tend to speak a great deal in order to feel happy or affirmed, we may find ourselves in a relationship with someone who prefers not to talk. If we have an exaggerated need for cleanliness and order, we may find ourselves with someone who does not give importance to these. We may have come to learn to be a little more relaxed about this and the other perhaps to be more mature and disciplined. We are together to learn.

Using these guidelines we can become more objective witnesses of our personality and become more detached from our body and mind.

DISCIPLINE

We have already mentioned the importance of discipline a number of times in various contexts. Let us simply add here that by performing various types of disciplines such as exercises, breathing techniques, meditation, fasting, silence etc., we have a continual opportunity to become the witness of the various mechanisms that operate within our psychological structure.

We can observe our laziness, our boredom, our need for variety, our feelings of suppression, and our negativity towards discipline. We can become witnesses to the various illusions and excuses that our mind creates in order to get out of keeping a discipline. Through discipline we have yet another opportunity to develop our witness.

RELAXATION AND MEDITATION

During the process of relaxation and meditation we are constantly confronted with our thought mechanisms and feelings which come in waves independently of our will. We can either fight these thoughts or we can learn to become their detached witness. We can learn to recognize these mechanisms and remember that we are not them. We gradually become the witnesses of all of our mental functions. This is our only real freedom; the total detachment from all of our mental functioning.

RETREATS

Nothing perhaps helps us more in cultivating the witness than retreat. By retreat we mean to be by ourselves, preferably somewhere in nature. Retreat can also be done in a group, but all should observe silence, and there should be no communication, so that each can focus deeply on himself and the present moment.

During retreats we usually engage in three types of activities. Many hours are spent in spiritual techniques such as exercises, breathing, meditation, relaxation and prayer. One might spend eight to twelve hours in such activities. (This should not be done without the guidance and approval of an experienced spiritual guide).

A second activity is contemplation and self-analysis. Often this is facilitated by some questionnaires that aid the inner search and clarification of life goals etc. The third basic activity is the contact and attunement with nature.

A meditation, which is especially useful for cultivating the witness, is called "NETI NETI", in which we allow every object of consciousness to pass out of consciousness, because we are not that, **we are not that.** By rejecting all mental phenomena we are left with the pure witness.

PHILOSOPHY

Through philosophical reasoning Socrates was able to attain the ability to be the unidentified witness of this body and mind, even at the moment of death. He realized that he, as consciousness or soul, could not be the body nor the mind. He realized that life must continue after leaving the physical body. He even concluded that this continuing life-energy-consciousness must most likely return to create another body and live again. He realized that the body is only the instrument of the soul. He likened that relationship to that between the guitarist and guitar. He realized that the guitarist remains unharmed and unchanged no matter what happens to his guitar. He learned to become the detached witness of his body and mind.

Through philosophy we can gain peace. We can learn to accept ourselves, others and life itself without fear. We begin to see the meaning in everything that happens.

Philosophy allows us to witness more clearly situations, events and our reactions to them.

GROUP WORK

Through working with a group of like-minded individuals we can receive help in seeing ourselves more clearly. The group acts like a mirror that helps us to see ourselves more objectively. When we realize that we have the same types of interactions with a variety of persons, then we can conclude that there is something within ourselves which is mirroring in those relationships and interactions. When such groups also take time to share feelings, impressions and thoughts, then we have an even greater opportunity, for the others can tell us how they feel with us, and we can begin to see ourselves more objectively through the eyes of the others.

CONSCIOUS COOPERATION

Conscious cooperative work with others is another excellent opportunity for self-observation. In some systems of spiritual growth this is a basic technique. We work together having a specific method of concentration for the duration of that work period. Each has a small notebook and pen. When a bell rings each stops his work and writes down the thoughts and feelings that were passing through his mind when the bell rang and during the last work period in general. In this way we learn to witness our mind while we are in activity. This is enhanced even more if after such a work experience all share what they have discovered about the way in which their mind works.

INNER SEARCHING

There are a wide variety of techniques available for working with the subconscious so as to become clearer about the inner hidden mental functioning. As they are many and really a subject for another book, we will only mention them by name here.

1. Regressions (through relaxation techniques or hypnosis) can reveal experiences from our childhood years that may be distorting our perception today, and thus, inhibiting the clear functioning of the witness or higher intellect.

2. Writing the story of our childhood years (preferably in the third person) can help in the same way.

3. Written affirmations in which we discover negative thought patterns and learn to reprogram them, freeing the mind from negative thought forms and allowing the witness to function with less obstacles.

4. Letters to persons who played important roles in our childhood years can free us from negative emotional reactions which usually shadow our logic, reasoning and, of course, our witness.

5. Letters can even be written **to the emotions** that usually disturb our inner peace and harmonious relationships with others.

6. Psychodrama is a method by which one can play out certain roles that he finds himself playing in his life and relationships. In such a setting with an experienced guide, he can be helped to see himself more objectively in those roles and thus can witness them more clearly, and gradually identify less with them, even if it is necessary to continue playing them in his life.

7. Dialogue between two conflicting roles which function within our own personality is another valuable technique for gaining more objectivity concerning the roles we play and games which we play with ourselves and others.

8. The previous two techniques require the help of an experienced guide and on our part some **role analysis,** which means to realize the types of roles we play in our lives with ourselves and with others.

All of these techniques will help us to gradually become less identified with our body and personality. We can gradually shift our focus from self to the witness, to the higher self. Thus we must remember that, although all of these are helpful, the basic tool is remembering the spiritual truths and meditation.

THE ELECTRICAL CURRENT
AND THE TAPE RECORDER

Before moving on to the results that we can expect as the witness becomes stronger, let us look at an example that helps us to understand the relationship between the spirit or witness and the body-mind. Take the example of the electrical current. There is a tape recorder through which the current passes and becomes sound. The type of sound the current will become depends on the quality of the tape player, the quality of the tape and the contents of the tape.

We might imagine that the player is the body, the tape is the mind and the contents of the tape are the contents of the mind. The electrical current is the witness. It exists independently of the player and tape. Its quality is not affected by the quality of the tape or sound. If the tape spoils or the player breaks down, the current remains unaffected. Neither its existence nor its value are affected by the condition or performance of the tape player and tape.

But there is another important point. This same current is playing through all tape players and tapes. It is the same current expressing itself through small and large, expensive and cheap, high quality and low quality, new and old, cassette players of all sizes and colors and brands. There is one power, one witness expressing itself through all of these various instruments. And not only through these but all the other types of electrical appliances and machines.

There is in reality only one spirit, one witness, one being which is the conscious reality in all beings. When we realize our own witness, our own spiritual consciousness, we will have come into contact with the same consciousness that is expressing itself through all other beings.

WHAT CAN WE EXPECT?

As we gain more detachment from our body and mind, and witness ourselves more objectively, we will obtain more spiritual discrimination. Thus we will have greater clarity concerning what is beneficial for our health and happiness. We will be free to develop disciplines that improve our health and state of mind.

As we will be freer from negative emotional mechanisms, we will be more effective and creative in our work and recreation. We will be more able to cooperate closely with other persons as we will have less need to protect our ego. Our relationships will be more honest, open and harmonious.

Being freer from negative emotional mechanisms, we begin to experience more love and unity with those around us. We will experience greater inner peace, which will be more stable and not easily shaken by events and situations.

Life in general will be much more beautiful and meaningful. With time, our minds will perceive to an ever greater degree the divine that exists in us all.

We will experience our real spiritual identity.

STAGES IN OUR SPIRITUAL PRACTICES

"Some whose hearts are purified, realize the Spirit within themselves through contemplation. Some realize the Spirit philosophically, by meditating upon its independence from the physical world. Others realize it by following the path of right action. Others, who do not know these paths, worship God as their teachers have taught them. If these faithfully practice what they have learned, they also will pass beyond death's power".

In the above passage from the Bhagavad Gita, Lord Krishna explains that there are many spiritual paths and techniques. These various spiritual paths may, or may not, be useful to a specific individual depending on his inclinations, conditioning, character, age, responsibilities, and other personal and social circumstances. A particular spiritual path, which may take one individual quickly towards Self-realization, may create only frustration for another. Also, as we mature physically, emotionally and mentally, we may find ourselves naturally moving from one spiritual technique to another.

The Indians understood this truth many thousands of years ago and developed the four "ashramas" which guided an individual through the various stages of his life. The first quarter of the life is spent in **preparation** for both material and spiritual life, and the development of a good character. One is taught to respect his teacher, parents, all elders and, of course, God. In addition to learning a trade, one is taught the various rituals and ceremonies belonging to his particular sect of worship.

The second quarter of his life is to be spent in **creating and selflessly sustaining and nurturing a family.** One is also responsible for the proper moral upbringing of his children and for performing the necessary rituals prescribed for a householder.

In the third quarter of the Life, the children have grown up and the individual begins to direct his energies toward **selfless service to the community** at large. Now he also has more time for reading, meditation and various rituals and prayers.

The last quarter of his life is spent in **study, meditation and prayer**. He gives up his contact with social events and worldly concerns, and concentrates deeply on God. He may even leave his family and live by himself, so that he can concentrate more deeply.

There is a great psychological wisdom in this system which allows the individual to fulfill his worldly and spiritual needs simultaneously all in one life. It is practical and spiritual. Each has a chance to fulfill his need for creating a family and succeeding in worldly life. Then he is able to let go of that worldly life and work toward Self-realization.

In our society, elderly people are not encouraged to do this. They have been conditioned to believe that they must, by all means, remain in the world and continue to occupy themselves with meaningless social activities, or become "work-alcoholics", who can find no meaning in life beyond their work. In the Indian system, everything has its time and place. There is a time for learning, making children, a time for working, a time for accumulating money and a time for letting go of all this and penetrating deeper into the meaning of life.

The Indians see no sin in desire or wealth. Desire is allowed to evolve over the years into desire for Liberation from the cycle of birth and death. The nature of the desire, which at first attaches

The Art of Meditation

itself to objects of momentary pleasure, gradually matures into a desire for a more deep and lasting peace that can come only through spiritual evolution.

Wealth is not seen as evil in itself; but rather is understood to be a great energy resource that can be properly used to improve the quality of life on earth for all beings equally. Money becomes an evil when it is hoarded and used for the benefit of a few at the expense of the many. Money becomes a spiritual force when used for the good of all equally.

From this point of view, all of life is a spiritual process. Every act can be a movement toward spiritual realization or a fall into greater ignorance and egotism. It is the **motive,** and not the act itself, which decides its effect on an individual's growth process.

VARIOUS PATHS OF GROWTH

Life's experiences are in themselves the first and most basic aspect of any spiritual path. Through our sufferings and joys we hopefully learn the lessons life is trying to teach us. Even if we do not consciously participate in any growth techniques, we can learn and arrive at the goal by simply observing and reflecting on life's experiences. This is, however, like trying to swim across a great rough sea. A boat would be safer and quicker. We may consider that the many growth techniques are like boats helping us to cross this great Sea of Life to the shores of Self-realization.

In addition it is seldom that one travels the whole distance in the same boat. We may disembark from one and embark on another. Some techniques such as physical exercises, breathing techniques or rituals may be more useful for us as we start out the journey. Later we may find that social service or disciplines of various types suit us more.

Still further along we may give less importance to the physical body and pay more attention to love for God, Scriptural studies and meditation. As we approach the other shore, the bottom is too shallow for boats to pass, and once again we must jump into the water and swim the final stretch without the help of any systems, teacher or techniques. But by now we are much stronger, wiser, more able to avoid undercurrents and whirlpools. If we had tried to jump into the water earlier in the journey, we would surely have drowned from an inability to cope with the ups and downs of the waves of Life.

The order in which one may pass from one mode of growth to another is not fixed in any definite pattern. A spirit may program his own individual curriculum plan starting with the more material and moving toward the more mental, and more subtle.

It is not to be thought, however, that techniques that are more physically oriented, or form-oriented, are in any way a lower type of techniques. They are simply techniques for a different time and place. We do not consider that what we learn in the second grade is lower than what we learn in the fourth grade. We do not consider that the second grader is a lower type of being than the fourth grader. We understand that without second graders, there cannot be any fourth graders. Someone who tries to go onto the fourth grade without having successfully mastered the second grade material will obviously have to eventually return to learn what he has failed to comprehend.

Let us take a look at some of these spiritual practices.

1) Health Oriented systems such as exercises, breathing techniques, deep relaxation and dietary guidelines are a good starting point for one who wants to proceed along the path of human development. Through such systems the body and mind can be purified, strengthened and harmonized so that the soul is not distracted in its efforts toward Self-realization.

It is not sufficient, however, to seek health as a goal in itself. That healthy body and mind must then be used for the purpose of personal and social improvement, and spiritual realization.

2) Rituals have been used over the ages by all religions as a way to communicate with, and gain the blessings of, the Divine. Rituals are usually addressed to a particular form of the Divine. They usually require a third party, such as a priest, to speak to God on behalf of the masses. In this type of ritual there may in some cases be an inherent feeling of unworthiness and isolation from God. Eventually the individual must remove this feeling of distance and unworthiness and realize his close relationship and ultimate oneness with God.

The atmosphere created by rituals is useful in helping many of us to concentrate on God and spiritual life. When this is repeated frequently, it gradually reconditions the subconscious mind in a spiritually oriented direction. Rituals, properly performed with concentration and sincerity, can bring upon the participants a flow of Divine Grace. The individual feels cleansed and is ready to start a new life with new determination.

Rituals also serve to bring a spiritual awareness into the simplest repetitive daily acts. Take for example the customary pre-meal prayer recited by the Indians:

"God is the ritual (the process of eating)
God is offering (the food itself)
God is he who offers (He who eats)
To the fire that is God (the digestive process)
If a man sees God
in every action
He will find God".

The unmanifest God is seen to be present in all aspects of the eating ritual. He is the process of eating, the food, the eater and even the digestive process. Everything, every being and every action, is an expression of the one God. When one realizes this, he realizes God.

You can imagine the power of repeating this ritual consciously and sincerely at each and every meal, making an attempt to really understand the full import of what is being said. It will undoubtedly transform one's way of thinking and living.

Each of us has grown up with certain rituals that we have taken for granted without deeply looking into their mystical significance. Many of these rituals have become empty for the average individual. There is very little attention given to them in the churches of today. Many of them have been distorted and abused.

We may benefit by reviewing and participating in some of the rituals that were impressed upon our minds as children in this new light. We may find many beautiful surprises in the way of worship that we thought was dead to us.

3) Disciplines and **control of behavior** have already been discussed frequently. We may briefly review, that through the control of behavior and desire, egotism is diminished and the individual comes into greater harmony with the beings and nature around him. He also is in more harmony with his own higher Self. Krishna explains in the Bhagavad Gita that "when a man is Self-controlled, his will is Spirit's friend. But the will of an uncontrolled man is hostile to spirit like an enemy". An uncontrolled man is a man at war with himself. His energies are divided against each other and he cannot succeed at any endeavor.

Disciplines also serve to purify and strengthen the body and mind so that they become more capable of understanding the higher truths. Some students asked a great sage some spiritual questions. He said to them, "live again a year more in penance, abstinence and faith; then you may ask questions according to your desire". This sage understood what Jesus meant by "do not throw pearls before swine". We cannot benefit from hearing great truths if we have not purified ourselves of the various desires and attachments which cloud our vision, understanding and discrimination.

An individual, who tries to follow the path of philosophy without having previously gained a certain control over his desires and selfish nature, treads a very dangerous path, which can be harmful to himself and his loved ones. However, the person who has overcome egotism needs no longer battle with his lower nature.

4) Selfless service, without attachment to the results, is perhaps one of the most important spiritual practices for today's world. It simultaneously benefits the individual and the society. What is good for a cell of a body is good for the whole body and what is good for the body is also good for the cell. Through selfless service an individual learns to transcend his overemphasis on personal needs and desires so rampant in today's society. He learns to think of others, and express his concern and love for others, through action.

It is important that the spiritual aspirant avoid seeking specific results from his actions. He must offer his service from his heart and not wait for gratitude. He must not even seek for a particular type of result from his action. He acts because he feels that the act must be performed, and then he leaves the result up to God.

Selfless action is also a way to remove impulses and tendencies from the mind so that the mind will be more able to meditate. Krishna explains this in the Bhagavad Gita.

"Let him who would like to climb in meditation
to the heights of the highest Union with God,
Take for his path the path of action:
Then when he nears the height of oneness,
His acts will fall from him,
His path will be tranquil".

Performing selfless actions, without attachment to the fruit of the action, purifies the mind so that it may meditate more deeply. If, however, the actions are performed with an attachment to a specific result, then the meditation will be disturbed.

Most of us will benefit ourselves and the society in which we live by spending more time involved in helping those in need in whatever way we can.

5) Devotion to God is a path of God realization complete unto itself. If one can completely surrender to God, and Love God with all his heart, mind and soul, then he needs no other spiritual technique to achieve union with the Universal Spirit. This is one boat that can carry one all the way to the other shore. Few today, however, have such devotion and love. Our devotion is to money, prestige, pleasure, power and material possessions. A mind full of so many other loyalties cannot be loyal to God.

Through surrender to God, the emotional nature is purified and focused as love for God as the inner resident of each and every being. This love leads eventually to a great wisdom, in which one sees that he is ultimately connected with all of creation.

Devotion may be expressed through prayer, chanting, hymns, rituals, disciplines of various types, through repeating the name of the form of God one has chosen, and other techniques. But basically it is a path without techniques. It is an inner path, which requires no outward show of devotion. It is the inner sincerity and devotion, which count. Outward show of devotion in public is often superficial.

This is the path of Surrender, in which the individual relinquishes his own personal will and accepts whatever God gives him in life. He has no fear, for he knows that God will give him exactly what the needs, whether it be pleasant or unpleasant.

6) Study of the Scriptures is another way in which individuals attempt to come close to God. By contemplating on the messages given in the various religious texts, they gradually grow in understanding of life. This knowledge must, however, be put into action, or else, it is not only useless, but even dangerous. Most of us, however, would benefit from reading each day a few pages or paragraphs from a spiritually oriented book. We could then contemplate on these truths throughout the day.

7) Through **meditation** the mind is purified, focused and merged with the universal Spirit. It is an advanced technique and one will likely have had to pass through other purifying techniques before starting with meditation. In meditation we go beyond form in order to realize the basic life principle behind all creation.

8) Pure **discriminative wisdom** uses no technique except for discrimination between what is the real unchanging reality of the spirit and the illusory ever-changing relative reality of the physical

The Art of Meditation

and mental world. At this stage of spiritual evolution, one practices no special exercises and observes no rules of behavior or rituals. He has gone beyond identification with his body and mind. He knows himself to be an eternal witness beyond the vehicles through which the spirit is experiencing the world.

This is an extremely advanced stage reserved for a very few remarkable souls. Most of us would be fooling ourselves to think that we can tread such a path without previous purification and preparation through other more tangible techniques.

Let each one of us consider what stages of sadhana are appealing and useful to him at this moment and begin to cross the sea of life so that we may soon arrive at our real destination. It is perfectly natural that a combination of these techniques will appeal to us.

Let us conclude with another statement by Sri Krishna from the Bhagavad Gita:

"Some yogis merely worship the minor Gods. Others are able, by the grace of the Spirit, to meditate on the identity of the Spirit with God. For these, the Spirit is the offering, and God is the sacrificial fire into which it is offered.

"Some withdraw all their senses from contact with exterior sense objects. For these, hearing and the other senses are the offering, and self-discipline is the sacrificial fire. Others allow their minds and senses to wander unchecked, and try to see God within all exterior sense objects. For these, sound and other sense objects are the offering, and sense enjoyment the sacrificial fire.

"Some renounce all the actions of the senses, and all the functions of the vital force. For these, such actions and functions are the offering, and the practice of self-control is the sacrificial fire, kindled by knowledge of the Spirit.

"Then there are others whose ways of worship is to renounce sense-objects and material possessions. Others set themselves austerities and spiritual disciplines; that is their way of worship.

Others worship through the practice of Meditation. Others, who are earnest seekers for perfection, and men of strict vows, study and meditate on the truths of scriptures. That is their way of worship.

"Others are intent to controlling the vital energy; so they practice breathing exercises-inhalation, exhalation and the stoppage of the breath. Others mortify their flesh by fasting, to weaken their desires, and thus achieve self-control.

"All these understand the meaning of sacrificial worship. Through worship their sins are consumed away".

Each technique, or system, is like a boat taking us a little closer to the goal.

The Final Stretch to enlightenment must be swum alone without the use of any technique or system.

When we arrive, we realize that we have always been there from the beginning. That it was a circular trip, from our Selves to our Selves.

CHAPTER 23

INNER CONFLICTS

I would like to complete this book with a brief discussion concerning some of the inner conflicts that develop as one follows any system of self-improvement or spiritual discipline. It is not absolutely necessary for such conflicts to arise, but in 98% of the cases they do. In some they manifest as subtle inner tensions, but in others as deep rooted inner conflicts which lead to self rejection, unhappiness and a resulting lack of stability on the path.

THE SPIRITUAL EGO AND THE MATERIAL EGO

Let us divide our ego structure for the purposes of this discussion into the part which wants to improve our character and life style and proceed spiritually and the other part which wants to remain in the familiar and conditioned types of behavior and activities where it finds security, pleasure and affirmation. Let's call the first part the spiritual ego and the second the material ego. In the end we want these two to meet, to open up to each other and become one.

We do not intend to imply that the spiritual ego is higher or more spiritual than the material ego. In some cases the opposite may be true, as the spiritual ego might be simply seeking security, pleasure and affirmation in other ways.

The spiritual ego may occasionally be even more afraid or more attached to persons and situations than the material ego. This is not always the case, however.

SOME SAMPLE CONFLICTS

Let us look at some examples of the inner conflicts that we may experience as a result of our desire to improve ourselves and grow spiritually.

1. We may have a desire for various objects or situations as a source of pleasure. Another part of ourselves may feel, however, that this is a sin, or that we are not spiritual if we partake in such pleasures. Or it may feel that this type of pleasure seeking is a waste of time and energy considering our spiritual goals. Thus these two aspects of our own being conflict.

2. One part of ourselves may feel the need to have an exclusive relationship, in which our happiness and security depend on another person (usually a mate). Another part of ourselves may find this an obstacle towards its need for independence, self-dependence, and freedom to move along the spiritual path without obstacles.

3. Similarly there may be a conflict between the need for personal love and the need to develop universal love.

4. The need to forgive and the need to hold on to negative feelings towards someone.

5. The need to employ various disciplines and the need to feel free to do what we want when we want to.

6. The need to follow our inner voice and the need to be like the others and be accepted by them.

7. The need to express our feelings as they are, and the need not to hurt anyone.

8. The need to express our real feelings and thoughts and the need to have the acceptance of those around us.

9. The need to follow a spiritual guide and the need to rebel against all types of advice or control.

10. The need to control persons and situations in order to feel secure and the need to let things flow and allow others to act freely.

11. The need to never show weakness and the need to share our weakness with others.

12. The need not to ask anything from others and the need to have their help and support.

13. The need for a stable routine for our balance and growth and the need for variety and change.

14. The need to play familiar emotional games in our relationships and the need to get free from them.

15. The need to face and overcome our fears and blockages and the need to avoid them and hide them.

There are many more conflicts that we haven't mentioned, but most will fall into these categories.

WHAT FORM DO THESE CONFLICTS TAKE

As we mentioned previously, these conflicts will manifest to varying degrees and in a variety of ways. But most have a common theme. The spiritual ego feels the conflict most intensely (if we didn't desire spiritual growth we would not have a conflict) and usually creates feelings of self rejection, failure and guilt, when we are unable to satisfy its requirements for it to feel that it is spiritual and it is worthy. If we do not feel that we are worthy, then we do not feel safe. We are programmed that whoever is not "good" or worthy in God's eyes is not safe, as he does not "deserve" God's protection.

These are not good reasons, however, to want to change something in ourselves. These are not spiritual motives. If we want to change because then we will be safe, or others will accept us, we are simply replacing the material ego with the spiritual ego. Nothing has really changed. In some cases our need to fulfill these spiritual "requirements" for our self-acceptance has more to do with our need to feel that we are **more** spiritual than the others. Thus we simply replace the need for affirmation and superiority on a material level with the same need on the spiritual level.

It is important to realize that our spiritual value is permanent and divine. We cannot be worth more or less in God's eyes. We are divine consciousness in the process of evolving its ability to express its divinity on the material planes. Our inherent spiritual value is not changed by our actions or spiritual growth. What is changed is our ability to express that value mentally, emotionally and physically.

Trying to be a better person because we believe that God will love us more is not the best motive for growth. Desiring to become a clearer channel for God's plan because we love God and all of His creation is a better motive. Seeking to purify ourselves so that we can experience that Divine Consciousness in every being and event that we encounter, is a useful motive. Seeking to remove all mental, emotional and physical obstacles so that we can merge into a continual awareness of the Divine and achieve total enlightenment, is also a useful motive.

These motives are free from the game of who is spiritual and who is not, or who is more spiritual, or who is good and who is bad, and whom God loves and whom God does not love. They are based on the presumption that God is a much higher type of consciousness, and thus is incapable of not loving anyone, no matter what he ever may do. This seems only logical since God, himself, has asked us, mere humans, to love even our enemies and those who ignore and harm us. Is it possible then that He himself is incapable of doing this?

This type of thinking also removes us from the game of spiritual pride in which we feel that we are higher, more important, more favored by God than others. It also removes us from feeling that we are lower, less important or less favored by God than others.

The Art of Meditation

The material ego, on the other hand, in such situations tends to react to the rejection and pressure it receives from the spiritual ego by rebelling and sabotaging the various efforts towards discipline and self-control.

Thus, the more we press ourselves, the more our material ego reacts and rebels. In such cases we experience instability in our spiritual efforts. We are usually, in these cases, playing the roles of parent and child with our own selves. The parent rejects the child for not being a "good child" and the child then reacts so as to undermine the parents' effort towards control.

In order to move more effectively towards our goal of spiritual transformation, these inner conflicts will have to be dealt with in a more mature manner. Rather than communicating within ourselves as child and parent, it would be more useful to develop a mature adult to adult type of conversation or dialogue.

UNDERSTANDING OUR CONFLICTING SELVES

The following technique is best done under the guidance of a person experienced in facilitating such dialogues with one's self. In the case that one cannot find such a facilitator, you can do this exercise in written form.

Our purpose is to allow these two parts of our selves to have a chance to reflect on what they really want, need, and desire and express all of this to the other part. It is best for one to begin with a written analysis. Here are some questions that may help you.

Take for example the Spiritual Ego:

1. What does it feel when it is unable to achieve or maintain a spiritual goal?

2. In which particular situations does it feel that? Give some examples.

3. What does it believe about those situations, and particularly about himself, which causes him to have the feelings, which he mentioned in answer to question 1.

4. Why does he believe those beliefs. Upon what basic beliefs are they founded?

5. What are his needs and desires?

6. What specifically does he ask from the Material ego?

7. What can he do in order to have a better relationship with his material ego and, thus, proceed with greater unity and stability?

And we can ask the Material Ego:

1. What does it need and desire in order to feel secure, happy and worthy? Let it make a list of what it needs (objects, persons, situations, behaviors from himself and others etc.).

2. Why does it believe that it needs each thing on the list made in answer to question 1? Let him answer in regard to each what it believes will happen if it is not able to fulfill one of those needs or desires.

3. What are the basic beliefs which underlie its dependency on these specific needs and desires?

4. What specifically does it ask from the spiritual ego in order to feel more unity with it, to establish greater cooperation between them and greater happiness for both?

5. What can the material ego do in order to create greater unity and harmony, since they both live in the same body and mind, and must share it?

Answer these questions as well as you can, giving sufficient time and thought in order to go deeply.

The Art of Meditation

THE DIALOGUE

As mentioned earlier this dialogue can be done verbally in the presence of an experienced guide or on paper, something like a scene in which two previously conflicting parties try to communicate more openly and honestly.

In the case that we do it verbally, we will have two chairs or pillows placed opposite each other. We will sit on the one chair and assume one of our two roles. We will imagine that the other part of ourselves is sitting in the opposite chair or on the opposite pillow. We will start the conversation explaining to the other part of ourselves how we feel, what our needs and desires are, and what our beliefs are which make us feel the way we do. Then sitting in the other chair, we will then give the opposite side of ourselves the opportunity to speak about itself, how it feels and what it needs. These two parts will speak back and forth as we get up and change positions whenever we change roles (it is important to change positions in order to help change mind - set and psychology).

This conversation goes on like any other conversation, as we ask questions and change positions to answer them. We may accuse, we may express feelings of tenderness and love. We may plead and ask for help. We may ask deeper questions which help the one part of ourselves understand the other part more deeply and clearly. This conversation goes on until we have sat in both positions and have nothing to say from either point of view. This is important, because we may not have anything more to say from the one side, but then sit on the other side and ask a question, which may open up a discussion, which might last another half an hour with many changes in position.

Throughout this process we do not speak at all to our guide. He is there only to facilitate in the case that we get blocked or off the track.

Once we have completed this dialogue, we then take a position between our two previous sitting positions and imagine that we are our higher self, or that we are an enlightened spiritual guide, and we give some advice to each part of ourselves, explaining to each what it needs to do in order to have greater harmony with the other and to proceed more effectively, and with less conflict, along the path of spiritual growth or self improvement.

Whether you perform this exercise verbally or in written form, I am sure that you will find it very useful in resolving such conflicts which are often obstacles in our progress.

EPILOGUE

I want to take this opportunity to express my deepest gratitude towards the technique called meditation and towards all of those who played a role in introducing and enhancing that technique in my life. It has literally saved me from much unhappiness and has helped me to bring forth beautiful parts of myself which otherwise would still be buried today. The only way in which I can imagine repaying for what I have received is to offer it to others by sharing with you my experience and to encourage you to employ this unique technique of coming into contact with your inner self, and thus, with whatever is most beautiful and wonderful within you and bringing it out into your daily life to share it with others.

I wish you every success in this endeavor and remind you that it requires daily practice and that it is the highest way in which you can manifest the purpose of your life which is to manifest your latent divine potential here on the earth plane.

I express to you my love and my wishes
for an abundantly happy, healthy and harmonious life
of evolution, and if you choose, service to mankind.

About Our Web Site **www.HolisticHarmony.com**

We have 30 years of experience in
helping people clarify and improve their lives

YOU MAY BE ABLE TO USE US TO:

1. Create **emotional harmony**
2. Improve your **health**
3. Develop inner **peace**
4. **Resolve** inner conflicts
5. **Communicate** more effectively and Harmoniously
6. Open your heart to **love**
7. **Accept** and love your self more
8. Develop **self confidence**
9. Cultivate **higher virtues**
10. Obtain greater **self-knowledge**
11. **Deal** with challenging tests
12. **Understand** what Life is asking you to learn
13. Develop your own **personal philosophy** of life
14. Clarify your **value system**
15. Make **decisions**
16. Strengthen the **truth** within
17. Increase your **creativity**
18. Become a **happier** person
19. **Overcome** fears
20. **Remove blockages** towards manifesting dreams
21. Improve your **meditation**
22. **Deal with death**, yours or loved ones
23. **Free** yourself from old emotional games
24. **Let go** of the past and future
25. **Accept your life** as it is
26. Develop your **relationship with the Divine**

And many others ways you might think of.

Support materials

1. Free Audio clips with Lectures and relaxation techniques:
http://www.HolisticHarmony.com/audioclips/index.asp

2. Free Articles on health, happiness, relationships, communication, etc.:
http://www.HolisticHarmony.com/ezines/index.asp

3. Books and ebooks at:
http://www.HolisticHarmony.com/ebookscb/index.asp

4. Learn About Energy Psychology at:
http://www.HolisticHarmony.com/eft/index.asp

5. Become Trained as a Life Coach over the internet at:
http://www.HolisticHarmony.com/introholisticcoach.asp

6. Free Teleclasses and lectures as audio files:
http://www.HolisticHarmony.com/teleclasses/index.asp

7. Free email courses
http://www.HolisticHarmony.com/courses/index.asp

8. Nine New Coaching Tools
http://www.HolisticHarmony.com/coachquestions/index.asp

9. Free Biweekly ezine "Clarity"
http://www.HolisticHarmony.com
* *

More about life coaching at:
http://www.HolisticHarmony.com/introholisticcoach.asp
http://www.HolisticHarmony.com/coachquestions/index.asp
* *

ABOUT THE AUTHOR

American born, Robert Elias Najemy is presently living in Athens Greece, were he has founded and is directing the **Center for Harmonious Living** since 1976 which serves 3500 members with classes and workshops designed to aid each in the improvement of his or her body, mind, relationships and life in general.

Robert has 20 books published in Greek, which have sold over 100,000 copies.

He is the author of hundreds of articles published in magazines in England, Australia, India and Greece.

He has developed a program of seminars for Self-Analysis, Self-Discovery, Self-Knowledge, Self-Improvement, Self-Transformation and Self-Realization. He has trained over 300 Life Coaches and does so now over the internet.

This system combines a wide variety of well-tested ancient and modern techniques and concepts

His teachings come from what he calls "Universal Philosophy" which is the basis of all religions and yet beyond and not limited by religions.

His seminars include a variety of experiences including:
1. Basic **psychological** and **philosophical teachings.**
2. Self analysis through specially designed questionnaires.
3. Methods of **contacting** and **releasing** the contents of the **subconscious** in a safe and gentle way.
4. **Exercises**, breathing, movement, **singing**, chanting and **dance** for expression and release.
5. Methods for **discovering and releasing** through **regressions** (in relaxation) the events of the past, which have programmed our minds negatively and thus, are obstructing our happiness and effectiveness in the present.
6. Techniques for **solving inner conflicts** and also for **solving conflicts with others**.
7. Methods for **calming the mind** and **creating positive mental states.**
8. Experiences for feeling greater unity with others and breaking through feelings of separateness.
9. Opportunities to **share with others** that which one is feeling and experiencing.
10. Emotional release techniques.
 11. Methods of meditation and transcendence of the mind for those who are ready.

Upcoming Teleclasses with Robert - you can view at:
http://www.HolisticHarmony.com/teleclasses/index.asp

1. More Effective Communication with Partners
2. More Effective Communication with Children .
3. Dealing Effectively with "Negative" People.
4. Clearing up the Confusion Concerning Responsibility in Relationships
5. Overcoming Fears
6. Discovering what we need to Learn from Close Relationships.
7. Manifesting our inner potential and important goals.
8. Increasing Self-acceptance
9. Resolving Relationship Need Conflicts
10. Dealing with the Death of Loved Ones.
11. Introduction to Energy psychology
12. Loving others (getting free from obstacles to love)
13. Forgiveness - Road to Freedom (forgiving ourselves & others)
14. Reconciling and Healing our Inner conflicts
15. Freedom from being controlled by the roles others play.
16. Getting Free from playing the roles we play.
17. Finding our life purpose
18. Pathways and Truths for Happiness
19. Practical Introduction to Meditation
20. Attitude therapy
21. Twelve steps to Co-commitment in Love Relationships
22. Helping the Dying to Pass Peacefully.
23. Stages of Love
24. Learning from Life Situations
25. Self-Analysis through Questionnaires
26. Relationships between the Sexes
27. Healing the inner child
28. Developing human and spiritual values.
29. Positive projection techniques.
30. Using Models and Parables to Emphasize our Concepts.
31. Perfecting Active Listening Techniques.
32. How Reality is created and how we can create a more positive one.
33. Resistance to change for the better– secondary gains and how to work with it.

Books and ebooks
by Robert Elias Najemy

1. Universal Philosophy

2. The Art of Meditation

3. Contemporary Parables

4. The Mystical Circle of Life

5. Relationships of Conscious Love

6. The Miracles of Love and Wisdom

7. Free to be Happy with Energy Psychology by Tapping on Acupuncture Points

8. Saram – The Adventures of a Soul and Insight into the Male Psyche

9. The Psychology of Happiness

10. The Adventures of Petro and the revelation of the Truth.

You can view them at:

www.HolisticHarmony.com/ebooks.index.asp

The Art of Meditation